D0021738

STUTTERIN'
BOY

Thanks

[signature]

STUTTERIN' BOY

by
Mel Tillis
with Walter Wager

RAWSON ASSOCIATES / NEW YORK

Tillis, Mel.
  Stutterin' boy.

  Includes index.
  1. Tillis, Mel.   2. Country musicians—United States—
Biography.   I. Wager, Walter H.   II. Title.
ML420.T53A3   1984   784.5'2'00924 [B]   83-43114
ISBN 0-89256-263-3

I figure we live in two worlds—public and private. It seems like I've got to prove myself in both all the time. I've got to climb mountains right to the top and then find new ones to climb. Whenever I finish writing a song, I always ask myself, "Well, Stutterin' Boy, is that all you've got?"

—M.T.

CHAPTER

1

My mama's a small, wonderful, God-fearing woman. She always has been. I couldn't have been more blessed.

My daddy was a good-looking man. He stood well over six feet tall. He was 210 pounds of romping, stomping redneck. Women noticed him and he noticed the women. I guess that was about the only thing I ever took after my daddy. He was a first-class self-taught baker who never was afraid of work. The heat and the long hours didn't bother him. He was very strong.

Well, he had been when I was a boy. Now I was the father of five children of my own and Daddy was seventy-four, and he wasn't strong anymore. He was a sick man. It was my turn to be strong. It wasn't just that he was my daddy, I wanted to help him.

There were hundreds of miles and a whole lot more between us. Divorced from Mama, Daddy had remarried and was living in a little house on Lake Arthur near Groveland, Florida. It was on a twenty-acre plot of ground that I'd bought back in 1962. Today my home's in Ashland City, Tennessee. It's a fourteen-hundred-acre working farm near Nashville. He'd never been to visit with us, and as a matter

of fact had never been out of the state except years ago
when he took a job with Wilson Truck Lines and they sent
him to Plainfield, New Jersey (he said he liked to have froze
his "Florida ass" off), and, later, a trip to Puerto Rico.

Daddy had been calling me quite a lot the past few
months, and I felt like he was trying to say something but it
never came out. Finally I said, "Daddy, why don't you
come up to Tennessee and visit with us on the farm? You've
never taken a vacation in your whole life. It's always been
work, work, work with you."

He hesitated for a few seconds. Then I told him,
"Whenever you want, I'll send *Stutter One*." I also wanted
him to know that I had my own King Air turboprop jet with
two full-time pilots. He'd never thought I could make a
living in music. He'd never believed in my dreams.

Lord knows I wasn't any overnight sensation. It took
many years . . . a lot of songs . . . thousands of performances at honky-tonks, dance halls, county fairs, and close to
two million miles of hard driving on back roads and highways, in all kinds of weather, before people began to care in
any numbers. For a long time the whole world of country
music was small change in terms of recognition and dollars.
So was I. Now things were different. It was time for Daddy
to see that his determined son, the one with the tangled
tongue, who couldn't talk straight or hold a regular job, had
made the "impossible dream" come true. I wouldn't just tell
him, I'd show him.

First he'd fly up to Nashville in *Stutter One*. Then I'd
drive him to every corner of the farm. He'd see all the
different animals and crops . . . the barns and machinery
. . . the ponds stocked with fish . . . the big log house and
swimming pool. Daddy had never saved enough money to
put down such roots. That farm was another one of my
dreams. I was sure it would impress him. I hoped it would
please him, too. I wanted him to stay with us in our home,
built out of 150-year-old logs, for as long as he liked. I

wanted him to see the hit records and the framed photos of his son with famous people like Ronald Reagan, Jimmy Carter, Frank Sinatra, Clint Eastwood, Roy Acuff, Burt Reynolds, Eddy Arnold, Governor Frank Clements, Governor Winfield Dunn, Governor Lamar Alexander, Senator Howard Baker, and Burl Ives.

It wasn't just a performer's vanity that moved me. It was something all men and women share: Like everyone else, I wanted my daddy to be proud of me. I needed my daddy to understand and respect me. Just as important, I wanted to understand and respect him. If we could both do that, we could share the success, enjoy it together, and be a family like other people.

Somehow I couldn't find the words to say all that to him, but maybe he heard something in my voice. He agreed to come up to Tennessee, where all four of his children by our mama lived. He'd never seen my youngest daughter, Carrie April, or any of his great-grandchildren.

I didn't just send the plane for him. A few days later my wife, Judy, and I flew down to Leesburg, Florida, to pick him up.

As *Stutter One* swooped down to the runway for a perfect landing, I wondered again why my daddy and I had never managed to get through to each other. After all those years, could we do it now?

A few minutes later, when we stepped down from the plane, I saw my daddy and smiled in hope.

I didn't know this would be our last chance. I had no idea that he'd be dead before Christmas.

CHAPTER

2

Let's start from the beginning. We're Southerners on both sides of the family. My mother is a Rogers, born on top of Sand Mountain, near Albertville, Alabama. Her daddy's first name was Tugalo. Some say his mother was a full-blooded Cherokee from South Carolina, while others say she was only a quarter. I can't even begin to describe how beautiful she was. You'd have to see the photographs of that woman yourself. Her long black hair tumbled down almost to the backs of her knees. I remember those wonderful evenings when Mama would take down the family picture album and us kids would all gather around her. She'd point out who was who and give each one's name. "Now, this is your great-grandmother, Johanna Virginia," she'd say. "She could sing like a bird, I'm told." I think I may get my singing from that side of the family. The Cherokees were one of the smartest and biggest tribes— spread across five southern states. Their names are all over that area of the map today. There's a Mississippi town called Tougaloo and a Tugaloo River on the border of South Carolina and northwest Georgia. My mama says her daddy was named after that river.

Mama's granddaddy, Jim Rogers, lived in that part of Georgia. He loved to hunt and fish; Mama said he used to go on hunting trips up to South Carolina, where some of the Cherokees lived.

One year, while on one of those trips, he met this beautiful Indian girl who lived near the Tugaloo River. He just couldn't forget her. The next year he *had* to go back for her. He married her and they headed west. I don't exactly know why. Maybe he wasn't sure folks in Georgia would welcome his Indian wife. Or maybe, like a lot of other good men, he wanted to start fresh with a new place. Anyway, the new couple settled in Alabama, where they had nine kids. One of them was Tugalo Rogers, my granddaddy.

He was a very independent man. My mama has that same kind of strength. There's a family story about why Tugalo Rogers, his wife, Carrie, and their kids left Alabama in 1921.

As I was told, it happened one hot Wednesday night during prayer meeting when Tugalo's old hound dog came right into the Canaan Baptist Church. I guess he thought he needed some preaching, too. One of the deacons didn't favor that, so he kicked that dog right out the door.

Now, it's not smart to kick another man's dog, never was. Granddaddy was a God-fearing man, but he couldn't abide by that. Granddaddy got fighting mad and threatened to whip that deacon's ass right there in the church house. Well, there was a big fuss in that little town. A lawsuit followed, and that made Granddaddy even madder.

So the Tugalo Rogers family decided to pull up stakes and move down to Florida. They had seven children. One of them was Burma Magdalene Rogers, my mama. She was fourteen at the time they moved. She tells that the reason they left Alabama was to get away from the cold winters, and because they weren't doing too well in Alabama, anyway. My mama's a woman of principle and good manners. She doesn't mention any fight with a deacon. I sure wouldn't argue with Mama. I wouldn't dispute her recollection, even about a thing that happened sixty-seven years ago. I still laugh and shake my head when I think of that other version I heard when I was a boy. Meaning no disrespect, I kind of *prefer* it.

Going back to 1921, when Tugalo Rogers and his family arrived in Florida, they started truck farming, raising strawberries and various other crops. It was near Plant City, about twenty miles east of Tampa. The land was rich and the weather was right and they worked real hard. They did all right. Some years later Granddaddy Tugalo was killed in a shotgun accident.

As for his pretty daughter, Burma, she got married in 1924. She was eighteen and deeply in love. So was her husband. He was Lonnie Lee Tillis, a strong, handsome man who wasn't afraid of anything. He was my daddy.

I believe that the Tillis clan originally came from Ireland, but there are some differences of opinion on that. That's not uncommon in the Tillis family. We all have our own ideas on lots of things. One of the most independent thinkers is my brother, Richard, thirteen months older than I am, and just as stubborn. He's a great talker, with only a slight stutter. Richard is a real hard worker. Aside from the ten years he was on the road with me, he has spent most of his working life as a bread truck driver and salesman for several bakeries. That's why the boys in the band nicknamed him "Breadman."

They all liked his good sense of humor, something very precious on long tours. Richard reads a lot of books, especially on religion and history. He strongly believes that some of the earlier settlers in Ireland were one of the lost tribes of Israel, and that there also had to be some ancient Greeks who got there. He's convinced that the name Tillis is Greek.

One of the other Tillises who cares about family history is my sister, Mildred Imogene Tillis Burdeshaw. We call her Imogene. She's been digging into our ancestry and has been in touch with another Tillis family in Reno, Nevada, who have been looking into it for years. As far as they can tell, the first Tillis on any written American records was a white male, between twenty-one and sixty, named Willoby Tillis. North Carolina's census for 1784 through 1786 shows he was there with two white females under the age of twenty-one, probably daughters. Now, Willoby Tillis and the two females, who came from somewhere in Ireland, were Protestants. An author I know says that this suggests their people were originally Scottish.

There's also a family legend about royalty. That story ties us to a handmaiden of an English queen, maybe a hundred years before Willoby Tillis. She's supposed to have come over when William of Orange was the English king. According to Imogene, there's a possibility this handmaiden was sent off, real quietly, to the American colonies because the king got her pregnant. We don't have papers to prove it, but as Imogene says, kings did mess around with handmaidens. They took it as their right back then. That handmaiden's child is rumored to be a branch on our Tillis family tree.

Now, where does all that leave me? Part Cherokee and a bit Greek perhaps, some English and a lot Irish probably, and Scotch-Irish definitely. Maybe descended from a royal bastard (I've been called worse). Possibly with some connection to those ancient Greeks.

Ancestry is interesting to think about but I've learned there's much more to people than who or where they came from. I've learned that lesson traveling back and forth across America hundreds of times. The U.S.A. isn't just a great nation, it's a wonderful education.

Who says so? Lonnie Melvin Tillis; born August 8, 1932, in a rented house on 2700 Morgan Street, Tampa, Florida. It wasn't the high-rent district, but it was near the Henderson Bakery, where Daddy worked.

I think I arrived early, before the doctor did. Even then, I was in a hurry.

CHAPTER

3

Nowadays my band and I are on the road about 250 working days a year. Maybe my childhood helped prepare me for that. We moved around a lot when I was a child. In fact, thirty-three times, my mama said. After about eight months living in Tampa, Daddy moved us to Dover, Florida, a small farming community eighteen miles east of Tampa. Mama, Richard, Imogene, and I all moved in with Aunt Erma (Mama's sister) and Uncle Alvin. In those days, with the Depression raging, that was quite common among kinfolks. We lived with them for about three months while Daddy took a job cooking and baking on a dredge boat out of Port Tampa. Then he moved us to the Bussey house and we lived there a couple of years. Daddy seldom came home and the money he earned hardly ever went for rent or groceries. Mama really had a hard time trying to make ends meet. It was 1935. I was three years old.

That's the year I almost died. It wasn't the mumps, measles, or any of the usual diseases that kids get. I'd have to say it was something more exotic.

I caught malaria. That's a fever you hardly ever hear about anymore. It killed a lot of workers during the digging of the Panama Canal back in 1904. But in 1935 there wasn't much malaria left because most of the stagnant waters where mosquitoes bred had been drained.

But "most" wasn't good enough, because one of those little devils bit me.

Mama said the fever burned me up day and night. My temperature went up and down like a yo-yo. There weren't any wonder drugs to treat malaria then. It was quinine the doctors used, a bitter drug made from the bark of the cinchona tree (I looked that up in the dictionary). I was a very sick little boy. They thought I was going to die for sure. Mama still has a clipping from the *Tampa Tribune* that says I was not expected to live.

But Mama saved my life. She took care of me around the clock, and she followed the doctor's orders to the letter. All she gave me was quinine on ice, with maybe just a little sugar or Coca-Cola, and very little food. Friends and relatives argued with her on that. "You've got to give the boy something more to eat, Burma. You're gonna starve that little fellow to death," they insisted.

Mama stuck to the doctor's orders, even though she was scared. Just as I began to get a little bit better, I came down with something else. It was serious, too. Before the malaria had completely broken, I was hit with a bad case of colitis, an inflammation of the colon.

The days dragged on and I was practically a skeleton, with hardly any strength left. Mama was completely worn out herself, what with nursing me, doing everything she could to make me comfortable, and taking care of her other kids. She cooked, cleaned, worried, prayed, and hardly slept at all. But Mama didn't give up. She didn't even consider it.

Being not too far from the Gulf of Mexico, you could almost touch the humidity in that little house. That was back before many folks had air-conditioning. Mama did everything she could do to keep me cool. Then one day the fever broke.

But the malaria wasn't gone, they say it stays with you for life in a dormant state, and can sometimes come back on you, but it did start to fade. I quit sweating, and the sheets weren't wet anymore. I was wrung out and completely exhausted. Though the battle was over, the war wasn't won yet. Mama and I still had to fight the colitis that was burning my belly. At least now I had a little bit of an appetite and could eat to build up my strength. I had to.

Colitis could do terrible damage, the doctors warned. It could kill a little boy already half dead from malaria.

Day by day, and week by week, I started to get better. First ounces, then pounds began to come back. Finally, after what seemed like months and months, and against all odds and expectations, I was well.

At least I thought I was. But I wasn't the same little boy. The beating my body had taken, or maybe the scariness of the whole thing, had left its mark. Doctors say malaria always leaves you with something.

Now I stuttered very badly, and I didn't even know it. Maybe my folks didn't want to hurt my feelings. It could be they thought I'd grow out of it. It isn't that rare for small children to stutter for a few years. Usually it ends on its own. Even today nobody can say for sure why it comes and goes.

These days most experts think it's a psychological problem, caused by some kind of stress. How do you get into the head and heart of a little child to find out? They're still working on that.

Back in 1935, nobody in Tampa, at least that my folks knew of, was that familiar with stuttering. Today stress is recognized as the main reason for lots of problems, mental and physical. It wasn't then. There also weren't as many speech therapists and psychological counselors that parents could call on.

I sure don't blame my folks, though—or anyone else, for that matter. Laying your problems on others has never been my way. It just puts off figuring out what's wrong and trying to do something about it.

I don't know if there was even one speech therapist in Tampa in 1935—or all of Hillsborough County, for that matter. That could have been why seeing one never occurred to my folks. Years later when there were more speech clinics and therapists around, I went to some. But between the ages of three and six, my family just treated me like an ordinary, healthy kid and waited for the stuttering to fade away.

We moved to Tampa and lived there for a while, and then Daddy moved us back to Dover. That was when he took off for New Jersey. We lived in one of Tom Jaudon's rental houses. I really liked that place. It was on a big curve in the road. Tom was a real nice man and, we found out later, was sweet on Mama. He wanted to marry her, and Mama's sister said, "She ought to if Lonnie keeps on acting the way he does." But Mama loved Daddy and that was that. I never saw or heard of my mama ever looking at another man, even after she and Daddy had divorced.

I hated to move again. We had made friends with all the other kids in that neck of the woods. We played all day long, and, when Richard and Imogene were in school and I was alone, Uncle Gabe Jaudon would let me sit up on top of his mule and ride while he plowed his strawberry patch. But Daddy came back and bought a house in Plant City, Florida, six miles east of Dover. Mama said Daddy only made one payment on that house. It was 1938. I was six years old and it was time to start school.

It was the Woodrow Wilson Elementary School, and I had a first-grade teacher named Miss Clark. I'll never forget my first day of school at Woodrow Wilson. That's when I found out that I stuttered.

I didn't have any idea I talked different. My family was used to my way of speaking, so they didn't say much about it. But some of the kids at Woodrow Wilson did. I ran into a couple, maybe more than that, the first day of school. They teased me plenty about my "funny" way of talking. I was really scared. In fact, I was so scared I messed in my britches. That day seemed a year long. I remember Richard, who was starting the second grade, taking me home early.

I remember Mama wouldn't let me come in the house. She made me stand under the hand water pump in the backyard to clean that doo-doo off me. Mama really scolded me for that.

I was still puzzled by what the other kids had said. I was still wet from that pump when I asked Mama if I stuttered. "Yes, you do, Melvin," she said. I don't recall what else she told me that day. It was a long time ago. When I tell that story now, I usually laugh, maybe because I've come so far from that wet, scared kid with the choked-up throat. I didn't laugh then. I couldn't. That water was too ca-ca-cold.

Now I knew that I had a problem, but I didn't know I'd have to cope with it for the rest of my life. That might have scared me even more.

I don't recall when I first began singing, but it probably started at home. Mama loved music, and so did Richard and Imogene. She used to take us to church every Sunday and also to Wednesday night prayer meetings. There was singing there, lots of it. Nobody had ever said anything special about my voice, so I had no notion I could even carry a tune.

Well, Miss Clark was the first to let me know I could sing. She had me stand up and sing a solo in front of my first grade class, and later she started taking me around to other classes to sing for the older kids. One of them was my sister, Imogene, who was in the fifth grade. She loved her little brother, but she sure was embarrassed at my being the focus of attention. Imogene slid down in her seat to hide that first time. Of course she's proud of me now, and I feel the same about her.

I wasn't scared or tense whenever I sang. I didn't stutter at all. The kids and teachers noticed that, and they talked about it. People still do today. They wonder how somebody who struggles so hard to get out a single sentence could sing so easily. There are other professional entertainers who can sing with no trouble, but stutter when they speak. *Why* is a mystery to me. Maybe it's the Lord's way of evening things out.

It could have something to do with confidence. You learn all the words before you start to sing a song, so you know where you're going. And, of course, the rhythm helps, too.

Going back to confidence, mine sure was helped when I went around to those different classes each week to sing. I felt good for days, but I still stuttered when I spoke and I knew it.

I didn't try to talk too much that first year, only when I had to. I daydreamed a lot. Usually it was about the good times we had playing in the woods near the house we had rented from Tom Jaudon, and about riding Uncle Gabe's mule.

Like Mama said, Daddy didn't make but one payment on that house, then he just up and left us again. Well, the owners of that house made us move, and Mama found a three-room garage apartment that she rented from Fred Gant, a Baptist minister who had a little church at Cork, Florida. We didn't have to change schools, though. That was one good thing.

It was better for Mama. It sure wasn't much, but it was clean and we ate okay. Daddy was sending us a little money now and then. Uncle Wiley (Daddy's oldest brother) and Aunt Eula used to come and bring us magazines and things. Oh, how I loved to see them come. Mama would always let me sing for them.

Things weren't entirely right between my parents. So I would get away from that, into a world where there was no stuttering, arguing, or other problems.

I remember a puppet show coming to Woodrow Wilson

Elementary. Well, that was it! You could say it was my first brush with show business. Today kids can escape into the make-believe of the television set, but nobody had television then. I made my own little theater out of a cardboard box. My performers were made of paper. For actors, I cut out pictures of men and women from the *Sears and Roebuck Catalog*. I even cut out pictures of furniture for my play-like productions.

I was alone a lot, so I did little plays on my make-believe stage downstairs beneath that garage apartment. Most of the time I was the whole audience, except one time when Mrs. Smith, an elderly lady who lived next door, came to one of my productions. She said she was very impressed and gave me and my paper actors a standing ovation.

For many years the *Sears and Roebuck Catalog* meant a great deal to me. It was a book of dreams. There were so many things I saw that I yearned for, and quite a few items that Mama wanted, too. I'm not talking about luxuries or fancy stuff. While Sears catalogues today offer a huge variety, in the 1930s and 1940s it was mostly basic things. We couldn't afford many of them, but that book has never left my mind. Even now, when I'm able to buy most anything from the local stores, I still like to order from that book. I buy all kinds of things like baby chicks, ducks, geese, farrowing pens for sows, horse bridles and saddles, beehive equipment, and lots of other stuff. Being able to order anything I want from Sears gives me a wonderful feeling. And if Mama, who lives in her own house on the farm with us, wants to order from that magical book, that's even better.

So my pretend theater, the *Sears and Roebuck Catalog*, and the singing at school helped me through that first year of Woodrow Wilson Elementary. I was feeling pretty good until the last day. That's when I learned that the teacher who liked my singing so much was failing me.

The other kids were moving up to the second grade, and I wanted so much to be like them and with them. We were getting to be real friends. But I had to stay back in the first grade. I remember I cried and cried. It wasn't my letters or numbers; it wasn't bad behavior, either. Miss Clark told Mama she was separating me from my friends because of the stutter. She thought it sounded "babyish," and figured that if I repeated the first grade, I might learn to speak "right."

I didn't.

CHAPTER

No one made any big fuss about my doing the first grade over again 'cept me. This was a farming area of Florida in 1939, and folks didn't worry a great deal if a child had to repeat. Lots of parents hadn't had that much schooling themselves. Now, don't get me wrong, they cared about their kids, but they sure didn't expect them to become brain surgeons. So there wasn't much tension when I started the first grade over, meeting a whole different bunch of kids and trying to make new friends. They noticed how I talked, of course, but only a few bothered me with tricks. Mama recalls how a couple of neighbors—two boys, Marvin and Junior Prevatt—used to ask me to say *fertilizer*. I didn't realize what they were doing. "Fuh . . fuh . . . fuh . . . ," I struggled. I gave it my best shot but I couldn't get past the first syllable. They thought that was real funny, and I guess it was.

Miss Clark tried her best to encourage me. She took me around to the classes to sing again, the same as she had the year before. She praised my drawing, too. She especially complimented the way I colored a picture of Santa Claus, saying it was so good I should color a much bigger one. To please her, I tried to do something original. I wanted to do it better, as well as bigger.

Well, I gave that lady a Santa Claus in a green suit instead of the regular red one. She didn't admire my creativeness that much, but she let me know kind of gently.

Some of the boys were hard on me at first, but by the end of the year I'd made friends with them.

This time I was promoted to the second grade with the others. I wasn't talking any better, but I was moving ahead.

But then I changed schools. I had no notion how much I'd be doing that in the years ahead. Our family was moving around so much that I only took half the second grade at the elementary school in Dover. All that moving was a sign of trouble at home. Things were going badly between my parents. Later they got a whole lot worse.

A big part of the trouble, and a main reason we moved around a lot, was Daddy couldn't manage money. He worked hard and earned enough, but he just threw his money away. And he was stubborn about it, which didn't help. He wasn't a bad man, nor a stupid man, but he sure was contrary.

He wouldn't look back to learn, because he couldn't face up to his mistakes. He wouldn't look ahead to plan, either. He didn't have any training or experience in handling money. He'd only gone to school seven years, Mama told me.

To the day he died, he never got much better at controlling money. It was a mystery to him, something he couldn't get a hold on. He couldn't admit that, so he wouldn't even talk about it. He'd get real mad whenever Mama said to save part of each week's pay so there'd be money to pay the rent at the end of the month. There were weeks she had no money for groceries because his whole check had to cover the rent or a car payment. Her family helped us more than once. Sometimes we lived with them for months, when we couldn't afford our own place.

It wasn't just the money problem between them. Daddy wouldn't take Mama's advice on anything. He was the head of the family. He said so. He'd do everything his way, which meant the opposite of anything she said. He was determined not to let her "boss" him. Thinking back, I don't recall Mama as ever being bossy, but it must have seemed different to him. Daddy's brother, Uncle Wiley, wasn't a bit like that. Although he had less schooling than the others, only three years I'm told, he had the best business head of all the Tillis brothers. He was a good man and a good manager. He worked hard and saved his money.

Uncle Wiley had started a bakery of his own down in Pahokee, Florida. Pahokee's a Seminole Indian word. They say it means "grassy waters." It was about 175 miles south of Plant City, where we lived, and right on the southeastern shore of Lake Okeechobee. God, that lake is big—730 square miles. It's the largest in the state, and the second largest freshwater lake wholly within the boundaries of the United States. The town was very small, practically surrounded by sugarcane fields on three sides and the lake on the other. They grew green beans, sweet corn, bell peppers, and other vegetables there. Pahokee only had a few thousand people, and most of them were black. Even now, the town's only got about seven thousand people, if the season's good.

One day in 1940, when I was in the second grade, Uncle Wiley wrote Daddy a letter. It could have been he'd heard things weren't going that good with us and he wanted to help. For a lot of years both the Tillises and the Rogerses pitched in to help us, as kinfolk sometimes do. I think Uncle Wiley's business was growing, too, so he could use another skilled baker. Well, Uncle Wiley asked Daddy to come down there and help him out in the bakery.

We went pretty quick. Uncle Alvin helped moved us. So, a new place to live, new school, new teachers, and new kids to make friends with.

Pahokee was a nice town. We moved into one of "Poop"

Thomas's little duplex houses, if you could call it that. What it was was one big eight-room house, with the doors nailed together in the middle to make two four-room apartments. We made a lot of new friends. I recall David and Phoebe Ann Ramey, Napola Thomas, Roger Jaudon, and Frank (Jellyroll) Tillis. Roger and Frank were our cousins. There was also Sammy and Johanna McKinstry. Johanna was later to become my brother's wife.

Our new town was a great place for kids to grow up in. There was swimming and fishing in the lake, frogs to gig in the swamps, and all kinds of strange birds and animals. Daddy was doing fine at Uncle Wiley's bakery. They called it Tillis' Hometown Bakery. I worked there myself, after school, some years later. Daddy taught me how to bake and I got pretty good at it. I wouldn't say as good as Daddy, because that man could bake, decorate fancy cakes, and everything.

Well, I started at the new elementary school in Pahokee. I was still in the second grade, and for the first time I could remember, our family was all together. We were doing okay.

We weren't there for more than three months when I came home from school one day and found Mama crying. "What is it, Mama, what's wrong?" I asked.

"Well, it's your daddy, son. He's gone."

He'd run off again. That wasn't the first time he'd left us, and certainly not the last. I think he was a good man who wanted to do right, but he was restless during those years. I never did figure out why. None of the family did.

We didn't stay in Pahokee long after he left us. Mama had a little money saved from working at the bakery, so she hired one of the bread truck drivers, Ruben Keller, to move us. He trucked our furniture back north to Grandmother Rogers's house in Dover, and for the second time that year I was back in Dover Elementary, where I finally finished the second grade.

It was December 1940. Mama found us a little house to

rent on Lee Street, in South Plant City, and some of our neighbors were W. L. and Bobby Woods, Edward and Letty Wilson, and Glen Crowley. We had great times playing on the railroad tracks that ran parallel to our neighborhood. We'd make slides out of old roofing tin and slide down a mountain of sawdust created by the local sawmill. We'd have marble tournaments, and Mama would let us go to the picture show on Saturdays, when she had the money. Eight miles away was a little country school at Turkey Creek where on April 2, 1941, I started the third grade. We had to ride the school bus every day. Mama got a job at the canning plant, stemming strawberries. We kids were working in the strawberries, too, but only in the picking season, and then only if Mama knew the people we'd be picking for. Those were "strawberry schools" in Turkey Creek and Dover. They held classes in the summer, so the kids could help pick berries in the winter months when they were in season. In a farming area you don't argue with the seasons. You can't.

We didn't mind working in the strawberries. It was a lot of fun. We got paid for whatever we could pick. Usually it was two to three cents a quart, and there was pride in earning money to help Mama.

Those "strawberry schools" changed to normal school months right after World War II. Now those kids have the same school year as those in the rest of the country. Adult migrant workers, usually from Mexico, do most of the picking today.

I recommend some field labor for children. I believe that having to work some when I was a kid didn't hurt me one bit. I think it helped make me a better person today. I mean, better than folks who don't know the value of a dollar. Picking those strawberries on a cold winter morning (yes, it does get cold in Florida) sure taught me that a nickel was a nickel and some other realities of life. It's worth knowing that berries grow on bushes, but dollars don't grow on trees.

I've seen singers who started poor and then made a lot of money—big names in country music—just squander it. Like my father, who never got near rich, they never learned how to handle it. It was years before I earned any good money, and when I did, I tried to pattern myself after guys like Mr. Eddy Arnold, one of country music's true stars. He's got wealth and talent and he lives well, but he doesn't abide waste. Even back when I was a kid of ten, picking strawberries, I never could. Today it's a guitar that I'm picking, and the wages are better, but the principle's the same. I tried to spell it out as best I could to my five kids. I think they listened and understood. I sure hope so.

CHAPTER

5

I passed the third grade at Turkey Creek in December, and the last day of school I brought home a note from my teacher that said the county was going to discontinue busing children from Plant City to Turkey Creek and we would have to go to our neighborhood schools. So after the Christmas holidays, Mama enrolled Richard and me into Burney Elementary, and Imogene went to Mary L. Tomlin Junior High. We had hardly any vacation at all.

My teacher was Miss Bowman. She was real pretty. I had my first crush on that lady. I was three and a half months behind the other kids, but Miss Bowman helped me catch up.

We were still living on Lee Street and Daddy was sending us postcards from Puerto Rico. That's where he went when he left us in Pahokee. Now he had a job as a chef and baker on another dredge boat. The Navy was building bases and ports in lots of places and that dredge was part of it. He'd send us a little money now and then, and I remember him sending us two huge straw *siesta* hats. Richard and I wore them to school one day. We were so proud of those big hats. We kept them around for years. Penny postcards weren't much comfort to Mama or to us, either, but at least we knew that Daddy was all right.

Music was our biggest comfort. I remember the evenings that we'd all sit on the front porch (back then, most everybody had front porches) and sing and sing. We'd sing until after dark and the mosquitoes got too bad, then Mama made us go in.

We're Southern Baptists, and Mama would take us to church as often as she could, especially if there was one close enough by where we could walk. Sometimes Uncle J.T. (Mama's only brother, who had a Model A Ford) would come and take us out to his church, the First Baptist Church in Dover, Florida. It's the largest rural Baptist church in America today.

I remember one time some folks came and set up a big tent in a vacant field near our house on Lee Street. Mama said they were going to have an old-fashioned two-week revival. She said they were Pentecostal or Holiness, but it was okay for us to go. She took us the first night. It was so exciting in that tent. They had banjos and guitars and fiddles and everything. Boy, I really loved that. I'm not knocking the southern Baptist music, but this was *something else*. You'd have to say it was a lot more . . . well, theatrical—no, dramatic. Anyway, we enjoyed it so much, she took us back for the prayer meeting the next night. I'll never forget that. I couldn't.

In the middle of the service two men came out dressed up in red suits just like the Devil. I'd heard about the Devil, though I didn't know there were two of them, but here they were. Those Devils seemed to be coming right after Richard and me. That scared us half to death. We ran out of that tent as fast as we could run and I was halfway home before Mama caught up with me.

"Where's Richard?" she said.

"He ran off and left me, Mama," I said.

He was waiting when we got to the house. Richard always could outrun me. Mama finally convinced us that it was only part of their program that night, and those Devils weren't real. Now, we didn't doubt our mama, but we didn't go back to that tent for a few days, either.

I thought those fiddles and guitars at the revival meeting were the prettiest things I'd ever seen in my life. They were shiny mahogany with sunbursts on them.

Mama was working at the canning plant, stemming strawberries, and when the berries ran out, they'd start shelling and canning black-eyed peas. Big truckloads of black-eyed peas were coming in from all over the Little Sandy Farms of Hillsborough County. The plant was short-handed because America was gearing up for war and lots of the men who worked there were being drafted. So the people in charge told the workers that were left to bring in their families, kids and all, to shell those peas for canning. It was the patriotic thing to do, and it paid some, too.

Mama took Richard, Imogene, and me up to that big building that the cannery had in Plant City. That old metal warehouse was really hot. Forty or fifty families came every day to sweat and shell peas. You had bushel hampers or baskets and you'd get paid according to how many peas you could shell. Each family was a team. We'd usually earn $3 or $4 a day. They also gave us plenty of free black-eyed peas to take home.

But there was something more than peas in that warehouse. It was music—hillbilly music, as it was called back then. I was ten years old and I'd hardly heard any music like that before. There were families all around us singing hillbilly songs and some gospel. Others joined in, and I learned the words, too. The plant owners had loudspeakers installed and played us the latest *records* of the times. Records were something else I was not familiar with—round 78 rpm celluloid discs. Bill Monroe, Eddy Arnold, and the Carter Family. What a wonderful discovery!

Their thinking, I suppose, was to make the job a little less boring. Using music to ease the burden has always been the way in the South. It was in that steaming warehouse that I first heard them, the records of Bob Wills, the King of Western Swing. I became a fan immediately. Kids at school didn't care for much country music back then. That "hillbilly stuff" wasn't worth bothering with. It wasn't on the radio much or in the movies.

The newspapers and magazines hardly ever mentioned country artists. Fact is, to 95 percent of the press, they didn't rate as artists at all. Who could take farmers' sons and daughters in overalls seriously? Who wanted to listen to cowhands in big strange-looking hats singing their "hayseed" songs?

So country talents had trouble getting record deals, and when they did, it was most always with small companies. Nobody was thinking of making any movies called *Nashville* in 1942. Nashville, now famous as a music center around the world, was then just another medium-sized southern city of no great importance. It didn't have any music activity, such as recording studios and publishing companies, and had just one radio station that cared about country music. WSM was broadcasting the Grand Ole Opry on Saturday nights, with strong clear channel signals that could be heard in many states, like a beacon in the darkness. But the big New York, Chicago, and Hollywood executives who ran show business didn't see that light for years.

I'd heard some country music from Mama's brothers and sisters. But it wasn't until those days in that warehouse, with Bob Wills and his fiddles making magic, that I got excited about it. I tried to tell my friends about my new discovery. Maybe it was my poor talking, or it could have been that the Sinatra, Tommy Dorsey, and Glenn Miller sounds were so popular no one cared about any other kind of music. My friends thought it was hick-y to like country, and they wouldn't listen to it.

Well, the summer ended, the pea crop was canned, and it was late in the year. I was missing Daddy. Mama said he was still working in the Islands at a place I could hardly pronounce. The other kids had their daddies at home. Why didn't I? I thought about that thirty years later when I was on the road so much, touring to earn money for my family. I'm still out on the road a lot and I still think about that.

I'm a friend of Willie Nelson's, and his song about being out on the road's a good one. But the road isn't good for families. Every touring musician can tell you that. It's bad if a father's away two-thirds of the year when his kids are growing up. And it's usually rough on a marriage. Plenty of times it's worse than rough. It can be fatal.

Well, Daddy did send us postcards occasionally. Some of them had real pretty photos. Later on, I co-wrote a song about that. Most songwriters draw a lot on their own experiences and feelings. Those feelings I had about him being so far away and sending those postcards stayed with me for a long time. The words of that song are still in my head:

> They say I'm like my daddy,
> Always on the roam,
> I know he loved my mama
> But he just couldn't stay at home.
> I vowed to not be like him,
> But somewhere I went wrong
> 'Cause I'm a thousand miles from nowhere
> And the girl I love's at home.
>
> One of these days
> I'm gonna quit my wandering,
> One of these days
> I'll wander back to you.
>
> My sweetheart writes me letters,
> They find me now and then,
> And I send her funny postcards
> To show her where I've been.
> She always writes "I love you"
> Altho' we're far apart,
> But a funny penny postcard
> Can't say what's in my heart.

One of these days
I'm gonna quit my wandering,
One of these days
*I'll wander back to you.**

Danny Dill, Fred Burch, and I wrote that song in 1963, and I'm still on the road. I've promised my wife, Judy, and my mama that I'll cut down on my touring around the country. If not next year, the year after.

*"I'll Wander Back to You" copyright © 1963 by Cedarwood Publishing Company (A Division of Musiplex, Inc.).

CHAPTER

Right after the first of the year, we moved from Lee Street one block over to Merrik Street. There were a few fruit trees and a chicken pen, so Mama could have her some chickens. She loved bantams. There was also a hand pump and an outhouse. We used kerosene lamps in the house at night. People were still talking about the Japanese bombing Pearl Harbor. It was 1942 and the whole world was at war, World War II.

I recall everybody was really patriotic. We had victory gardens at home, and victory drives at school. We brought tinfoil from chewing gum wrappers and empty cigarette packs to school, and rolled it into big balls. We collected copper wire, rags, paper, scrap iron, old aluminum pots and pans, and all kinds of things that could be recycled to help fight the war against Hitler and Tojo. It was a real good feeling to know that, in a small way, we helped some.

One day out of the clear blue sky Daddy came home. I remember I was out sweeping the yard with a sagebrush broom. We didn't have much grass in our yard, if any. It was mostly sand and sandspurs. A taxicab pulled up and this big tanned man got out. I always thought that Daddy

looked a lot like John Wayne, and he did. I was in a pair of
old anvil overalls, the kind with the galluses, no shirt, and
bare feet. I was just about as dirty as I could be that
afternoon. Boy, I dropped that broom and tore off a-
running. I jumped right up into his arms and he hugged me
and kissed me. We went inside. Mama was so glad, and so
were my sister and brother. He'd brought us some little
gifts from Puerto Rico. Then he told us he'd gotten a job at
the shipyards in Tampa, building wartime ships.

Our daddy had come home. He started to work at the
shipyards as a riveter, and for a while everything was
okay. But I didn't know a lot about liquor and what it can
do to a man. It wasn't long before I found out. Late one
payday afternoon he came home drunk. I saw him before he
got to the house. I was out in the yard playing kick-the-can
with Edward Wilson. Daddy was staggering, falling down,
and making noises. I don't know how he ever found his way
home. Speaking of home, Edward *headed* for his. I was
really embarrassed and scared so bad I ran out behind the
house and climbed up in the tallest grapefruit tree in the
backyard. I'd never seen anyone acting like that. Was he
having a fit or something? Would he hurt us?

I was really shaking the leaves on that grapefruit tree, I
was so scared, and I didn't know who to call for help. My
throat was choked up and my heart was pounding. Well, I
stayed up in that tree 'til after dark, hoping my daddy
wouldn't miss me. I didn't come down until I knew he'd
fallen asleep. I hoped that what had happened was something rare, and wouldn't happen again. But it did. It became a regular ordeal.

Whenever it was payday, we all knew he'd come home
drunk, if he came home at all. Some times were worse than
others. Mama used to tell us that it wasn't so bad when all
he'd had to drink was beer, but she said, "He just can't
handle that cheap white port wine." He really got the devil
in him when he drank that.

Generally he only got drunk on payday. He'd work hard

the rest of the week and there were no complaints about his work. He could do almost anything, but that man just couldn't control whatever was burning and churning inside of him. He was a generous man with a big heart, but he didn't think family. He meant us no harm, but we paid the price.

Sometimes on payday he wouldn't come home at all. We'd worry ourselves almost to death when he didn't come home, and then worry about what he'd do when he got there. He'd go out drinking with some of the shipyard workers. I think some girls went, too. Women were always after that big, good-looking man. He didn't exactly fight them off, either. We didn't know about his weakness in that area for some time. Well, I didn't anyway.

We had a pretty good Christmas that year. Everything was jolly. The family got a Majestic radio. We'd listen to all the shows that came on in the evenings, like "Henry Aldridge," "The Great Gildersleeve," "Corliss Archer," and "Amos 'n' Andy." Mama liked "December Bride," but Richard and I didn't care too much for that one. It was a radio soap opera.

Saturday night was my night. At least I thought it was. I'd stay up and listen to the "Grand Ole Opry" until it went off the air at midnight. I remember I'd run out to the hand pump during those Prince Albert commercials and fill my little tin cup full of water and dab it on my eyes whenever I'd start to nod off to sleep.

I didn't want to miss a thing, especially Jamup and Honey, a blackface comedy team. I liked Pee Wee King and the Golden West Cowboys, Eddy Arnold, Roy Acuff, Bill Monroe, the Fruitjar Drinkers, and Clyde Moody. I loved them all and I loved that battery radio.

Then Uncle Wiley wrote Daddy and asked him to come back to the bakery in Pahokee. None of us said anything, but we all wondered how long we would stay this time.

Daddy rented a truck and we packed up everything we owned except Mama's chickens. Richard and I tried to catch them, but they all flew up into the grapefruit trees. Daddy said, "The hell with them chickens, Melvin, run next door and tell Old Man Perkins he can have your mama's bantams." Well, I ran over and tried to tell him he could have the chickens, but nothing would come out. Daddy, impatient as always, was hollering, "Let's go! Let's go!" So I ran back. The truck was all loaded except for me and Richard. He put us in the back end and then tied a bed-spring to it to keep us from falling out. That's how we rode for more than five hours down to Pahokee, looking out the back end through those springs, singing songs, and wondering if Old Man Perkins would ever find out that he was eleven chickens richer.

So we started all over again. Soon we had a baby sister, a pretty little curly-headed girl named Linda Gay. We all loved her so much, especially Daddy. Richard and I didn't have any experience with baby sisters, though. We treated her like a boy for a while.

One day Mama was out behind the house washing clothes. She had Linda in her baby carriage real close by so she could keep an eye on her. I asked her several times if I could push the baby up and down the alley in front of the house. I promised her I would go real slow. Finally she said, "Yes, you can, Melvin, but be careful." I pushed her back and forth a few times, and then Linda fell asleep. Well, that got boring real fast, so I speeded up a little bit, then a little bit more. Finally, Mama said she looked up and saw that baby carriage and me go by the house as fast as I could run. The left front wheel came off. Mama screamed, Linda went a-flying through the air and landed on top of a cherry hedge. She never even woke up. That was one of the first whippings Daddy gave me that I would really appreciate.

Mama says when Linda was just four years old, she caught us showing her how to shoot tin cans with a .22 rifle. She wasn't a bad shot, either. Then a few years after that, we had our little sister in boxing gloves, "fighting" Ronnie

Crosby, a boy her same age. She whipped him, then Mama whipped us. She laid the law down after that and we stopped doing those things, permanently.

During the first year we were back in Pahokee, I was in the fifth grade and having some problems at school. It wasn't that I couldn't learn or remember, it was my talking. I had questions, and sometimes answers, that I couldn't get out of my mouth. It got more and more frustrating. I didn't complain, and I guess I didn't explain, either. I wasn't looking for pity. I hadn't figured out yet the difference between pity and sympathy. Well, it probably wouldn't have mattered. I wanted to do it on my own. I was a boy in south-central Florida, just as strong and healthy as the others in every way but one. I was a good athlete, not bad at fishing, and dead set to learn how to swim in that great big lake nearby.

But I was still blocked and trapped, a prisoner of my thoughts and choking throat. When it got too hard for one angry boy to handle, I'd go up on the levee that surrounds Lake Okeechobee, alone. I'd make sure nobody was near and then I'd practice talking. I'd talk to the lake. Boys weren't supposed to cry. That was a sign of weakness and I didn't see myself as weak, but I cried a lot inside.

I was changing in many ways, starting the trip from child to adult. Once a stout little boy, I was beginning to shoot up tall and skinny. Even my voice was turning different, deeper. Since the age of four, people had been telling us not to worry because the stuttering would go away by itself. Lord only knows the remedies that people have told me and my folks about over the years. One that I will never forget: "You catch young Melvin walking alone at night on some dark sidewalk (he'll already be scared), then you jump out of the bushes and hit him right in the face with a deceased, wet squirrel." I think my answer to that was, "Does the squirrel have to be w-w-w-w-wet?"

But the stutter hadn't gone away. How long would I have to wait? The answer came to me slowly. I didn't have to wait. Whatever my problem was, I could go on living. I could move ahead in other things. I knew that I had the energy. From my early boyhood days in central Florida, I'd never been one to sit still. I had always been a very active person, always doing.

There was one way I was like my daddy. I was a real hard worker. I was always at something, even before I started to school. Since we didn't have the money but for an occasional toy, I made my own toys and forms of play. I'd use whatever I could find. Mama used to give me her empty thread spools and I'd cut notches in the ends to get some traction. Then I'd put a rubber band through the center of the spool, attach it to Diamond matchsticks on each end, with one match longer than the other, and wind it up and let 'er go. That was my tractor. It would crawl until the rubber band had unwound. We'd make Tom-Walkers or stilts and walk all over the place. Standing ten feet tall, we could pick the best hard-to-get-to oranges. I'd build sand castles in our yard. I was really good at that. Richard used to sit back and watch me work building sand castles. Then he'd say, "Mehin, build me one, just like yours." I didn't mind. It was a chance to show what I could do, and doing has always been important to me.

I stopped going out, alone, to the levee to talk to the lake. It never said anything back, anyway. I quit crying inside, at least for a while.

I got me a job at Julian Chandler's drugstore along about that time, and I became a soda jerk. I learned to make all the good sundaes that the school kids loved. Cherry smashes, ammonia Cokes, banana splits, sodas—you name it, I could make it. I got to meet everybody in town that way, including most of the black folks. I loved to read all the new magazines that came in once a month, like *Country Song Roundup*. They published the latest hit song lyrics and you could read about your favorite country music stars. *Billboard*, another favorite of mine, still is considered the bible of the music entertainment business.

I worked at the drugstore on weekends and after school. I kept that job for about two and a half years, and then one summer (the only way you knew it was summer in Pahokee was when they let us out of school in June and told us not to come back until September) the Boy Scouts were all going to Fish Eating Creek, about forty miles from Pahokee, to camp out for a whole week. I wanted to go with my buddies real bad, so I asked Julian if he cared if I went, and he said, "No, go ahead." But I don't think he wanted me to leave because when I came back, R. D. Hickman had my job. For a while I felt bad about losing that job, but I never did hold it against Julian or R.D. We were still buddies. Julian Chandler died a few years after that. I still see Merdis, his widow, out in California from time to time. We still talk about those days.

With my soda jerk days over, I found other ways to make money. I delivered the *Miami Daily News* for a while. Then I dug up and sold earthworms to the black folks in town. I had my regular customers who bought fishing worms from me every week. I even had me a baby-sitting service. I did all the sitting, though, because I couldn't get Richard to pay me my commission on the jobs I got him, so I quit using him. I worked for Orin Bacon at Pahokee's only hardware store for a while. Then Danny Hitchcock and I made some real good money selling parched peanuts at all the Pahokee home football games. We'd buy the peanuts on credit from Danny's father's grocery store. They came in three-hundred-pound bags. We'd drag that bag of peanuts to the bakery and my daddy would parch them in the bread oven. Danny and I were making a killing, until some of the school authorities noticed and made us quit. The school sold peanuts after that, but not with as much pride.

Since my childhood productions of little plays in that garage, I'd always been fascinated by theatrical things. Many years later, when they were doing the junior play at Pahokee High School, I made up my mind I'd be part of it. Nothing was going to stop me. I went to the teacher who

was producing and directing the play, and told her I
wanted a part in *Here Comes Charlie*. She was surprised
and somewhat uneasy. She didn't want to hurt my feelings.
She tried to be tactful. "I'm sure you'd be good, Melvin,"
she said, "but . . . uh . . . you see . . . the speaking parts
might . . . well, be difficult for you."

I thought about that for a few seconds. I was disappointed, yes, but I could understand. Still, I wasn't about
to quit. "Then . . . then . . . let me puh . . . puh . . . pull the
curtain," I answered. "I'll be the best curtain puller you
ever had."

She smiled, and then she nodded. She could understand,
too.

So I was part of the play. I'd won. That stutterin' didn't
keep me out—no sir! I was with Richard and the others for
all the rehearsals, and when people applauded at the end of
the show, I felt I'd earned my piece of that. The teacher
even introduced me.

Sometimes I remember that experience when I'm onstage or working in a movie or television production. Beginnings are something that stars, executives, and others
shouldn't lose track of, no matter how important they become. The curtain pullers of the world count, too. There's
no show without them. They're doing their share, and
they're entitled to respect like everyone else.

CHAPTER

7

I'm getting a little ahead of myself, so let's go back and pick up here.

As things got better for me that second year in Pahokee, another change was improving life for the whole family. Daddy wasn't drinking much anymore. What turned him away from that, he never said. He wasn't a great talker about his inner feelings, and we didn't want to stir him up by asking. He was still a stubborn man with a short fuse and, I suppose, trying to be a good father.

It was 1945 now and World War II was over. Richard and I celebrated by smoking a cigar that made us plenty sick. Less than a year after the Japanese surrendered, another guy who was different came to Pahokee. He just showed up one day. He was short, and he looked like the character called Louie in the Dead End Kids movies. He didn't speak English too well, and he had an East European accent a foot thick. Maybe a foot and a half.

Some say he was a survivor of those Nazi death camps. He'd come with his wife, to start a new life in the United States. How in the Good Lord's name he ever found the little town of Pahokee, Florida, still beats me. Nothing beat him, though. He wouldn't let it. Maybe that's why I liked him so.

He'd rented a little old store next door to the poolroom and started a small business. We boys ran into him the day he was unloading some boxes to carry into that little store. Since it was obvious one guy couldn't do all that hauling, we pitched in to help. When he started to open the cartons inside, we got a look at what he hoped to sell. It was all kinds of war surplus stuff.

You can imagine what the sight of that army and navy gear did to us teenage boys. We got all excited and began to hold up the different things, trying on helmets and ammo belts, and then we started sword fighting with bayonets. For a minute or two he got flustered. "Boys! Boys!" he pleaded.

Then we told him we'd help him put the stuff on the shelves. He saw we weren't trying to trouble him, so he started to give us instructions.

"All right, boys, over there with the shirts, please, the canteens and mess kits by the boots, and you can put the forks and spoons by the fatigues." We didn't know his name. He'd said it, but it was so foreign to our ears that we couldn't make it out.

Paul Hawkins said, "Since this is army stuff, let's call him Sarge." Why not?

"Sure, Sarge," one of us hollered.

"Right away, Sarge," another sang out.

You know, that name stuck. He liked it himself. So the next day he put up a sign outside his store, and from then on, that place was "Sarge's Army and Navy Store." Everybody called him Sarge after that. It was a lot easier for people in Pahokee to say than his real name.

He was an honest, hard-working person, and so was his wife. They wanted so much to make it in America . . . and to become part of our little town. They weren't looking for favors—just a chance. Folks in Pahokee got to wandering into that little store, and liked what they found. Business grew and kept getting bigger. In a while, Sarge and his wife had to expand their quarters. They built a much bigger store a few years later, and they worked hard outside their store, too. They were going to be Americans, full members of our town. Sarge wanted to know everything, so he could be part of it. Well, in Pahokee football was one of the few things that involved the whole community. Everybody rooted, loud and proud, for the Pahokee High School Blue Devils. Sarge came to every game, learned the cheers, and yelled for the home team. This new place was his home, but for the first few games, I doubt if he knew a football from a cow turd. That didn't last long, and he became a real fan.

He also became a friend. He didn't forget the boys who'd helped him unload that first day in town. When my brother and later I played football, he rooted for us louder than almost anybody. And when Richard and I graduated from high school, Sarge and his wife came to the ceremony with gifts for us.

I don't recall that man's proper name. He was always Sarge to us. We lost touch when I went into the Air Force. A few years ago he sold the business and retired. I heard he was living near West Palm Beach. I hope he and Mrs. Sarge are well. They earned it.

I'm glad that man and his wife came to Pahokee when they did. They proved what Mama had been telling me. Mama always believed that people could overcome obstacles . . . that I could do anything. Just as important, she let me know it.

"You can do whatever you want, son, if you work hard enough, pray hard enough, and if you keep trying," she told me at least a thousand times.

Mama had some of her own ideas on what I could or should do. She wanted me to play the violin. It didn't sound like a bad idea, but I wasn't sure. I was still a great admirer of Bob Wills and the great sounds of his fiddles. He always had fiddlers—good ones. The thing was, I wasn't exactly confident I could get the hang of that instrument and I wasn't entirely ready to give up even a few hours playing with my pals. My heart was in football and fishing at thirteen—not Beethoven.

But Mama talked me into it. My Aunt Eula, Jellyroll's mama, bought me a fiddle in West Palm Beach and I took lessons on it from Mrs. Osteen for two years. Mama says the squeaky sounds I scratched out on that fiddle made everybody real nervous. Even the neighbors complained. All I ever learned to play right was "Hot Cross Buns" and "Three Blind Mice."

The other kids—my buddies—would all make fun of me. I'd be in the house, going over the scales, and I'd look out the window and see them laughing their asses off at me. It was really embarrassing. Then one day, while walking home from one of those dreaded weekly fiddle lessons, I saw Paul Hawkins and Joe Kent Carr coming up the sidewalk on their bicycles. I knew I was in for a ribbing if they saw me with that fiddle case. So I jumped into the nearest cherry hedge and waited until they passed by.

I guess I didn't have what it took to be a fiddle player. Mama suspected that, too, and finally let me quit. I still love the fiddle, but it wasn't my instrument. That was one thing I definitely learned, and so did the neighbors. The other, which I didn't see until later, was that Mama was right. I could do anything I wanted. But I do poorly at things I don't really want, the things I'm talked into. If I'm not convinced or enthusiastic, it usually doesn't work out. Now, I'm not boasting about that, it's just the way I am.

I was still interested in music. It was just a question of finding the right instrument. After the fiddle lessons in junior high, I moved up to high school and heard they needed a drummer for the band. I'm talking about the marching band that played at all the Pahokee football games.

"I'll do it," I said, and I did.

To tell the truth, I had two reasons. One was I liked the

idea of marching with the others and playing music, and the other was you'd get out of a study hall or two if you went to band practice. I was never too fond of study halls or homework, either. Mama used to ask me why Richard and Imogene did homework and I didn't. "Well, I pay close attention in class and remember it so I don't have to," I'd answer.

Mama will tell you I spoke the truth about my memory. It's one of my stronger qualities. Of course, time does play tricks and maybe my memory was better then than it is now. More than once in the past couple of years I've asked my wife, Judy, to cook up something the way Mama used to, and Mama says she never cooked that dish. One of us has got to be remembering wrong.

There's no dispute about my drumming, though. I became a pretty good marching drummer, a snare drummer. I played two years in the band. Seeing all those football games stirred me up to try out for the team. I knew I wasn't as heavy as most, but I just had to play football. The second year that I was in the band was when I began.

Maybe it sounds strange, but I was doing both. On the same night and in the same game.

It was my junior year. I'd play the drum and march with the band up through the first half of the game. And then before the second half started, I'd go inside to the locker room and suit up in my football uniform. I played end that first year, mostly as a substitute. I wasn't on the A team— the first team—yet.

But one day I got mad at the other drummer during band practice. He was a big guy, a lot bigger than me, and obviously out for trouble that day. He kept hitting me with his drum stick and changing the cadence as we marched along. I got tired of that real fast. I took off my drum and, with the strap, put a little red in that bully's fat ass. But I gave him what he was asking for.

Then along came R. O. Lampe (Fess), the band director, and he gave my ass a little color, too. I didn't think that was fair. The big guy had started the whole thing. "Well, that's it, I quit," I said, and I played football full time from then on—the rest of the season. The next year I did pretty good—made first-team right halfback. I was Number 23.

I never did play drums again, but I still felt the need to make music.

My brother had bought a guitar from Sears and Roebuck, and he wouldn't let me touch it. He messed with it for a few weeks, but he never could get anything out of it. As a matter of fact, he couldn't even tune it. He knew that I wanted to get my hands on it real bad, so he had this good idea. One day he offered to sell it to me. "Mebin," he said, "you can have it for twenty-five dollars." To this day, he's never been able to say my name right.

"You've got a deal," I told him about one second later. And brother, I didn't stutter, either.

I told Uncle Wiley about our deal, and he gave me a job helping Otis Allen on the bread truck. I worked weekday mornings and all day Saturday. I usually would have to get up around 3:30 A.M., be at the bakery by 4:00, have the truck loaded by 5:00, and be in Belle Glade nine miles away by 5:30. We'd deliver the bakery products that had been ordered the day before, and by 7:30 Otis would let me out on the road to Pahokee, and I'd hitchhike back home, bathe, eat, and be in school by the time the bell rang at 8:30. My little sister said a lot of times I'd pass her, running a hundred miles an hour. That job almost killed me, but I raised the money and bought that Silvertone guitar from Richard. I didn't know how to tune it, either, but there were several people in Pahokee that could—Jackie Sullivan, Thomas Elliot, Mr. Snyder, Sheldon Upthegrove, and his mama. I learned a little from all those nice folks.

It wasn't long before I was playing just about anything I could sing. I never had any lessons or anything. With the help I'd gotten from the others, I basically taught myself, as most country musicians do. I enjoyed every minute of it.

I learned how to play all kinds of songs. Some were the

songs the big stars, like Sinatra, were recording—the records I heard on the radio. Others were those country songs I'd learned in the canning plant when we were shelling peas. And I'd picked up a few other country songs here and there.

After a while I could handle that ole Silvertone guitar pretty well, and my buddies said so. Kids at school began to invite me to parties so I could sing and play my guitar. Soon I was being asked to two or three parties a month, grown-ups heard about me. I was invited to perform at the Lions Club and the local Women's Club, where they all applauded. I was getting all kinds of compliments, which certainly helped a stutterin' boy's confidence.

It was only a small town and I wasn't getting paid or anything.

But it was a beginning.

CHAPTER

Those were good years. Pahokee was a wonderful place to be young. You remember those famous books Mark Twain wrote about Tom Sawyer and Huckleberry Finn? Their adventures on the Mississippi? At times, I think of how Tom and Huck must have felt. South-central Florida was still mostly open and hardly developed, with plenty of woods and streams and a few farms. There was hunting and fishing and lots of places for kids to get out on their own. That great big lake was our Mississippi.

We didn't have the steamboats and barges Twain wrote about. But Okeechobee's wide waters were bursting with all kinds of fish, snakes, alligators, otters, and there were many different birds, like egrets, herons, Florida kites, turkey, ducks, coots, and many other creatures.

Okeechobee Lake was where my brother and I learned to swim. A boy never forgets that experience—the first time he manages to stay afloat and move in control of his direction. That's an important day in a kid's life. It was a painful one for Mel and Richard Tillis, though. But you pay a price for most everything worthwhile, so we didn't mind.

Mama had told us not to go into the lake. Besides the chance of drowning, she said we could get fungus in our ears, and Lord knows we didn't need any more doctor's bills. We didn't live too far from the shore, and she realized her boys were hungry to get into that cool water. I knew in my head she was only trying to protect us. Maybe there are boys today—somewhere on this planet—who live in a tropical place and obey their mother's orders to stay out of the lake. I doubt it, though, because there was a real shortage of such kids in central Florida in the late 1940s.

One day Richard and I made our way to the shore of Lake Okeechobee and in we went. Naked as the day we came into the world, we thrashed and splashed around, kicked and swallowed muddy water, got strangled a few times, whooped and hollered and laughed and had a glorious time. Oh, yes, we figured out how to swim—in a primitive way, sort of like a dog. We called it dog paddling.

This was one of the few times that either Richard or I went against Mama's instructions. We weren't boys who got into much trouble at home or at school. Oh, there was that time Richard and a buddy of his tossed some dead fish up onto the high-school roof and the janitor went half crazy trying to find what was stinking so bad. But in general, Richard and I were what most parents would call "good" boys.

Now, my mama's always had a ton of common sense. She was, and still is, full of what city folks call street smarts. She's got sharp eyes and she never was anyone's fool. No, not nearly. When we got home that day, she asked us whether we'd been in the lake.

We tried to hide the fact that we had, but the truth was our hair was still wet, our eyes were blood-red, and our skin had wrinkled so much that we looked like walking prunes. Mama could see the truth. She told Daddy, and he whipped both of our asses with an Australian pine switch about a half-inch thick. He whipped us twice, once for disobeying Mama and another for lying. Well, we didn't go back into the lake, at least not until the swelling went down. But now we were free to swim because we'd learned how.

My brother likes to remind me about the time we acted up in front of our older sister's date—using some bad language. I knew that we'd surely get it from Mama for those words, so before Imogene's date left, I hurried and put on three or four pair of pants. They were supposed to cushion the impact of that belt. Mama noticed that I had gained weight. It only took her ten seconds to figure out I had lots of extra clothes on—but she wasn't sure of the reason.

"Melvin, why are you all dressed up like that?" she asked.

"Because I'm freezing to death," I answered with as straight a face as I could muster.

I'm afraid she didn't buy that. It was August, ninety-five degrees, and "dog days".

Most of what we did was plain high-spirited things that didn't bother anybody. We used to get long sheets of tin off the roofs of old disregarded sheds and such. We'd get some scrap lumber to make a bow, fold the tin into a hull, and pick up old lard cans from the Tillis bakery for pontoons. Our buddies did the same, so there were fifteen or twenty of those metal canoes out on the lake. We called it the "Muck Armada." You wanta know what muck is? Well, muck is the topsoil found in about a twenty-mile-wide band on the southeastern shores of Lake Okeechobee. Some places the muck is twenty feet deep. It gets in your shoes and blood, too.

We'd read about the Spanish Armada in our history books at school, and who could not want to be like Errol Flynn and Tyrone Power, who were our favorite pirates? We paddled our homemade pontoon canoes all over Lake Okeechobee, imitating their exploits.

Sometimes I'd go over to the Saint Lucie Canal with my

cousin Frank (Jellyroll) Tillis and another buddy of ours, Gene Herring. After we fished for a while we'd find a tall skinny pine tree, and then one of them, usually Gene, would climb to the top and bend it all the way to the ground. They'd tie it down with a rope and then, like a fool, and since I was the lightest, I'd let them set me on top of it and they'd cut the rope. That tree would sling me about fifty feet into space and I'd land out in the middle of the Saint Lucie Canal. I was a human cannonball.

We boys never did anything bad, like stealing or harming anyone. We didn't damage property, except once by accident. One night I was out with Frank, joyriding in Uncle Wiley's army truck. Always in Pahokee you had to go up on the dike (levee) before you went home, or you hadn't done much. On that night Frank got to talking, and, not looking, ran right into one of the many Army Corps of Engineers gates that are on the levee. I think Uncle Wiley had to buy a new gate. (He got to keep the old one.) We like to have drove that man crazy.

One night Frank asked me to spend the night with him. The next day was the Fourth of July and he said he had a bunch of firecrackers we could pop. Well, we didn't sleep much that night and Frank said, "Let's get up and go down to the lake."

Well, friends, it was four o'clock in the morning, but I wanted to pop those firecrackers just as much as he did, so I said, "Let's go."

We climbed out his bedroom window and headed for the lake. We probably wouldn't have got caught if we hadn't popped two firecrackers and set off a roman candle right in front of the Bank of Pahokee. Chief Morgan nailed us just about as fast as a duck nails a June bug. I thought they'd put us in jail for that one for sure, but they let us go. Frank and I were both crying.

Then Frank and I had a water-drinking contest. He was three years older than I was and weighed about three hundred pounds. It would have taken a giant sequoia redwood tree to sling Jellyroll three feet out into the Saint Lucie

Canal. Well, I didn't know Frank was throwing his water over his shoulder, so I kept drinking and drinking—at least three quarts. I almost drowned on dry land.

Of course, we did a lot of hunting and fishing. I learned early to use a .22 rifle that my brother had bought. But one bird I didn't shoot at was the screech owl. A couple of years back, I'd had this idea of being a taxidermist. Trouble was, I didn't have any idea how it worked. I loved to read, and had noticed an advertisement in several magazines, "How to Be a Taxidermist." Well, I sent off for the course, and one day the first lesson arrived.

I'd never heard of formaldehyde or studied any books on the subject. I just shot this screech owl, took out the guts and innards, and stuffed it up with big wads of cotton soaked in a solution that came with those lessons. It didn't take long for the experiment to smell something terrible. Daddy told me to get that damn thing out of the house right now—which I did. I gave up the dream of a career stuffing animals, which was probably a wise decision. Science and machinery were never my strong points.

I was curious about machinery, though. The big levee around Lake Okeechobee was built after the 1926 and 1928 hurricanes, which killed thousands of people, mostly blacks. That big lake just came up over Pahokee and Belle Glade, so President Hoover said, "We've got to stop this," and had the Corps of Engineers build the dike. It was so big that the first Pahokee airport was built up on top of it.

There was a Mexican guy who moved into town with his family and started a crop-dusting business. He had a Piper Cub. One day he made Charles Holmes and me an offer. "If you boys'll wash the crop dust off my airplane, I'll take you up for a little spin."

So we got some buckets and we hauled water from the lake below. That plane was covered with dust and dirt. Heck, we washed it for four or five hours. Then we noticed the plane only had one seat in it. "Where we gonna sit?" Charles asked when the pilot came back.

"It's okay," he told us confidently. Then he instructed us

to sit on the cockpit edge on either side of him, half-ass inside the cockpit and half-ass out. We were told to hold on to the struts, and hold on good, so we wouldn't fall out.

Well, we did. We didn't even hesitate. The chance to fly was something we couldn't resist.

So we took off over the lake and flew around for about fifteen minutes. We weren't up all that high, but it sure was fun. Maybe too much so, since I began to get airsick. So our pilot friend landed.

When my folks found out, they didn't appreciate our adventure. Daddy beat my ass for that. I guess I deserved it. As a father, I'd do the same.

My teenage years in Pahokee weren't all pranks. I was always interested in raising animals and growing vegetables—the same things we do on our farm today. Since we didn't have any place to garden, my brother and I joined the FFA—the Future Farmers of America. In a while we were given the use of some small pieces of land to grow vegetables. The idea was to learn by doing—as we did with the swimming. We thought about growing green beans, but Daddy said the market looked better for cabbage. We could sell whatever we grew. That was another incentive to do a good job. My brother and Bobby Peacock went in together and farmed a half-acre plot, while I farmed a quarter-acre by myself. They took really good care of their cabbage patch, I mean, not one weed could be found. But then a drought came and their cabbage split open from the heat and rotted. I'd been sort of busy with other things, including football. My brother says I plumb forgot my cabbages, and my neglect let the weeds grow up and shade the crop. By the time I picked the cabbages, the price was way up. I made a nice little piece of money, plus an A in FFA.

I tried my hand raising a rabbit, too. Somebody gave me this young buck—that's a male—and I fed him, took care of him, and kept him looking good. He got real big and healthy. When I heard they'd be judging rabbits and other animals at the Belle Glade Experiment Station, I figured there'd be no harm in seeing how he rated.

There'd be grown-ups who were in the business of raising rabbits, and folks who had hundreds of them, competing. I'd get a look at some of the best rabbits in south Florida, plus a chance to have some fun at the judging. It was bound to be a lively change from life in little Pahokee though Belle Glade wasn't much bigger and only nine miles away.

Well, my rabbit won first prize—best in his class.

Nobody was more surprised than I, unless it was Richard and Bobby Peacock. I didn't do nearly as well with that little red piglet I was given by Orin Bacon, the owner of the hardware store where I worked after school. On Mama's advice, I hid that little pig in the closet until I could bring up the subject with Daddy. We didn't even get to say the blessing at supper that night. Daddy heard the porker squealing before we sat down to eat, found him, and made me take him back.

Would you believe he did the same thing with the baby goat Mr. McCurdy gave me a few months later?

CHAPTER

Being determined, I wasn't nearly ready to give up on talking right. When I was fourteen or fifteen, I was told at school about a speech therapy clinic ninety miles away at the University of Miami in Coral Gables. A man named Dr. Raymond Van Deusan ran it. He was a good man and he seemed to care. He understood how to deal gently but honestly with people who stuttered or had other speech-related problems. I respect that man to this day.

The clinic was free, and perhaps the treatment, although late, could help. So I signed up and hoped. Once a week volunteer ladies from the Pahokee Red Cross Chapter would come and pick us up at school and drive us kids with speech problems down to Coral Gables in a Red Cross station wagon. You remember the kind, the ones with the wooden doors. I don't think they make them anymore. This was the ladies' good deed, and they meant well, but while we were in the clinic, they'd go shopping or go see a movie or whatever. Sometimes we'd have to wait a long time for them to show up. Once we waited three hours on a street corner for the ride back home. But how could we get to

Pahokee without them? After a few late pickups, I stopped going to that clinic.

It was 1949 and I was sixteen. I had plenty of buddies at school. We did all kinds of things together, including enlisting in the National Guard. A bit of it was patriotism, for the Korean War was going on, but most of the reason my brother and I joined was the pay. I think we got $150 every three months. We could use the extra money because we were starting to date the girls. We liked the uniforms, but best of all we could get out of the house on Wednesday nights for Guard meetings.

We went to a few meetings over in Belle Glade, and found them really dull. Richard and I were both listed as cooks, and that duty added to our discomfort. So we started to skip the Wednesday night meetings. Others did the same thing. Then the company commander and his lieutenants came up with a way to fix that. No, it wasn't anything from the National Guard manual. It was definitely unofficial, and maybe not original. They decided to end each meeting by showing what the older guardsmen called f--- films, known today as hardcore porno pictures, XXXX. They had 100 percent attendance from then on, on the nights they were showing those films. Sometimes they would trick us and tell us they were going to show the films, but didn't, and we felt cheated.

Well, one night after a meeting when the films had been shown, we were all leaving the armory when James Sims, Jack Cromarty, Kenneth Johnson, and some others told me about this girl who lived out on Kramer Island, a little archipelago in Lake Okeechobee. It's connected to the mainland by a long wooden bridge. There were a few acres of beans planted out there, but mostly cows were being pastured on the island. Well, they told me her husband was never home. They said he drove a refrigerated produce truck, hauling green beans and other produce up to New York. They said she lived out on the island in a big old white house and she was very, very *lonely*.

I'd seen that old white house many times while fishing, duck hunting, or paddling around that island in our homemade Muck Armada, but never knew that anybody lived there.

Well, like I said, we'd just seen one of those XXXX films and the sixteen-year-old defenders of our country were horny as hell. All of us had problems at that age, and my problem wasn't all stuttering.

So, Dopey Floyd (a skinny little guy who looked exactly like Beetle Bailey with his uniform on), Sonny Phillips (everyone called him that, and another name, too, even though his real name was Charles), and I listened when the others told us about this girl.

"We've got it all lined up for you young studs to go out there," they said. "She's expecting you tonight."

We didn't see the wink. Well, we couldn't wait to get out there. I'd never been with a girl before, but had thought about it a lot. Neither had Dopey. Sonny had, he *said*, but Sonny could tell a lie with the best of them. "Boys, since I've got experience and it's my car and my gas, it's only fair that I be first, okay?"

Well, that was all right with Dopey and me.

"Now, all you have to do when you get there," Sims continued, "is get out of the car and holler, 'Hey, Mabel!' Don't honk the horn, just yell, 'Hey, Mabel, we're here!' Got that?"

We were scared to death on that ride. We were all shaking like a dog passing a peach seed. There were a few clouds, but a full moon was peeping through and the night air was calm. On the left of the dirt road that led from the bridge on the island side was a drainage canal about twelve feet deep and full of water hyacinths. This was usually the undisturbed home for cottonmouth moccasin snakes, alligators, streaked-head turtles, and such—until tonight! On the other side was that big old white house that I thought had been abandoned since the two big hurricanes in 1926 and 1928. That should have been the tip-off. But I didn't care. I wasn't thinking about anything but what I was there for. As I heard the guys say when I was in the Air Force on Okinawa, "All my brains wasn't under my hat."

So, we finally got out there and Sonny, just a-grinning, climbed out of the car. "Hey, Mabel! We're here!" he hollered.

Dopey got out on his side of the car, and I was halfway out, when a shotgun went off. I mean, folks, I saw fire coming out the end of those double barrels, and the noise was loud as a cannon. *Boom! Boom!* Egrets left their rookeries by the thousands. Ducks and coots were flying in every direction. What a rude awakening, I thought.

"Goddamn you sons-of-bitches!" a man's voice roared.

"Run, boys, run!" I heard the girl scream. "He's home, he's gonna kill all of us. Run! Run! Run for your lives."

Sonny made one leap about twenty feet over into the canal and went down under the hyacinths and hid with the snakes and 'gators. Dopey froze, he got buck fever and stood there in flat-out terror and pissed in his pants. "Please don't shoot me, mister!" he begged. "Don't shoot me!"

Me, I took off running and I didn't stop. I could hear that shotgun blasting away. *Boom! Boom! Boom!* "I'll kill every one of you little bastards," the man with the shotgun was hollering. I was running just as hard as I could run. I couldn't see much in that darkness and I didn't care. I ran right into a barbed-wire fence. It went *boinnng*.

Well, I didn't pause to consider. It was no time for reflection. I backed up and somehow jumped clean over it. I found myself in a big pasture full of Brahma cows and bulls. Normally I would have been scared to death of them because a Brahma bull is nothing to mess with, especially when he's sleeping. But this time I ran right through, over, and under those animals, all the way to the other side of that pasture. I found some burrows beneath the tall Johnson grass that muck rabbits had made and used on their nocturnal journeys. I hid in one of them.

My heart was pounding, I was completely out of breath,

and I was sick to my stomach. If this is what sex is all about, I thought, I can't take many more trips like this. I knew I had to be calm and not panic. It was my only chance to survive. I figured I had to be on the end of the island. Pahokee wasn't far away. I could see the water tank and the lights from that little town shining like a beacon of hope. The water wasn't deep here—about three to four feet—and I knew that I could wade until I got to the channel, and then I'd have to swim about a hundred yards. After that, I could walk the rest of the way. If I was lucky!

Oh, how I prayed out there. I didn't have to get down on my knees, I was already down. Soaked in guilt, sweat, and fear. "Mama, you always told me never to mess around with lower class people," I confessed, "and here I am a-fixin' to get killed! Oh, God help me, Lord Jesus, please help me!" Then I heard a whole bunch of people calling out.

"Hey, Gus. Hey, Gus!" That was my nickname. I think I got it because I looked like Beetle Bailey, too, but Richard says it was because I looked like a distant relative with that name. "Hey, Gus!"

I recognized some of the voices and slowly but cautiously I came out of my rabbit burrow. Then I heard something else. It was awful. "Sonny is dead! Blowed his head clean off and a 'gator got it!"

"Oh, God! Oh, Jesus! Don't let Sonny die," I pleaded. I was so shook up I didn't even want to hear what happened to Dopey.

Finally a bunch of kids from my school came out of the darkness. I couldn't understand what was going on. They were laughing their asses off. When I got up close enough, I saw they had asked most of the Pahokee and Belle Glade high schools out there. They were really laughing at the joke they'd pulled on us.

That wasn't the end of it. I went home with my National Guard uniform wet and filthy. I smelled like muck rabbit shit. I wouldn't tell Mama what had happened, for obvious reasons, but I made the mistake of telling my brother-in-law, Johnny Burdeshaw, about it. The whole school knew, anyway. Next day, all of Pahokee and Belle Glade were laughing at us and joking us. I still carry the scars from that barbed wire, Sonny has an ear fungus to this day, and I hope Dopey has learned to control his bladder. People still kid me about it when I go back. They say, "Hey, Gus, where's Mabel?"

I stayed in the National Guard, and so did my brother. We had no choice. That summer we went with our company, Company E, 211th Infantry, 51st Division, to National Guard Camp at Fort Jackson, South Carolina. I'd done a lot more singing by then, and playing the guitar that I had bought from Richard for $25. I entered all the local talent shows, entertained at parties, dances, Boy Scout camps, the Lions Club, and also the Rotary Club.

One night, while at camp, Company E had a dance on the base and hired a local band, called the Hired Hands, to provide the music. They were very good. I had read about them in *Country Song Roundup* when I was working for Julian Chandler at the drugstore. They were a well-known country music group with quite a reputation in their neck of the woods. They had their own midday radio show on a Columbia radio station called WIS. When they played at our dance, Sergeant James Sims, one of the fellows who had sent us to that island, asked if I could get up and sing a song with them. "Sure," they said.

Well, I did a couple of songs. One was a Hank Williams hit, "Why Don't You Love Me Like You Used to Do?" I guess they kinda liked my singing because they invited me to come into town the next day and be on their noontime radio show. Boy, I thought I was gonna come down with Dopey's bladder problem. Being only a buck private, I had to ask Captain Hooker if I could go, and he said, "Sure, Gus, go."

"I'll act as your manager," Sonny announced.

"Okay, I'll need somebody to help me talk," I agreed.

So we went into town and I did the show. It was my first

time to sing on radio, and I was just tickled to death. I sang "Why Don't You Love Me Like You Used to Do?" again and when I got back to camp, all the guys were calling me a radio star. It sounded great and I knew they were proud of me. I liked it. I still grin when I remember.

Next year, we took our summer camp at Fort McClellan in Alabama. That was a real hot place for training, just full of insects. Some of the boys got poison ivy and they didn't have to march. But I was marching my ass off in that Alabama heat, which I didn't appreciate one bit.

My brother and I talked it over. We decided how to beat that marching. We went out, found some poison ivy, took off our clothes and wallered in it, did most everything but eat it. Do you know, we couldn't get it. We really tried to catch that itchy rash, but it didn't work. While we were wallering though, we were completely unaware that an army of redbugs (chiggers) were invading the tender areas of our bodies. I must have got a thousand bites myself. I looked like I had the measles. So I went to the captain and told him I couldn't march and scratch at the same time with all those chigger bites. He'd heard what Richard and I had done, so he made us march anyway.

I don't think marching was for me. I never did get to like it, even in the marching band. Fact is, I had trouble just putting up with it. A few years later, when I decided to enlist in the service, I picked the Air Force to avoid that footwork. I was surprised to find that they march, too, at least during basic training. I never did get the hang of marching too well. Matter of fact, it got me into trouble.

When I was just starting in the Air Force as a recruit, they asked if anybody had any ROTC—Reserve Officers' Training Corps—or National Guard. I'd put in a few months of ROTC at the University of Forida, and had had three years with the Guard, so they made me a flight leader. One morning I was out marching my "flight" of guys to the chow hall, barking out the cadence like I was sup-

posed to do; "Hup . . . Hup . . . three . . . four . . . Hup . . .
Hup . . . three . . . four . . ."

It was a sunny January day in San Antonio, Texas, and everything was going fine. I was feeling right proud with myself until it happened. It was really funny, but not at the time. I could see it coming, as stutterers sometimes do: the word *halt* would not come out. I ran those guys right into the side of the mess hall. I couldn't prevent it. I just couldn't get out "Ha . . . Ha . . . Ha . . . Halt." I was trying hard, but I didn't make it in time.

Those new recruits took it better than the Air Force. The men I was leading rolled on the ground, laughing like crazy. I ran into one of them in Vegas a couple of years ago, his name is Johnny Sundquist, and he still thought it was funny. The Air Force took it otherwise. After that, I wasn't a leader anymore. I didn't get to be a leader again until I had my own band about thirteen years later.

CHAPTER

10

It was 1950, and back in high school, after that summer training at Fort McClellan, my senior year went well. I made the A team in football, playing right halfback. I was not big by any means—about 145 pounds—but I had decent speed, so I got good yardage running. In a small way, I was getting pretty popular in that little town.

I was being invited to all the parties, as a halfback and as a singer. I was doing some jokes and humor, too. It never came to mind that I'd be a professional singer or entertainer. I was good-natured and added some fun to our parties, sometimes doing imitations of Sinatra and other top singers of the day.

I was getting up my courage with the girls, too. I'd start asking them out about two weeks before a dance to go with me. It usually took that long for them to figure out what I was trying to say. I got dates. There was one special girl, named Mary Hall, who I went out with a lot. We were in love—my first real love. One time, for my birthday, she

Mel's mother, Burma Tillis

Mel's father, Lonnie Lee Tillis

Mel at age four

Mel at fifteen

The house where Mel was born, in Tampa, Florida *(Gladys Jeffcoat's Photo Studio and Camera Shop)*

Mel with *(from left)* Cindy, Connie, Mel Jr., and Pam

A Tillis family reunion at Lake Alfred, Florida in 1956. *From left:* Richard, Mel, Lonnie, Burma, Imogene, and Linda

Mel's first new tour bus *(Russell Ray Studios, Nashville, Tennessee)*

Mel Tillis and the Westerners at the Stateside Club in Okinawa in 1952

Bob Wills and the Texas Playboys *(Courtesy of the Country Music Foundation Library and Media Center, Nashville, Tennessee)*

Jamup and Honey, the Grand Ole Opry *(Courtesy of the Country Music Foundation Library and Media Center, Nashville, Tennessee)*

Mel singing "State-side" to the troops in Germany in 1967

Mel with brother Richard *(Bob Davidoff Studios)*

The house where
Mel and Judy
live today *(Alan
Messer)*

Mel and Judy

gave me a nice cigarette case and lighter. She hadn't known that Daddy didn't know I was smoking cigarettes? Well, I thanked her for the gifts and when she left, I gave my present to Daddy. I smoked for about twelve years. I puffed away until July 19, 1962, when Mel, Jr., was born, and I began to take the surgeon general seriously. It wasn't only the risk of lung cancer. I'd come to appreciate that a singer's throat is his business, not-to be abused.

Though I didn't take it too seriously at the time, I'd had some encouragement as a singer and an entertainer. I'd been entering some local talent shows in town for a couple of years. A fellow named Malcolm Millar, God bless him, had started them in Pahokee's movie theater. The Prince Theater, it was called. It became a big traditional thing there. There wasn't much other entertainment in town.

The first year Mr. Millar had his talent show, a buddy of mine named Charles Holmes (the one who took the plane ride with me out over the lake) and I dressed up as a blackface act. At that time there was a minstrel team called Jamup and Honey on the "Grand Ole Opry Radio Show"— they were really funny and very popular. One of them still lives in Louisville, Kentucky. They were big stars. I'd listen to them on Radio WSM on Saturday nights, memorize all their jokes, and the next day teach them to Charles.

Mama would blacken our faces with burnt cork, and we'd wear black stockings over our heads. I doubt anybody'd do that kind of act in America today. But Charles and I didn't know about racial things back then. We didn't mean any harm. We lived in a small town that was 70 percent black and we young people got along well with those folks. I'd say that the atmosphere in town back then was racist because of the older white people who'd been raised that way.

It was never explained to us why we should keep apart, or the reasons they had to maintain those rules, you just did. I found out on my own. Years later I wrote a song about that, called "Quarters":

My heart's a-pounding in my chest,
Night's so hot a man can't rest,
August moon yellow as gold,
God forgive me and save my soul.

Chorus
'Cause I can't stay away from them quarters,
Can't stay away from them quarters.
Jump down, turn around, pick a bale of cotton.
"Hey, boy, hey, boy, where you been?"
"Down in them quarters and I'm goin' again."

Well, Papa told me that a man's real low
To mess around with a mandingo,
But I've hid and I've watched 'til two and three,
Papa come home from a drinking spree.

Oh, Papa's been down in them quarters,
Papa's been down in them quarters.
Jump down, turn around, pick a bale of cotton.
"Hey, boy, hey, boy, where you been?"
"Down in them quarters and I'm goin' again."

Well, she sure looks good in her cotton patch,
Makes a man forget where he's at.
Crowders and conchs and black-eyed peas,
Honey, can I help you with your cotton sack please?

Repeat chorus

Well, one of these days they're gonna find out
And they're gonna catch me and there's no doubt,
But I don't worry 'cause I don't care,
'Cause if you ain't been there you ain't been nowhere.

Repeat chorus*

When I was growing up in Pahokee, the black part of town was still called the colored quarters. In my song I wrote about some of the whites who told us kids to stay away from the quarters. I had all kinds of jobs to make me my spending money. Some of my pocket cash came from a newspaper route, which is how I found out at least some of the grown-ups' reasons.

When I used to deliver the *Miami Daily News* and *Palm Beach Post* all over the black part of town early in the morning, I'd see some of those whites visiting the quarters or leaving. They were sneaking down there, messing around with some black women, and they didn't want us to know that.

I held on to that song for a long time, not quite sure what to do with it. Eight or nine years ago, on a flight to Los Angeles, I found myself sitting beside Alex Haley, the black author who wrote *Roots*. I told him the story, and how I'd written about some of those goings-on. I sang him the song. Then I asked him whether he thought people, black or white, might now be ready to accept that song. He took a few seconds to answer.

"Maybe it's a little too soon," he told me.

Well, I've recorded that song, but it's one I've never released. Maybe I could put it out now.

Charles and I won first place that year at the Prince Theater. It was 1951 now, and I guess that the other kids in town and I weren't exactly concentrating on the race question during that last year of high school. I was feeling good about almost everything, for the first time. Daddy had straightened himself out, Richard and I were looking ahead to graduating, and I was getting on well with everyone, including the girls. I was coming out of the lanky, awkward stage. I was even a good dancer. The school yearbook teasingly described me as "God's gift to women." 'Course, I wrote those lines myself.

Soon there was another talent contest coming up. I looked forward to that. On the big night Mama had to stay

home to look after my younger sister, but Daddy came.
When he got back, Mama could hardly wait to get the
news.

"Did he win again?" she asked. "Did he get the first
prize?"

Daddy, who'd never been impressed with my ability as a
performer, shrugged before he answered. "They gave him
the prize," he told her. "But he didn't deserve it. There was
a little girl who sang better."

That hurt her, but maybe it shouldn't have surprised
her. Two years earlier, Malcolm Millar had told my father,
"That boy could go somewhere if you gave him a little
encouragement," but Daddy had ignored him. After all,
nobody we knew had ever known anyone who'd become an
entertainer. How could a boy with no musical training or
connections—and a stutter—even get started, let alone
make a living?

Or maybe he just didn't believe in me.

Or was it he expected his sons to join him in the bakery,
doing honest labor as he and his four brothers had done for
so long?

I wasn't about to break the peace by getting into an
argument. So I went about my school and my odd jobs,
wondering what I'd do after I graduated. Richard was getting married to Johanna McKinstry, and going into the
bakery. I'd worked in the bakery off and on after school and
I didn't mind it, but I couldn't see spending the rest of my
life glazing doughnuts and slicing bread with Dober Gray.

Well, some people had noticed my ability.

Not the singing, the running.

I had tryout offers at the University of North Carolina
and Florida State University. A fast halfback had a chance
to get a college scholarship, if he passed the tryout. A few
of my buddies were going off to the University of Florida.
One of my best friends, Bobby Peacock, and I decided to
try out for Florida State University up in Tallahassee. We
were hoping to make the football team. His family was in

the fish business, so we drove their old fish truck up there, stinking every mile. No air-conditioning or anything like that.

It was a long, hot ride to Tallahassee. When we got there and tried out, Bobby made the Seminole Team as a kicker. He was getting off fifty- and sixty-yard punts. I was proud of Bobby. They let me suit up in pads and work out with the other players that were a lot bigger than me. I tried, but I was just too small.

They offered Bobby a scholarship, but he wouldn't accept it. "If you don't take Gus"—as he called me—"you can't have me," he said.

Well, after that ordeal I decided to go to the University of Florida in Gainesville, where most of my classmates were heading. I'm still a diehard fan of the University of Florida football team, and organize a big country music concert each year to raise money for their athletic programs. We call it the Orange Blossom Special. Bobby went back to Pahokee and married Bonnie Faye Meeks, and I went to Gainesville.

I had no scholarship, but there was a "campus call," where anybody could walk on and try out for the football team. I went out to see what I could do. Boy, the competition was rough and huge. Those were big boys. I met Rick Casares and Buford Long, who later played some good pro ball with the Chicago Bears, and lots of other big, heavy football players.

"I'm just not big enough," I said realistically. So I went to school and hung around for about three months. I wasn't failing or anything, but I realized that everything for me seemed to be leaning toward music. There was a young man from Lakeland, Florida, named Ernest Cumby. One day he was playing his mandolin in the dorm. We were rooming in the same hall at school, so we got to playing together, mandolin and guitar. The Mayflower Hotel in Jacksonville, Florida, asked us to entertain at the roof garden during the Gator Bowl in late December 1951.

I made $5 that night. My first professional pay. I thought about the future then, and I guess I decided that music was going to be the door for me. Country music was really coming on good. It was growing, picking up speed. I feel like I had a little something to do with that. World War II had helped expose a whole lot of people to country songs. Soldiers from all over America—big cities, too—served with boys from the South and West. That was the first time a lot of young men ever heard of country music, and many of them learned to like it. The seeds were planted.

It took a while for the interest in country music to grow, but it was beginning to get a little bigger. As recently as 1961, there were only eighty-one radio stations in the entire U.S.A. offering country music full time. Today more than one thousand do that, and more than three thousand broadcast at least five hours of country music every day.

Back when I was at the University of Florida, western music was probably better known to most Americans, since artists such as Gene Autry, Roy Rogers, Tex Ritter, and other singing movie stars were making records that sold well. Country is a lot bigger now, but those of us who play and sing it haven't forgotten the great western sounds. You still can hear it in lots of records today, if you listen. I do western songs in every one of my shows, and so do others.

One of the country singers to get big recognition back then was a man I admired a lot, then and now, Hank Williams. He was writing and singing a mixture of country and Negro blues. Pop fans loved him, and so did black people. His great honky-tonk songs are still classics. He was a man who could reach all kinds of audiences, so much so that the Hadacol folks—they made a patent medicine—sponsored a tour that brought together Bob Hope, Milton Berle, and Hank Williams. Hank's "Lovesick Blues" had been on the charts for months. He was *hot*. The first night, I'm told, some lesser-known act opened, and Berle slipped out onstage behind him, cutting up, as he does. Hank decided to

have a word with Mr. Berle. "If you try that while I'm on,
I'll wrap this Martin guitar around your head."

So Milton behaved when Hank came on, and Hank
knocked 'em dead. They wouldn't let him off—nine or ten
encores. Well, the next night Milton went on before Hank,
and Hank still came out best.

When they moved on to the third city, Bob Hope was
smart enough to recognize who it was that the crowd loved.
"Hello, I'm Hank Hope," he said with a smile. Everybody
laughed.

The promoters had to change the order of the acts to
keep the folks in those audiences happy. From then on, the
top spot went to Hank Williams.

That's what was happening as I headed home from college that Christmas. Country stars Hank Williams, Red
Foley, Carl Smith, and Lefty Frizzell were all making it
big. Maybe I'd try to sing something like Red Foley. He
wasn't as country as Hank, but had a style that my voice
could handle better.

There were a lot of maybes in my head as I rode south to
Pahokee with Dale Maxwell and Bobby Mackey, but I had
no earthly idea as to how or where to start. Maybe I'd
audition for that new little station playing country music
over in Belle Glade, WSWN—"the little station with the
long reach." No, you needed a record before that, I
guessed.

I'd have to work at it for a bit, so I needed a job until I
had something going. When I got home for Christmas, I
talked to Daddy about it.

"I'd like to drive a bread truck, like Richard," I said.

He shook his head. "You can be a helper on a truck," he
answered.

"But I know how to drive a truck, Daddy."

"No, you can either be a helper on the truck or work in
the bakery. I'll pay you twenty-five dollars a week, and you
give fifteen dollars of that to your mother for room and
board."

I was nineteen years old, and the idea of working for $10 a week didn't set too well with me. I got sort of rebellious. Richard believes he wouldn't let me drive because the driver was also a salesman, and a salesman has to talk. I'm not sure. Even if my brother's right, it wasn't fair to deal with me like I was still a kid. It just reminded me of some other things Daddy had said and done.

Was he ashamed of me? No one else in town or in our family was.

"Well, I ain't gonna do that," I told him.

I walked across the street to Chandler's drugstore, where I'd worked as a boy. It was next door to the post office. There was a sign outside the post office that said, "The Air Force Needs You." The Korean War was going on. The idea that I was needed appealed to me . . . I liked that.

So I went in and signed up.

If I wasn't good enough to drive a bakery truck, I could serve my country, and I did. I served them cakes, cookies, pies, and doughnuts.

On Christmas Day I left West Palm Beach on a troop train. Mama was crying, of course. Daddy didn't say much . . . "Just behave yourself, son," he finally said.

We were going to Lackland Air Force Base near San Antonio, Texas, and as the train pulled out, I wondered what they'd have me doing when we got there. Whatever it was, it would be a whole lot better than sweating in that bakery.

CHAPTER

11

During the first few weeks after leaving Pahokee, I kept hearing the records of a new singer on the radio. Webb Pierce was that singer's name; he had feeling, and he had a style. I really loved his singing, especially on a big hit called "Wandering." So there was a chance for new guys, I thought. I wrote home and asked Mama to send me my guitar, she did. In January 1952 the Air Force put me in a flight group with a bunch of boys, most of them from Wisconsin. There were seven of us from the South, six from Tennessee, and myself from Florida.

Well, those Yankee boys called me Reb. It was a friendly nickname. We had black guys in our flight group. That was the first time I had ever slept in the same place, eaten with, and used the same bathroom with blacks. It was a new experience for me but not a bad one.

Well, they'd join in with me and sing. We liked the same songs, including Hank Williams's blues and his honky-tonk songs. It wasn't long before we became good friends. That's one of the things music can do.

San Antonio had a nightclub called the Barn, where you could hear country music. I went out there one night and met George Morgan, a good singer who later had a big part in my beginnings in the music business in Nashville. I tried to ask him to sing "Candy Kisses," one of his big hits, but I stuttered so badly he couldn't understand what I was saying.

Then I had my short adventure as "flight leader," which ended when I ran my barrack buddies into the side of that mess hall. We finished the basic training, and everybody's orders came through except mine. All my buddies shipped out, but I stayed at Lackland for another six weeks before I got my new assignment. I was rarin' to go. "Boy, I'm gonna get the hell out of San Antonio now," I told myself.

I didn't.

They shipped me eight miles across town, to Fort Sam Houston. That wasn't the worst part of it. They sent me to Bakers' School. Daddy's gonna laugh his ass off when he hears this, I thought.

I already knew how to bake, but the Air Force said I had to learn it their way. So I learned the "proper" names of the utensils I'd been using in the Tillis bakery for years, but not much else. I breezed through that course, went home for thirty days' leave, and left for Okinawa, via Camp Stoneman, near Pittsburgh, California.

That was when I first started trying to write. Waiting at Camp Stoneman to ship overseas, I had a weekend off, so I went into Vallejo, a little town outside of San Francisco, for some fun. I wasn't old enough to get into the clubs, but I found one, the Hitching Post, that had a band that played country music and I stood listening in the doorway for a couple of hours. Then I checked into the little hotel above it to sleep.

That little country band kept me awake all night. They went full blast until four o'clock in the morning. Just twang-twang, honky-tonk this and honky-tonk that, real loud. I'd get my pillow and cover up my head, but it didn't help. They were blasting so hard, I felt the bed rocking. Later I wrote a song about that place—"Honky-Tonk

Song"—which became a big hit for Webb Pierce. It went to Number One in 1957.

Well, I got me a room in cheap motel,
My head was a-spinning and I didn't feel well.
I laid right down and I tried to go to sleep,
But a band kept playing in a joint underneath.
I picked up my pillow and I covered up my head,
But the band kept a-playing and a-shaking my bed.
Honky-tonk all night long,
*Honky-tonk same old songs.**

I don't write down the notes. I never did learn that. I work out the song in my head and on my guitar, then play it into a tape recorder. I can read notes some. I used to read the notes in the fiddle instruction book, and I learned to read rhythm notes when I played snare drum in the Pahokee High School Marching Band. It's not that rare for songwriters not to read or write notes these days. That's because quite a few didn't have a regular music education. Some good ones did, some good ones didn't.

Not long after that night in Vallejo I was fed up with Camp Stoneman. A month of KP every day will do that. Yes, I wrote a song about that, too—"The K.P. Rhythm of a Soldier Man." About the worst thing you ever heard in your life. Well, finally they shipped us out to Okinawa, on the USS *General Mitchell*. There were over two thousand of us, plus dependents, on that troopship.

The trip took about twenty-three days. When we arrived, all the others were met by buses and trucks, and off they went. I was standing there wondering what in the cat hair was going on, when an Air Force sergeant wearing short khaki pants and a pith helmet walked up to me. The Okinawans called him Mitama, which means "Big Blue

---

*"Honky-Tonk Song" copyright © 1957 by Cedarwood Publishing Company (A Division of Musiplex, Inc.) and Tree Publishing Company.

Eyes." He sure had them all right. He was definitely a squirrel.

"Are you Airman Third Class Lonnie M. Tillis— AF24625111?" he asked.

"Y-y-yes, s-sir, that's me."

"Well, your orders are to come with me. You've been assigned to the Filipino compound," he said.

I looked around and saw I was the only one going with him.

Ole Blue Eyes got up front in the truck. There was plenty enough room up there for me, but he told me to get my ass in the back with my duffel bag.

He took off, driving like a bat out of hell, dust just a-flying. We went as far as the road went. Then he dumped me at this bunch of Quonset huts, where 150 Filipino construction workers were housed. Some of them also worked in a thirty-five-piece band that played pop music all over the island.

Across from the compound was a small anti-aircraft site, with seven or eight American soldiers.

"What's your MOS?" the mess sergeant asked. In case you don't know the term, MOS means military occupational specialty.

"I'm a ba-ba-baker," I said.

"Like hell you are, you're a cook now," he growled.

Don't ever try to argue with a sergeant if you're wearing but one stripe (I'd been promoted to airman third class after my basic training was completed). I'd never cooked before—my stint as a cook in the National Guard had been a laugh—but I learned fast.

It wasn't hard feeding those Filipinos once you mastered rice. It was just like cooking grits—all you did was boil the water out of them. They ate rice with almost everything. Every now and then, Sergeant Eckler would let me bake a little bit, usually on special occasions and holidays. I remember one time, after I had moved on down to the main air base (Kadena) I had to bake nine hundred individual pumpkin pies for Thanksgiving. I only had one helper, a little Okinawan named Ehaw. Would you believe we had to open over six hundred little cans of pumpkin? We even had a friendly little pumpkin fight that night, to make matters worse. We had pumpkin all over the mess hall, and us, too. We finally got all the pies baked, though.

You need vegetable shortening to do proper pastries. It's much lighter than pure lard, which was what we usually had to bake with. It came in from Australia in big five-gallon cans. Boy, was that stuff rank. I kept trying, in spite of that. I even wrote home and asked Mama to send me some decorating tubes so I could decorate cakes for the guys' birthdays. Pretty soon I was making cakes for the whole base. Officers' children's birthday cakes, wedding cakes, party cakes—you name it, I did it.

One day I'd had an easy menu. I'd gotten my baking done real fast, so I went down to a little village called New Koza to get me a massage at one of them there geisha houses. They were everywhere. I knew the *mamasan* (madam) at this one particular house. I went there all the time. She had the prettiest geisha girls. That lady called me Tillison. She liked the way I talked—southern.

Well, that time I stayed there a little too long, and Mamasan was getting all over my ass to get out of there. She said, "Tillison, AP [airmen police] come pretty soon, you must hubba hubba and leave."

I told her, "Okay, okay, no sweat. I'll leave as soon as I have my bath."

I'd no sooner set my skinny butt down in that big hot tub when Mamasan went crazy. "Tillison, Tillison, *eee-kay, eee-kay*," she said (meaning "Get the hell out of here"). "AP come."

I crawled out of that big tubful of warm water, and left two of the prettiest girls you ever laid your eyes on in there. Where's my clothes? was my first thought. I found them but I didn't have time to put them on. I jumped right out of the back window of that bamboo house. I didn't think

I'd ever quit falling. That house was built right up to the edge of a forty-five-degree bluff and it was about a hundred feet to the bottom.

I rolled and tumbled all the way down and landed on top of about a million beer cans and bottles that GIs before me had thrown out the windows of that geisha house. I was lucky, I only cut my hand in one little place. I quickly regained what little sense I had, found my clothes and brogans, grabbed them in one arm, and ran as hard as I could run. I came to a dead end. All the Okinawans had little fowl pens behind their bamboo shacks. I found one of those pens I thought was empty, but it wasn't. There was a big ole goose in there, and he was mad. I guess I must have awakened my new feathered friend. I was naked as an earthworm. That gander came after me, and anything hanging loose. I was plenty scared. I grabbed that ugly duckling by the neck and held on tight. We went round and round. And, you know, if the APs hadn't heard all that racket and come to my rescue, I believe that old gander might have whipped me.

By that time the whole village was up and had gathered to see what was going on. Those two airmen police told me to come out of there, with my hands over my head.

I told them, "I can't, I'm naked."

"Well, put your clothes on," one of them barked.

"Yes, sir," I nervously answered. "If one of you guys will hold the g-g-g-goose."

I paid the Okinawan who owned the gander for any damages done. There weren't any, but he took my money anyway—2800 yen (about $20 at that time). Those airmen police probably needed a good laugh because they let me off the hook, and I ran all the way back to Kadena Air Force Base, three miles away. I stayed away from those geisha houses for two or three days.

We had more time than recreation to fill it on Okinawa. On the armed forces' Far Eastern network radio station, I heard a band called the Westerners. They did a country and western program on the air once a week, and played dances for U.S. service clubs all over the island. One day I heard their guitar player, Tommy Sparks, say, "Our singer, Lefty Hale, is going home to North Carolina." Then he said something that really caught my attention. "We're gonna be needing a new singer, and from your cards and letters, you don't seem to take too kindly to my singing."

Right away I asked my buddy, Airman First Class Raymond F. Roberts, from Galax, Virginia, if he'd take me in to audition for the singing job. And he did. We hitched a ride on a supply truck down to the NCO club at Kadena Air Force Base. I was tense and scared to death. I didn't know what I'd say, or whether I'd get the words out at all.

So I started drinking beer, a pleasant habit of mine from my brief college days. I was getting up my nerve. I had about eight bottles of San Miguel beer, and I really got to feeling good. The band was playing "Salty Dog Rag" and other good dance songs, so I cut loose dancing—*alone*. I had on khakis and my Air Force brogans, and I was really kicking up my heels. After they finished the next number, I walked up to the bandstand, trying to act cool.

"Can I sing a song with ya'll?" I asked in a voice that wasn't my normal sound. Fact is, it was more like Ted Knight.

"Sure. What do you want to sing?" the leader answered.

That's when I got to stuttering. I couldn't get it out. So I had to hum the song. I hummed him a little bit of "Alabama Jubilee," and Tommy recognized it. I sang it with the band, and they all loved it. I mean, the folks dancing and the musicians, too. They said I sounded like Red Foley. Boy, did my chest swell! So I did another Red Foley song, "Tennessee Saturday Night," and they liked that too. Then they offered me the job. They didn't care if I could talk or not, it was what I could do—*sing*—that mattered, they needed a singer.

Lord, I was happy.

A regular job singing country music, and getting paid for

it. I was lucky in my cooking and baking schedule. I had twenty-four hours on and forty-eight hours off. The other guys in that band all were cooks, except the fiddle player, Pee Wee Adkins. He was a tech sergeant in the Air Force. Tommy Sparks, who was an Army mess sergeant, from Sikeston, Missouri, remembers the night I met the Westerners. "First time I saw Mel Tillis, he was dancing by himself," he tells people. It was clog dancing, country style.

We bought an old green Hudson and drove it all over that island, playing at officers clubs, NCO clubs, and airmen clubs. Depending on the place, we each made $5 or $10 a night. I learned how to play rhythm guitar with the band. Tommy Sparks helped me with my chords. He taught me how to play bar chords. I did that for two years, we made a lot of folks happy on that island. I've heard the Westerners are still together today on Okinawa, different pickers, of course.

After two years on Okinawa I went home.

When I got back stateside, I had to ride a Greyhound bus from San Francisco to Pahokee, Florida. Now that's a long haul, my friends—about thirty-four hundred miles. I had a thirty-day leave, and I was happy I was going home, but I had a problem ordering what I wanted to eat at bus terminals. It was the stutter. Usually the waitress was some pretty young girl, and it really embarrassed me to try and order, although most of those girls were patient with me. There were two things that I could order without stuttering, and that was a grilled cheese and a large Coke. Between San Francisco and Pahokee, I had forty-nine grilled cheeses and Lord only knows the amount of Cokes. When I finally got home, I felt like one big log. I told Mama what had happened, and after several doses of milk of magnesia, I lost weight. I lived. Mama had saved my life again.

I was twenty-one—1953—and I had a great time on that leave. I learned to water-ski. We'd go out in groups—they

called them "boat-a-cades"—from Pahokee up the Kissim-
mee River. We'd camp overnight on the riverbank, having
some of the greatest times I've had in my life.

It only lasted a month, though. Then the Air Force sent
me to a SAC base at Lincoln, Nebraska. I'd saved enough
money in Okinawa to buy me a new car, a '53 Belair Chevrolet. One of my Air Force buddies I had met in Okinawa,
Fred R. Morris, had been assigned to a base in Salina,
Kansas, and had bought a new car, too. We'd kept in touch
and decided to meet in Sumter, South Carolina, his
hometown, so we could drive most of the way, together.
But after only fifty miles on the road, we lost each other.

I found someone in Lincoln, though. Her name was Lauri
Sullivan, but everyone called her Butch. I went with her
for almost the whole two years I was stationed there. I was
playing and singing in little bars around the base, but not
as a paid act. When my buddies and I wanted some beer,
I'd get out the old guitar and entertain. The bar owners
would always give us plenty of beer.

I liked that Butch a lot. I almost married her. I bought
her a ring and everything. I wrote my mama and told her
that I was gonna get married. She raised Cain. Why? Well,
Butch was a Catholic and we're Baptists. Now I'd say the
hell with that, but to them it was a bigger issue back then. I
felt I should honor my folks' decision. So Butch gave me
back the ring. She's got another one. Every now and then I
see her and her husband in Salem, Oregon. They're both
fine people.

I was already planning to make it as a musician-singer.
I'd even told my buddies and some girls we knew. I wanted
it so bad that I'd take an MGM record of Hank Williams,
print up a label with my name on it, and put it on top. I'd
just sit there and look at it, thinking how it would be. It had
to be.

I guess it was kind of silly, like those pretend plays I'd
done with the pictures I cut from the Sears catalogue. But

seeing my name on the record seemed to make it almost real. It said that the dream didn't have to be impossible, even if the odds were very strong against it.

My folks had moved from Pahokee back to Dover. Daddy had bought a bakery in Sarasota and was commuting back and forth, about forty miles. When I got out of the service, I joined my folks in Dover. I had my Air Force separation money, and was working on local farms. I picked strawberries, worked in some pepper patches, painted houses—did anything I could. I wasn't loafing, never did. I was making $100 a week, and that was good money.

Then my cousin, James Simmons, got me a job with the Atlantic Coastline Railroad as a fireman. I worked on a diesel electric engine. Steam engines were being phased out.

I ran into that same problem—my talking. One of my duties was to call out the signals on the main line up ahead, to keep the engineer alert. I had to let him know if the signal was red, green, amber, or if it was a spring switch coming up. But usually, I more than likely couldn't get the words out. Those signals were always a mile behind us before I could say what color they were. Well, they fired me.

It was a good job, but what bothered me most about losing it was the feeling I'd let my cousin, James, down. I continued doing odd jobs, with my daddy on my back to get a regular permanent job. He'd get real mad when I talked about being a singer, which he thought was just crazy. He'd get so torked-off he'd threaten to bust my guitar, and my ass, too, if I didn't give up that foolishness.

I was still a kid to him, although I was twenty-four.

Mama was urging him to give me a chance to find my own way. She pointed out that I was only a few months out of the service, but he didn't seem to listen. He seemed to have his mind made up.

My Air Force separation pay ran out, so I was helping James and Juanita Simmons with the watering of their pepper patch. One day I tried to refill the tractor's gas tank with the motor running. It was a careless thing to do. Some of the gasoline dripped over on the battery, and it exploded. *Boom!!*

That explosion blew me about twenty feet into the air. And then the tractor caught fire. I got down digging in the dirt like a dog, throwing dirt backwards through my legs, up on that fire. I put it out. But James got all over me. First I'd lost the railroad job he got for me, and now I'd messed up his tractor.

"L-l-l-look, I sa-sa-saved the tractor," I stammered.

"You had no business putting in gas like that. Ain't you got no damn sense?" he said.

So we had a falling-out (that means not talking to each other for a while). I started dreaming more and more about getting to Nashville, which was now a growing music center. Every month I'd buy a new *Country Song Roundup*, look at the pictures of the stars, and read about their latest hits. Now and then, I'd put my hands on a copy of *Billboard*, the music business weekly. Today it has pages and pages on country music, written by a whole staff of writers based in Nashville, but back then, country music didn't get much space. As country grew in popularity and record sales soared, so did the coverage in the trade papers and magazines.

I read in *Country Song Roundup* about this talent scout over in Tampa who'd discovered a new talent named Buddy Thompson, and how he had gotten him on RCA Victor in Nashville.

That coming Sunday I was in church, and after the services, on my way out, I mentioned to my cousin Louise's husband, Bill McClellan, that I'd read about this talent scout, a man called Buck Peddy.

"I know him," he said. "He does business with us at the GAC Finance Company." I wondered for a moment about that.

Then Bill said he'd arrange for me to meet Mr. Peddy.

While I was waiting for that meeting to take place, I read where there was a job opening at the Miller Candy Company in Plant City. I went to see Mr. Miller, the owner. He was a nice man and recognized the stutter immediately. He told me he'd had a speech problem himself at one time.

"I like you," he said. "But I don't have anything open right now, nothing that is, that you could handle. Let me give you some advice." He opened his desk drawer and took out a piece of paper. "Take this piece of paper home and read it—read it ten, twenty times. When you wake up tomorrow, you should have a different attitude."

I didn't realize that my feelings were so clear to others. I was kind of depressed about everything, but that piece of paper he gave me helped. It was the creed used by Alcoholics Anonymous. I wasn't an alcoholic, but Mr. Miller said, "It works for everybody, no matter what problem you might have." Here—roughly—is that creed:

God grant me the courage to change the things I can change,
The serenity to accept those I cannot change,
And the wisdom to know the difference.
But, God, grant me the courage not to give up on what
    I think is right
Even though I think it is hopeless.

CHAPTER

12

I think that's how it goes. I've remembered it for thirty years. Deal with what you can, accept the rest, and find the wisdom to know the difference between the two. It makes a lot of sense for all of us.

I read that creed over and over, and I began to get a different outlook on life. There are things I can't change. I told myself that I've got to accept me the way I am. I was pretty down then, out of work, and the stutter seemed to be getting worse. It was a real bad time for me, so I needed that creed.

Well, the day came for me to meet Buck Peddy, I went to his house in Tampa. At first, I couldn't make any sense out of it. The address was an auto paint and body shop. The sign said "A. R. 'Honest John' Peddy." He had an old metal building for his shop, and I found him there sanding a car. He was wearing shorts, and he had paint and grease all over him. He was short, with a little mustache, and a cigar hanging out of his mouth.

I tried to tell him who I was. I stumbled and stuttered and finally managed to get out two words: "B-B-Bill McClellan?"

"Oh, you must be Melvin. Bill phoned me yesterday about you. I got a new boy coming over for supper tonight. You can stick around and eat with us if you like, Lucille's made a Key lime pie."

As I soon learned, that lady sure could bake and cook. Then he asked if I'd written any songs. I told him I hadn't because I didn't think the ones I'd written were professional enough for him to hear.

When his new protégé, Larry Kirby, arrived, I sat back and listened while they taped some songs on Buck's Wollensack recorder. They planned to take them to Nashville in two weeks. Then "Honest John" Peddy—friends called him Buck—auditioned my singing. I wasn't too good. I had too much adrenaline. I was too scared. I really felt shitty. I knew I'd bombed.

He shook his head. "I don't think so, Melvin," he told me. "I'm gonna put all my marbles on Larry. *He's* really going places."

Larry Kirby was a nice guy, but somehow he and the songs he wrote just didn't get beyond small clubs. Of course, there was no way of knowing that then.

"If I p-p-pay my own expenses and help on the g-g-gas, can I go up to Nashville with you?"

"Well, Melvin, if you want to go that bad, be here a week from Tuesday."

I think I cried going back to Dover.

Back home, I apologized to James, and he let me work in his pepper patch again. I painted Aunt Mozell's house. I did anything to make an honest dollar.

I was determined to go to Nashville with Buck, his wife, Lucille, and Larry Kirby. And we did. It was Summer of 1956. We checked into the Holman Motel, just outside Nashville, which was cheaper than the places in town, nothin' fancy, but nice, and we went into town every day.

First we went around to the more active music publishers. There only were about three that mattered in those days. (Now there are thousands, and I own four myself.

That's something I'm very proud of, because I worked so hard to get them.) I could see that Buck Peddy was hardly an expert on the town himself. He'd only been there a few times before and we were sort of feeling our way around together.

We went into the Acuff-Rose Publishing Company, and I met Mr. Wesley Rose. He was a nice man, and he listened while I sang. He seemed to like me, but told me I needed to write my own songs. Then we went to Tree Publishing, where Buddy Killen told us he needed songwriters, not singers. Back then the company was owned by Jack Stapp and some man in New York. Today Buddy Killen's the sole owner, and I am very proud for Buddy. They only had about three big songs then. I think one of them was the theme song for the "$64,000 Question" quiz show, on network television. Another was "Heartbreak Hotel," a big hit song for Elvis Presley. Today Acuff-Rose and Tree are multimillion-dollar corporations, known all around the music world.

The third publishing house we went to was Cedarwood. We couldn't get past the pretty red-headed receptionist, Dollie Denny.

She was a very nice woman, who later became one of my good friends, but she wasn't letting in three amateurs of whom she'd never heard, to waste her boss's time. With my stuttering, she might have thought it'd take forever.

One of the music publishers we met on that trip to Nashville put it bluntly. "Don't see how anyone could record you as a singer," he said. "With a stutter like that, the record would have to be as big as a washtub." Everybody laughed and so did I, and maybe he was half joking, but I felt it.

Not enough to discourage me, though.

Finally we went to see a lady named Mae Boren Axton, one of the writers of "Heartbreak Hotel" and a good journalist, who did, and still does, public relations. She's the mother of Hoyt Axton, the singer-songwriter-actor. I think Buck Peddy had met her before, back when she'd lived in

Florida. Anyway, he asked her if she could help us get in to see any music publishers.

"How about Jim Denny at Cedarwood, boys?" she answered.

"We-we-we-we tried," I said, "but cou-couldn't get past the receptionist."

"Let me see what I can do," Mae Axton suggested.

Meeting with Jim Denny would be a big break. He was a man the whole Nashville music world respected. He'd been in charge of artist relations for the Grand Ole Opry before he started Cedarwood with Webb Pierce and another partner, Carl Smith. The big acts and top record producers all liked him. Every young songwriter and singer in town wanted to get in to see Jim Denny.

Thanks to Mae Axton, we did. She fixed it with one phone call.

She knew most everybody in the Nashville music scene, and still does. I'm not the only young talent she helped get his or her foot in the door. There was a singer named Presley who got his first important tour, the one that brought him together with the great manager Colonel Parker, through Mae Axton.

"As a personal favor, Jim, just give this nice young man half an hour," she asked, as she spoke about me, "and be patient with him. He stutters, but not when he sings. He's a good singer."

Denny agreed. It is hard to say no to that charming lady.

Then she hung up the phone and turned to us. "Buck, he'll see your boys at two o'clock. Don't be nervous, Mel. If you find you can't get the words out when you're talking, why, just sing them."

And I did. Jim Denny didn't mind a bit.

He and I hit it off right away. He was a great music man and a true gentleman, one of the finest I ever met. He and his wife, Dollie, were kind to me. I'll never forget them. He was encouraging from the start. He told me he'd be happy to hear any songs I wrote. I couldn't believe it. I felt good when we walked out of his office.

Years later, there was another time I had to sing because I couldn't get a word out. During one of the early country music weeks, I was out partying for two or three days with Wayne Walker, a great lyricist and my best buddy. After all the parties and no sleep to speak of, we got real tired. So we went to the room we'd rented at the Capitol Park Inn. He fell onto one bed, I dropped onto another. The window was open wide that hot October night, which was unusual. We had no air-conditioning. It had been turned off for the winter.

We were on the ground floor. Our friend, Johnny Paycheck, who later hit with "Take This Job and Shove It" and other big records, was looking for Wayne's car keys. Johnny didn't want to wake us up, so he came in through the ground-floor window and went through our pants to find those keys.

I heard him fumbling around. I was half asleep, kind of half in and half out of it. I saw a figure, but didn't know who it was. Well, that scared the hell out of me. When that happens, I choke up. Who wouldn't?

I tried and tried to say something, but no words came out. Finally, in desperation, I sang out, "Wayne . . . Wayne, we're being robbed."

We were all laughing a minute later. It really happened, just like that. That story's been told in lots of different ways. So have a bunch of others about Mel Tillis, his stuttering, and his wild escapades.

Well, that visit to Cedarwood Publishing Company made a big impression on Buck Peddy. He'd seen that Jim Denny and some of the other music publishers we'd met were more interested in me than in his new protégé, Larry. Now that was important because music publishers are important. What they do in the business is important. They're the ones who encourage and support songwriters, give them cash advances, or sometimes weekly "draws" against future royalties, and make demos. Demos are demonstration records publishers take to artists, record company executives, and independent producers. Demos lead to regular records.

Records are half the source of a songwriter's income. There are royalties from record sales, and royalties from radio play of those records. If the record hits, there'll be sheet music sales and royalties on that. That money's collected under the copyright law. Fortunately for songwriters, there are such laws in just about every country. Otherwise songwriters couldn't support their families, or even afford to go on writing. The publisher is the writer's business partner, the one who gets the records cut and looks after collecting the various kinds of royalties.

The slogan of the Nashville Songwriters' Association is: "It all starts with the song." And that's right. But without publishers, the writers wouldn't get their rightful money. So the writers create, and the publishers market the creations, and they split the income fifty-fifty.

A good publisher earns his or her 50 percent by working the song for more than one record, here and in other countries, for years and years to come.

Seeing that several good publishers seemed to like me, Buck Peddy signed me up *immediately*. The contract gave him 50 percent of my earnings as a songwriter, and 25 percent of whatever I'd be paid as a singer. For that, he'd be my manager, push my songs, and try to get me bookings.

I was happy, for now I had a manager.

I didn't think about the percentages, and I didn't realize he'd be putting his name on my songs as co-writer. Before long, other people would be putting their names on my compositions as co-writers, too. There used to be quite a bit of that. Long before I got to Nashville, I'm told that bigtime pop stars were putting their names on Tin Pan Alley writers' songs and taking half the profits in exchange for singing them on network radio shows.

Now, I'm not saying Buck was a bad guy, or that he tricked me. He didn't. I signed that contract of my own free will. I was over twenty-one, but being so eager to get moving as a professional writer and singer, I guess I didn't think it all out. All I had on my mind was writing some good songs and bringing them back to Nashville as soon as I could.

Buck, Lucille, Larry, and I went back home to Florida. I intended to write some songs. That was what they all seemed to want the most. Along about that time, I met a pretty girl who was selling tickets at the Dover drive-in theater, and I asked her to have a Coca-Cola with me on her break. I didn't have much money for anything else. I was seeing a few girls, but began to see more and more of her than the others. She was sixteen, and her name was Doris Duckworth. We liked each other, and I didn't consider that the eight-year difference in our ages mattered that much.

I was doing different kinds of work around Dover to earn enough money to get back up to Nashville. One hot day I was out watering newly planted strawberry plants. Now that's hard work, so I wrote a song called "I'm Tired." I did it as a love song, but the last line said what I felt: "Oh, Lord, I'm tired—tired of livin' this-a-way!"

I'd written a couple of others after I got back from Nashville, but Mama really liked this one the best. Ray Price was performing with Red Sovine and Benny Martin at the Florida State Barn Dance in Tampa. I went over with Buck, who'd met Ray and Red earlier at the Grand Ole Opry. Buck got us in without paying to see Ray backstage, and played him a tape of "I'm Tired."

"Yeah, I like that one, Buck," Price said.

Buck said that *he* and I had written the song together. Ray Price took it back to Nashville to think about recording it and I just about worried Buck to death. Every day I'd call him, and ask if he'd heard anything from Ray about recording the song.

"Not yet, Melvin," he'd say.

"Why don't you call up there and find out if anything's happening?" I pushed.

I kept aggravating Buck, and he kept telling me to be patient. Ray Price was a big country act, a regular at the Grand Ole Opry, and he toured a lot with his Cherokee Cowboys Band. A record by a star like him would be *something*.

One night I was home in bed, feeling really down. I couldn't sleep, so I turned on the radio and tuned in WSM. I heard the voice of Smiling Eddie Hall, the all-night disk jockey in Nashville. "Well, I've got Webb Pierce here tonight, folks, and he's brought us his brand-new single, hot off the presses. So let's give it a listen, right now."

It was "I'm Tired"!

I went bananas. I jumped out of bed and hollered, "We're gonna be *rich*, Mama! We're gonna be *rich!* I'm going to Nashville."

Then I got to listening real close to that song, and there was something strange. The music was mine, and so was the first verse of the lyrics, but the other two verses were different. "Well, it's almost my song!" I said.

So I got Buck to call up to Cedarwood the next day and find out from Webb what had happened. How in the world did Webb Pierce get to record my song?

"Ray Price was singing it backstage at the Opry," Webb said, "and I told him I liked it. He didn't need a new song then, because 'Crazy Arms' was still Number One on the charts. So I kind of talked him into giving it to me. But all he'd give me was the first verse."

Price had another version of what happened.

"I changed my mind about giving it to him after I sang the one verse," he said. "But he went and got Wayne Walker to write the other two verses."

Sounds crazy, doesn't it?

Well, Wayne Walker, who was later to become my friend and songwriting partner, didn't get a cent for his work. It ended up that I got one-third, Buck got one-third, and Ray Price got one-third. Price hadn't done anything but bring the song up to Nashville. But I appreciated that. That's when I learned you don't get something for nothing.

I was still bananas when Mae Axton called Buck and told him she had liked an earlier song of mine called "Wild, Wild Mind." She'd gotten it recorded by an almost-unknown midwestern disc jockey named Johnny T. Talley who worked for a radio station in Minneapolis. I've still got the first and only royalty check I received for that song—twelve cents. But that didn't count at all compared to the record by Webb Pierce, a major artist.

I remember being parked in the car one night and showing a copy of the "Wild, Wild Mind" record to Doris, I was really proud. I showed her my name, in small print, on the record label and told her that I had written the song. That was the first time I took my guitar from out of the backseat and played her some of my new songs. I guess that was when she understood I really was a songwriter.

Now I had a record by a star like Webb Pierce, a record on a major label. I was somebody, or would be soon. So I got together some more songs and went back up to Nashville with Buck. Yes, the Webb Pierce recording had been noticed. We signed a contract with Tree Publishing.

I was on my way.

CHAPTER

13

It was Buddy Killen, of Tree Publishing, who got me an interview with Don Law, who produced records for Columbia. Mr. Law lived up in Bridgeport, Connecticut, but he'd come down to Nashville every few months to record at a little studio in Owen Bradley's Quonset hut. I think it closed only a couple of years ago, out of date compared to the state-of-the-art studios all over town today.

Country artists from all over came in for Mr. Law to record them. It could be Lefty Frizzell, in from California, or Little Jimmy Dickens, both now in the Country Music Hall of Fame, George Morgan, Carl Smith, Freddy Hart, or other big singers. I went up to the James Robertson Hotel, with Buck and my guitar. Mr. Law, an Englishman with those ever-present glasses down near the end of his nose, was talking to a man named Troy Martin, who worked for Peer International Publishing, and a red hot singer whose name was Johnny Horton. Mr. Law invited us to sit down.

We talked for a few minutes. And then Mr. Law said in his British accent, "Sing—hell, I haven't got all day."

Everybody in the room laughed, including me. I sang a couple of songs, and then he said, "How would you like to record for Columbia Records?"

I had to sit down. I couldn't believe that was all there was to it. This was it—my big break!

Ole Buck couldn't believe it either. He was just a-grinning.

"I'll be back in Nashville in three months," Mr. Law said. "You be here and I'll record you."

So I went home, and they mailed me the recording contract. When I returned to Nashville three months later, I wasn't sure he'd even remember me, but he did. "I have the same feeling about you that I had for Lefty Frizzell, when I first signed him," he told me.

Mr. Law shortened my name to Mel. I asked him why, and he said, "So you can say it."

So I recorded my first song, "Honky-Tonk Song," the one I'd written in Vallejo, California, when I was in the Air Force.

It must have sounded pretty good, because it wasn't out two weeks before Webb Pierce "covered" me on it. *Cover* is the word for one artist doing a record of a song that another has just cut and released. It's a fact of life in the commercial music business—okay for the songwriter, but not good for the original singer. If the artist doing the cover is better known, or has a stronger record company to push his version, the first singer's effort can easily get lost.

Around that time Buck Peddy decided that Cedarwood Publishing might be better for me than Tree. So one day we went in to see Buddy Killen at Tree. Now, you've got to understand Buck. He wanted me to succeed as much as I did.

"Can I have a look at Mel's contract?" Buck asked.

"Sure," Buddy agreed and took it from his desk.

Buck read it over, to make sure he had the right paper. Then he just tore it apart and ran out the door with it. I couldn't believe what I had just seen. Finally I collected my senses and hauled-ass too. We signed with Jim Denny at Cedarwood.

Ripping up the paper didn't mean a thing legally, of course. "But if you guys are that damned stupid," Killen said in disgust, "good riddance."

What Buck Peddy did wasn't the usual or kosher way to do things, but there were a lot of pretty wild things going on in country music then. Songwriters and musicians, never a very disciplined or orderly group, are more impulsive and less inhibited than business folks. A whole lot of the guys who rolled into Nashville in the 1950s and 1960s, and some who came later, didn't have any idea what was happening. (I know I didn't.) In that sense, you could say they were something like most of the black musicians and songwriters of that time. Both groups had two things in common. Being ignorant of the music business, they would get ripped off, or at least they made bad deals. And there was quite a bit of drinking and hell-raising.

There really weren't an awful lot of music lawyers in Nashville who could teach the writers and musicians about the business side. Only a few accountants in town had any experience with the money and legal aspects of music. Now that's changed completely. As the dollars grew, and the number and size of contracts exploded, a whole class of managers, accountants, executives, lawyers, and other specialists developed to deal with the boom.

The musicians and writers now know more about business than they used to. Probably less than they should, but artists are like that. And they still live life a little harder and faster than most folks who have steady nine-to-five jobs with regular paychecks. I've done some of that myself. You pay for your fun, of course, and, as Glen Turner would say, "There are no free lunches."

And there's no lunch at all for a songwriter who doesn't pay attention to business. One of the first things I heard when I signed with Tree was that there were two outfits that would collect the money for songwriters and publishers from radio and TV stations, nightclubs, concert halls, and the like. They license music "users" all over the country, and even collect for you if your song or symphony is performed in foreign countries. Put short and simply—if you get played, you get paid.

I had to learn about such things. I'd made up my mind I was going to manage my money better than my daddy had handled his. I was going to be a real professional, which meant learning the business side, as well as writing better songs. At that time I think the only outfit licensing "performing rights" that had a Nashville office was Broadcast Music, Incorporated. The outstanding woman who ran, and still runs, that office is Mrs. Frances Preston, now a BMI vice president, and my friend.

Well, I joined BMI. I had only a rough idea about how things worked when I cut that first single for Columbia. What I did know was that Don Law was mad as hell that Webb had "covered" us. He said so in plain words.

"Columbia isn't going to be a showcase for Mel Tillis songs," he warned, as I prepared to leave town. "We're not in the business of cutting demos for Webb Pierce to cover." Heck, I couldn't stop it and he couldn't, either. Once the record is out to the public, the song is free game.

After he set a date for me to come back to Nashville to record again, I went home to Florida to write some new songs. Doris phoned the house the first night I was back and said she wanted to talk to me. I picked her up and we went to the local recreation park, where we always parked. She came straight to the point. "I'm pregnant," she said.

That was quite a shock. I didn't know what to say or do. I thought about it a few days before I told Mama my problem. Her suggestion came as a real surprise to me: "Son, you get on a train heading north, and don't get off till that Canadian border's way behind you."

"Mama, I can't do that," I answered. "I love her."

So I went and talked to our preacher, Brother Durrough, and then I spoke to my Uncle Alvin about it. He was a deacon and a good man. I wanted to do the right thing.

I couldn't just leave a pregnant girl not yet out of high school and barely seventeen. I didn't have much money, but that wasn't the important thing. I talked it over with Buck Peddy next, as he was my manager and friend. Then I made the decision myself.

We took the blood tests and got married at Buck's house in Tampa. He was the best man. We had a very short honeymoon—one night in a motor court at Lake Alfred, Florida—then we drove back to Dover the next morning.

Now I had to raise some money right away. There was only one thing to do, something I didn't care for at all. But as a married man, I had responsibilities to meet. So I sold my 1953 Chevrolet and bought a cheaper car. I ended up with $50 in cash and a '49 Mercury that had a hole in the right side of the windshield. The heater worked but the blowers didn't. I couldn't do much about that, but I stuffed my high-school football jersey, Number 23, into that hole in the windshield. It wasn't too pretty, but it kept out the rain and wind.

Doris and I took off in that old car for Nashville. I stopped on the way in Dothan, Alabama, Bobby Goldsboro's hometown, and bought her a $9 wedding band, all I could afford. We reached Nashville the next day.

I arrived with a pregnant teenage wife, a tired '49 Mercury with a busted windshield, and $28 in cash.

No house, no furniture, and not much in the way of clothes.

Well, Buck and Lucille came up in their car, too, and we rented a little old house together in Woodbine. Both couples in one house. Buck had dropped Larry, his other protégé, and was concentrating on me. Thanks to my contract with Cedarwood, I was getting a $50 a week "draw," to be deducted from future songwriting royalties. So I got busy writing.

And I began to get songs cut left and right.

One seemed to inspire the other. It was just crazy.

Young songwriters didn't get records cut this fast, but it was happening to me.

First it was Webb Pierce who recorded almost everything I wrote. Then Ray Price began to cut my songs, one after another.

Now, it takes quite a while—many months—before a songwriter actually gets his hands on the royalties that his record sales and performances earn. Jim Denny knew that, so he treated us right. He raised the weekly advance to $75, showing his confidence and support.

Doris cried for a whole week for me to let her go back home. I said, "Hell, Doris, we just got here." She and Lucille weren't getting along, she was throwing up a lot, and she was homesick. Finally I let her go home.

I saw that living with Buck and Lucille in that small house wasn't working out at all. So I talked it over with them. They moved to a house trailer, and I found a two-room apartment on Peachtree Street in Woodbine. Not much, but all ours. I went down to Florida and brought Doris back. We were getting to know each other. It didn't come that easy, but we were trying to make a go of our new life together.

I was hoping to do some singing and road work, since I had always wanted to make it as a singer, not as a writer. What's more, as a singer, you got paid right away, not months later, as in song and record royalties. Suddenly, out of a clear blue sky, I got my first road booking as a singer at the National Guard Armory in Memphis with Johnny Horton.

I got paid $50. That was more money than I'd ever seen for only thirty minutes' work. I was tickled pink as we drove over to Memphis with Buck and Lucille, stopping every thirty miles for Doris to throw up. I felt for her, but there was nothing I could do about it but hold her hand. It was the pregnancy and car sickness together, and I'd caused both. The concert went well, which pleased the local Columbia Records man. I don't recall his name. He invited us to go to church with him the next morning.

Doris said she couldn't because she didn't have the proper clothes to wear, so we went without her. It was Sunday, March 17, her birthday. When we got back from church, Doris was sitting up in the middle of the bed, wearing a big corsage of flowers.

My first thought was they looked real pretty.

My second was to wonder where she got them.

Well, she'd taken some of that $50 I'd been paid for singing the night before and bought the corsage.

"Doris, you know we can't afford that," I said, as patient as I could be. "We've barely got enough to get back to Nashville and buy a few groceries. We sure can't eat flowers!"

Maybe it was her age. Whatever, she wasn't interested in such facts.

"Well, it's my birthday and I thought I deserved some flowers," she answered in a bold, almost defiant voice.

I could see there was no point in talking further, so I did what a lot of married folks have done before and since. I just *accepted*, and moved on to another subject.

We drove back to Nashville, and the next day we went out to buy a few things for our little two-room apartment— just the essentials. We stopped by the local supermarket for some aluminum pots and pans and a sack of groceries. When we got back to the apartment, we checked the grocery bill because every penny counted. I found we hadn't been charged for one of the pots. So I went back to the store to pay the clerk. He seemed surprised that a customer, a new one at that, would do this. "Well, if we're gonna start out doing business together, let's start out honest," I told him.

I have a very strong feeling on that. On fairness, too.

Now a couple of weeks after that show in Memphis, Jim Denny booked me for another singing job. George Morgan was going into the hospital for an eye operation. He was the main, or lead, singer for the Duke of Paducah Road

Show. The Duke's real name was Whitey Ford, same as the famous baseball pitcher. Mr. Denny, who was the booking agent for the Duke and his show, said, "I've got you a singer," and that's all he told him. Finally we met each other and the Duke phoned Jim Denny the next day.

"What's going on, Jim?" he said. "First, you send me a singer with a bad eye, and now you send me a singer who can't talk!"

No, I couldn't talk very good, but I could sing, so the Duke hired me for the job.

My first trip was a ten-day tour down in Florida. Can you believe it? My first road tour, and it was back to Florida. I was getting more confidence with every show, and the Duke pulled good crowds. One of the people who came to hear me sing was my daddy. He was living down in Fort Myers, working at the Snack House there. Things were getting worse between him and Mama. It wasn't drinking—he wasn't doing that anymore. The problem was other women, one in particular.

Yes, Daddy was on the prowl again.

I don't think he meant to hurt Mama, but he did. I don't believe he ever meant to hurt anybody. He was just a restless guy who didn't think ahead. He didn't grasp that what he'd do would touch Mama and us. She took that for a lot of years.

Well, Daddy came to our show in Fort Myers with my brother, and I was really glad to see them. Maybe it was Richard's idea for them to see me working as a professional with the Duke, who wasn't exactly a nobody. Maybe Daddy was curious as to how good his stutterin' son might do. Whatever it was, we did well. We drew a pretty big crowd, and we were getting a nice reaction.

That was one of the very few times since the Prince Theater in Pahokee that my daddy ever saw me perform. I'm not exactly sure how much he enjoyed it, or whether he thought I might be on the right road, but Richard liked it fine. Years later Richard went out on the road with me and my band. Being a bread salesman who could, as they say, practically talk the birds out of the trees, my brother ran our souvenir and concession sales, selling albums, T-shirts, and the like. He was good at it, quick and funny.

Well, not long after Daddy and Richard saw that show, things got worse between him and Mama. I guess it was the end of the line. That's what my mama told him when she heard that the woman he was seeing might be pregnant. Now, he hadn't *intended* to do that, but Mama decided to separate from him.

So they got a divorce. That was a painful thing for all of us. Daddy married the woman, and they had two children, Allen and Mary Ellen. I think he stopped his roving after that. They were still married and living together some twenty-four years later, when he died.

CHAPTER

I didn't make much money on that tour with the Duke and his band. I think it was only $25 or $28 a night. Those were the kinds of wages that country musicians who weren't stars pulled in those days. You stayed in second- or third-rate hotels and motor courts, rode from town to town in cars or station wagons, and sometimes, after a long ride, when you got there, you'd look like a question mark. I didn't have much money left for Doris and me when that tour was over.

It wasn't the least bit glamorous. But I loved it.

That was my first time on the road, so it was exciting. I was learning from the other pickers in the band, and from the audiences, too. That was valuable in the long run. I figured I had plenty to learn.

Back in Nashville, I went on writing songs and cut some more records. My records were not accepted as well as my songs were, in the beginning. In a while another touring job came up. Jim Denny heard that Minnie Pearl, already a star, and a funny one, was going out on a long summer tour. She needed two musicians, so he got me on as her rhythm guitar player and singer. The pay was about the same as for Duke's show. It wasn't much, but it would be regular, and we sure needed that. I was going to be a father pretty soon.

Minnie also needed a fiddle player.

"I know a guy who plays the fiddle," I told her. "He's just out of the Army. I met him down at the old Clarkston Hotel coffee shop."

That was where all of the musicians hung out in those days. It was the only place back then, except Mom's, behind the Opry House. The coffee shop was close to the offices of WSM, which did the Grand Ole Opry broadcasts.

"I'll go and see if I can find him," I said.

So I ran down the street, and there he sat in the coffee shop, singing his crazy songs to Vic McAlpine, another Nashville songwriter, now deceased.

"Roger, you want a job?" I asked.

"Doin' what?"

"Playing fiddle for Minnie Pearl."

"Sure—any port in a storm."

That young man was Roger Miller, just getting started himself. He didn't have the experience to write "King of the Road" yet, but he learned some on that tour. So did I. Learning and traveling together, we got to be friends.

Roger quit his job as bellhop at the Andrew Jackson Hotel, and we went on the road with Minnie, playing all through Iowa and around the Midwest. It seemed like we played every little county fair in the country. In those days it was all one-nighters for country acts. Do your show and then pile into cars and station wagons and drive all night to the next town. That was tiring, but we were all young and sorta half slept as the miles rolled by.

Minnie would sometimes let Roger and me fly in her and her husband, Henry's, plane with them. Henry was also Minnie's manager and pilot, and one good human being. Years later, when I bought my plane, I arranged for some of the boys in my band to fly in and out one flight, and others on the next. You've got to rotate to keep it fair, something the musicians appreciate.

Minnie did something else for me. She heard me joking with Roger, and she noticed that I could be funny, even if I stuttered. And I sure stuttered a lot.

"Mel, you could do some funny stuff as part of your act," she said. "It might be real good for you to talk onstage."

"You think so?" I wondered.

"Sure. It'd be good for the show, too. And it might give you more confidence. That might help your regular talking, Melvin." She sometimes called me that.

Minnie was right. That first step was an important one. I started to talk and joke some—a beginning. It took a long time before I made much progress, but it did happen over the years. It came real slowly. Still, just the idea that I could dare to talk in front of crowds of people was great. It helped. Minnie kept on encouraging me all through that long tour. She was like an older sister to me.

Doris had gone back to my mother's house in Florida to have the baby. One day, as we were coming into Bowling Green, Kentucky, I heard Bill Morgan, a disc jockey, on WMAK. He's the brother of George Morgan, the singer I'd replaced on the Duke's show.

"Well," he said, "if Mel Tillis is in the listening area, I want him to know he's now the father of a six-pound eight-ounce baby boy!"

We stopped the car at the next pay phone, and I got Roger to help me call home. He put the dime in this time, but I gave it to him. With my stuttering, I couldn't be sure a long-distance operator would understand what I was saying. I was so nervous I could hardly talk. I was tickled to death, too.

Well, Roger made the call. He got my daddy, who was still home at the time, on the phone, and handed it to me. It was Daddy who'd put out the first word on the baby.

Would you believe he'd been mistaken?

It was a girl, a very, very pretty baby girl.

We named her Pam. She's quite a singer and songwriter herself now, and getting attention, too. Recently there was a story on her in *People* magazine, and my wife, Judy, joked about me being a proud father.

"Watch out, Melvin," she said. "Someday you may be known as Pam Tillis's father!"

"Well, that will be all right with me," I told her.

It could happen. Anything could, in this world of country music. I've seen it myself!

CHAPTER

15

Before I went down to Florida to bring back Doris and our new daughter, Pam—Lord, she was a pretty baby—I realized we couldn't go on in that little two-room apartment. There just wasn't enough room for us there. So I began looking for a small house, with a yard for Pam to play in. I sure didn't have the cash in the bank for that, but I'd served my country for four years in the Air Force, and veterans could get government loans to buy homes.

So I bought us a house in the Tusculum Whispering Hills area, on my GI loan. I paid $8,000 for it (right now it would go for $50,000). I bought basic furniture from Morrison's Furniture, just enough to get by with. I moved my family in, and went back to writing songs. Then I went into the Cedarwood offices, permanently, as a staff writer. It was like a job, going in every day to write.

I still didn't have much money. My old '49 Mercury had conked out, so I'd hitch a ride into town every morning. I was writing songs with a great person from Shrevesport, Louisiana, that I'd met earlier at Cedarwood, Wayne Walker. I learned so much from that man. Owen Bradley, the great record producer, who is still a legend in Nashville, used to call us the Rodgers and Hammerstein of country music.

Wayne Walker and I wrote a lot of successful songs together. He was my partner, my teacher, and my best buddy. He taught me how to construct a song, and showed me everything about a song. He'd take me to the Grand Ole Opry, and to recording studios, introduce me to the artists he knew, and to some he'd just met. I'd been over to visit with the folks at the Opry earlier. That was standard for every songwriter in town. Since the Opry show broadcasts had a big audience, and the acts who performed there also did lots of recording, they were always looking for new songs.

At first the people at the Opry looked on me as almost a curiosity—I guess that was the word for it. Well, someone unusual. They were just fascinated that I stuttered so bad but sang and wrote songs, too—some good ones. They were always friendly. Some years later, after I'd built a little reputation as a performer, I got to sing at the Grand Ole Opry. That meant I was accepted as a real professional, a member of the country music family. It was a big moment for me.

It still doesn't pay a lot, just scale. But every performer in the country music world just loves the Opry, what it stands for, and what it's done. It's kept the faith, and spread the music. It's presented so many artists, young and old, and still does. And at a time when very few live country radio shows were on the air, it helped us with both audiences and promoters. It was easier to get bookings from a promoter or club owner who had never seen you perform if he knew folks had heard you sing on the Grand Ole Opry.

The Opry has always been a warm and informal gathering of dedicated country musicians, singers, and comedians—not a show planned months in advance, for the most part. The very able people who run it may have some regulars and a star or two lined up, but others are booked in the week before the broadcast. It's friendly fun—so much fun that even top acts, like my buddies Roy Clark and Roger Miller, still enjoy working the Opry for that reason.

Coming in with Wayne, I soon knew those Opry folks and other established music people a lot better. Everybody liked Wayne Walker, including me. He was a fine lyricist, a bright person, and very decent to everyone. Being friends, and both under contract to Cedarwood, we wrote a lot of songs together that artists cut. We had quite a few on the charts.

One of the good singers who recorded lots of our songs was the man who cut my first song, "I'm Tired," Webb Pierce. For some years Wayne and I spent a lot of time drinking and generally roaring with Webb, a very sociable guy, to say the least. That was one of the ways you got your songs recorded in those days. You went drinking and partying with the recording stars.

Wayne and I liked Webb, which wasn't hard to do. He was a big-hearted and generous man in most ways. He was good company, and he'd usually buy the drinks. Wayne and I couldn't afford to buy a round yet. That wasn't a strain on Webb, since he commanded big money, and was earning more every month. I don't talk about other folks' business, but Webb Pierce, whose big house and guitar-shaped swimming pool are on the tour for Nashville visitors, will tell you himself that he's a millionaire. I think he may have been among the first country millionaires. Wayne's passed on now, but I'm still Webb's friend, and he's mine. Webb's been semi-retired for a while, but our adventures together are fresh as this morning in my mind.

Now, picture what it was like in those wild and woolly years of the 1950s, when Nashville was growing up. For us in the music world, it was like a boomtown. Not many were thinking about tomorrow. Today was it. There were great raw talents—giants like Hank Williams. He was a monster of a songwriter and artist, who hit the bottle hard. The man was a truly inspired genius, who died before he was thirty.

He became a legend and the guru of country music, not only to the fans but to so many young songwriters and artists as well. "He lived fast, died young, and left a beautiful corpse," his talented son wrote a few years ago in his book.

During my early years in Nashville, lots of guys wanted to be like Hank Williams, so they carried their little pints of liquor with them. I was as guilty as the next man. It seemed like the romantic thing to do, the *in* thing, cool. Well, plenty of songwriters are sort of romantic, which may explain all those love songs. Of course, a hungry gut and grocery bills can be a fine inspiration, too.

So, a lot of us would-be's and not-to-be's were drinking as hard and often as possible, sometimes going on for several days. I was doing my share of that roaring for both business and pleasure, and when I didn't come home some nights, that didn't please my wife very much. But she generally knew where I was, and that I was plugging songs. It wasn't every week, but I partied my share. Sometimes Wayne Walker might be with me, but I drank with others and wrote with some others, too.

I recall roaring more than a few times with another singer songwriter named Warner Mack, and Webb. Once we drank all afternoon and night in Webb's office, and then some. Well, we got drunker'n an outhouse rat. I could barely drive to my house in Donelson, where we all passed out in exhaustion. Too much Seagram's V.O. and not enough sleep will do that to a feller every time if he's not careful.

Doris had gone out shopping, and when she came back, there we lay looking like hammered goat shit, just wrecked. She was getting real fed up with this kind of crap. Well, she decided to put a stop to us, at least for a while. So, she called over the other wives. They were ticked off at us, and the drinking, too. To make sure we didn't go back to town when we woke up, those ladies took our clothes, which we'd slung on chairs and on the floor. And that wasn't all.

They carried out of that house every piece of men's clothing, and hauled ass. I guess they figured that way, we'd have to stay there until we sobered up.

After a few hours' sleep, we just came to, instead of waking up. When we saw what they had done, we were livid. We sure weren't going to put up with that sneaky stuff. Maybe they had left us half naked, but there was no way we were going to let them tell us what to do. They had a smart idea. Well, so did we.

I don't recall who thought of it first, but it worked. We just went and put on some of Doris's clothes. Whatever we found in her closet would do. Webb put on a pair of pajamas, Warner a housedress, and I something fancy. Could have been a cocktail outfit or one of those BMI dinner dresses, but it sure looked crazy on me. I suppose we were feeling a bit hung over, but whatever, we didn't care how we looked.

So, looking very strange, we called a cab and went downtown and checked into a suite at the James Robertson Hotel.

I thought that room clerk would faint. He stared at us as we registered, but didn't ask any questions. He'd probably already seen his share of wildness pulled off by drinking entertainers, and this was just one more bit. He didn't put up any fuss at all.

When we got into that big suite, Webb telephoned his tailor shop. They made fine business suits for lots of the stars.

"Mr. Levy," he said real friendly, "we're over here at the James Robertson Hotel. There's three of us. We need suits, shirts, ties, drawers, shoes, and socks, and we need them now!"

"Now?" Mr. Levy asked.

"Yes. Would you be kind enough to send over your man, Guido, to take our measurements? We're in a big hurry."

"You mean *right now*, Mr. Pierce?"

"Yup, and one more thing."

"Yes?"

"On his way over, could Guido pick me up a couple of fifths of Seagram's V.O.?"

So we drank for another day. We felt mighty proud we'd outfoxed our wives. They'd always forgive us. I don't know why, though. Maybe they loved us. It seemed real smart then—drinking and doing what you pleased was the thing for musicians, singers, and writers in Nashville. Singers lived and partied in high style.

One night, some years later, when I was out sipping with Webb Pierce and some others, we were at a place called the Jungle, when Webb decided he didn't like the closing hours. Why should he let those blue laws stop him and his friends from drinking? So Webb Pierce just went and bought that bar, right on the spot. Then he and his cohorts could lock up the doors whenever they wanted and use it for private parties, day or night, as they pleased.

Now, when songwriters got to be friends with the singers who cut their songs, they might go out with them on short trips, in a social way. That was usually fun. Once it was dangerous. I went down to Memphis for two days with Webb and Red Sovine, to work a show for a disc jockey named Eddie Bond. Webb was the main attraction. It was a lot of years later before I earned top billing.

After the show we stayed up late, partying as usual. When you finish a high-energy performance at eleven o'clock at night, there's no way you can come down enough to sleep before two or three, or sometimes later in the morning. I'll bet that's true for anybody whose work ends at midnight—factory workers, waiters, newspaper or radio people, police or firemen or whatever. I don't know what those folks do to unwind until they can doze off, but lots of musicians—country, jazz, or rock, probably symphonic, too—if they're working late, on the road or in their hometown, will eat or drink some. And they party together, since most everybody else sleeps "normal" hours.

Yes, the entertainment world does attract people who aren't exactly like the folks who buy the tickets and records, but we're not all hell-raising sinners. We do have more guys who are less conventional, some free spirits, and a number I'd have to call squirrels. A little bit nutty, but nothing too bad. From what I've read and seen, there are plenty of squirrels outside show business, too.

Going back to that night in Memphis, we should have driven back to Nashville, but we didn't. We stayed up late after the show, and finally went to sleep in the hotel at around four in the morning. Webb awoke in his room first, around noon. After he'd dressed and started downstairs for breakfast, he found the elevator was jammed with people.

The reason for that crowd was clear a few seconds later—heavy smoke, as they passed the second floor. The door opened there, and they saw why. The kitchen was on fire. When Webb reached the lobby, he phoned my room right away.

"Wake up Eddie and Red, and get out, Mel. The hotel is burning!"

"You're shitting me!" I said.

"Hell no, I'm not, get your asses out of there!"

So I jumped up and put on my clothes as fast as I could. I ran to Eddie's room, and at first, like me, he didn't believe what I was trying to tell him. I had to tell him twice. He still wasn't sure that I wasn't kidding him.

"Okay, I'll get my shoes."

"The hell with your sh-sh-shoes!" I told him. "The hotel's on fire! What room is Red in?"

I couldn't find Red's room. I panicked. I was in such a hurry, I didn't wait for the elevator. I ran down the backstairs, opened a door on the second floor, and—oh, God! There was that deadly smoke. I'd come out at the burning kitchen. I could hardly see a thing. There was smoke all around.

Oh, Lord, I never wanted to go this way, I thought. My

mind suddenly flashed back to the night Dopey and I went to Kramer Island to lose our virginity. Then I saw a place where I thought I could jump. I might bust up a few bones, but it was better than ending up ashes. I never was a quitter. I was just about to jump when two firemen walked through the smoke.

"W-we g-g-gonna die?" I asked.

"Not if you take those stairs," one answered calmly.

Feeling foolish but much relieved, I turned around and walked a dozen stairs down to the lobby. They put the fire out a few minutes later. Red and Eddie, who had stayed calm, had beat me down.

So I went home, back to that peaceful shelter and my family, back to writing more songs with Wayne Walker. As we wrote more hits—one sold 500,000 records for Pierce— we got sort of a reputation in Nashville. I was tall and thin, so people got to calling me "Bones." Being shorter and fatter, Wayne was tagged "Fluffo."

Once after I got back to Nashville from a road trip, I went over to our new hangout, a bar called Tootsie's Orchid Lounge. It used to be called Mom's, but she retired and sold it to Tootsie Bess. It was the main gathering place for country music folks. Now, it was across the alley from the Ryman Auditorium, where they did the Opry shows for so many years. When the big new Opryland opened and the Ryman finally closed, people actually bought the seats from that aging auditorium, for memories and souvenirs.

As soon as I walked through the door that day, Tootsie hollered to me, "You'd better get over to the jail, Bones. They've had Fluffo locked up for three hours."

"W-w-what for?" I asked.

"For racing Hank Garland down Broadway in his T-Bird," she said.

So they had Fluffo in jail for racing down Broadway. Well, I went over to get him out. That wasn't too hard, but another problem came up while I was doing it.

It had to do with my stuttering. When I was living in

Dover, I'd gone to a lady speech therapist in Tampa. We'd worked together, but I didn't seem to get much confidence. I think she saw that. To show me how much I could improve myself, she told me we'd go out into the street for a test. I was to go up to the first person I met and ask them the way to the Greyhound bus station.

I sure tried. Hard as I could, and then some. But the words just didn't come out. That man must have thought my bread wasn't done or something. He didn't even stop. He just walked right on by me.

That woman speech therapist was right. Confidence was a very big part of it.

The problem was how to get that confidence—that inner something. It took me many years to come even close. Over those years I tried different things I'd read about. Demosthenes, an ancient Greek who stuttered, had cured himself by practicing speaking with a mouthful of pebbles. He became a top orator. Well, I tried pebbles, too.

"What the hell you doing that for? You'll swallow one and choke to death, Bones," Wayne told me.

"So I can t-t-talk right."

"Forget the stones, Bones. Your stuttering is an asset. Artists notice it and remember us. They pay more attention to our songs."

I don't know if that was so, but the rocks didn't do much for my talking. I'd given them up weeks before I went to the jail to get Wayne out. They thought because of the stutter that I was drunk. Hell, I had only had half a beer.

They locked me up for a couple of hours, until Bill Morgan could get me out. The story got all over town. People still laugh about it, and I can laugh now, too. It wasn't funny when it happened, though. Not to me.

My home life wasn't that cheery, either. Pam was growing up tall. I was restless. I wanted a different atmosphere. I was doing all right with my songwriting, so I decided to buy a new house with a little land. That would be better for kids, I figured. So I bought us a little ten-acre farm right

off Bell Road, a bit further from town. It had an old house
on it. Everything looked fine, I thought.

I'd never lived on a farm before, and didn't know what to
look out for. The real-estate man must have recognized
that, because the day we moved in, we found out we had no
water.

The well was dry—not a drop.

So I hired a man to come in and drill another well. He
knew there was no water on the property, because he'd
drilled the other hole. But he took my money, just the
same, to dig another hole. He wasn't gone fifteen minutes
when Pam used the bathroom and I heard the sputtering.
First it was air belching in the pipes. Then the faucets
started spitting out grit and stones.

It didn't set too well with Doris that her brilliant stuttering husband had moved the family and all our belongings to
a barn with no water. "Nobody can live in a house with no
water," she cried.

It could be that she was also mad about all the time I was
spending in town, song plugging and socializing.

"I have to compete with my competitors," I had told her,
but she didn't accept that at all.

Doris really lost her cool about that dry well, and we got
into quite a fuss about it.

That blew off some steam, but it sure didn't help our
water situation any. I raised Cain with the real-estate man
who'd sold us the place, and then had to take a loss when
we sold it to buy another house. This one had plenty of
water, but Doris was still unhappy. She missed something,
and wasn't feeling good about me or her life in Nashville. I
think she was nineteen at the time.

So she left me. She took Pam and went back to Florida.

It looked as if we couldn't put it all together. I didn't
know what to do. I didn't want any divorce. I wanted the
marriage to work, and I wanted my family. I wanted to be
together.

Well, Mother Nature stepped in, as she'll sometimes do, and I got a phone call from Doris with some very important news. "I'm pregnant again."

So I made another trip to Florida to bring her back.

Things calmed down some, and about six months later we were the parents of another pretty little girl. We named her Connie Lynn.

I don't know whether it's inherited or not, but she has at least one exceptional gift. Even as a child, she had a beautiful singing voice. I loved to hear her sing "The Yellow Brick Road."

CHAPTER

16

Around the time that Connie Lynn was born, I began getting unhappy with Buck Peddy, my manager. He wasn't contributing much to the songs he got half of. But I'd turn on the radio and hear ole Buck talking about how Mel and he had written those hit songs—*my* songs.

I didn't like that at all, but I figured I could put up with it if he did his job. I owed him something. Buck Peddy did write some songs, and he gave me half, but he was supposed to be pushing me, not himself. So I decided to get out of the deal. It cost me a lot to buy my way free. I had to give Buck rights to a number of songs. He moved back to Florida, since he had no more reason to stay in Nashville. He's still living down there in Groveland, with no grudges between us. I don't forget that he helped me get started.

I also recall the problem I had before we signed that paper to split up. I was living off my song royalties, and all my money was tied up until the court settled the legal thing. Well, I had to support my wife and two small daughters somehow. I had written hit songs, some on records still being played and sold, but I had to do something else. I mean I needed income right now for bread and milk, all those things. I faced up to the fact that I had to get a job. I decided to leave music for a while. You can't eat pride. I'd never backed away from work, and this was no time to start.

We moved down to Pahokee, where we could live cheaper, and I hoped to get a job. I knew a lot of folks there, and I figured they'd give me some kind of work. Maybe I could have borrowed money from friends in Nashville or got a job there, but I had no idea how long I would be tied up in court, which meant I didn't know when I'd be able to pay them back. I couldn't do that. I'd always supported myself and paid my own way. Finding a job in Pahokee was better. I wanted to go home, anyway.

Within a day or two after Doris, the girls, and I got to Pahokee, I found a job driving a cookie truck. The Tillis bakery had long been sold and was now a car lot. I drove for a company called Harry's Cookies.

I drove for Harry for about three weeks. I'd thought all my old buddies in Pahokee and Belle Glade who owned grocery stores would buy from me. Surely Bobby Peacock would. But Jack's Cookies had the competition all sewed up. So I failed as a cookie truck driver–salesman. I was fired. And you know what? They didn't even give me notice.

I joke about that onstage sometimes.

I got me another job driving a milk truck. One morning I was in Your Food Store in Belle Glade, which was owned by Rooster Edwards. I was unloading the sweet milk, buttermilk, and cottage cheese when I looked up to see an old girlfriend, Sue Armstrong, now Mrs. Bill Bailey. My records were being played on the jukebox at the Elks Club, and here I was working as a milkman. I just knew Bill Bailey was an Elk.

Boy, was I embarrassed. Too embarrassed to explain my legal problems back in Nashville. I got over and hid behind the Coca-Cola cases. I sat on a case of peaches on the floor for forty-five minutes until she finally left the store. She really took her own sweet time.

Finally the court in Tennessee settled my lawsuit and I started drawing my royalties again. So we packed up and went back to Nashville. I thought about the many times my family had moved when I was a boy and hoped we wouldn't be doing the same. In no time at all, I was back at the Cedarwood offices, writing more songs.

I wasn't doing nearly as well with my recording. Other artists were more successful with my songs than I was back then. The Columbia Records people lost interest, so I looked for another label deal. I had this idea that I could make it as a recording artist. I'd wanted to be a performer when I first came to Nashville, and I still did.

I had another dream, too. I wanted to meet the man whose magic first turned me on to western swing music—Bob Wills.

To my surprise, the two things came together.

I had recorded a few sides for Decca Records (now MCA), without any huge success. I just wasn't known as a singer yet. Decca was a strong label in the country field, with stars like Red Foley, Webb Pierce, Jimmie Davis, and Kitty Wells. Well, a friend of mine, a producer named Paul Cohen, left Decca and went to Kapp Records. Kapp was owned by a good man named David Kapp, from New York City. I'd left Decca myself, after an incident that happened when Red Foley came to town to record some new songs. Red and Grady Martin and I all gathered at the Anchor Motel and stayed there for three days. Red missed his sessions, and I guess I got the blame, so Decca asked me to leave. I was now recording for a small label named Ric (since gone). Grady Martin was my producer.

When Paul Cohen asked me to come over to Kapp, I was interested. One afternoon I went to see Paul at the little RCA studio where Elvis made his recordings.

"Who're you cutting today?" I asked.

"Bob Wills."

"You are!" I gasped. "I'd like to meet that man. I've always loved his style."

"Well, let's go out there and meet him now."

I did. And he was just as impressive as his music. There he stood, wearing that big white cowboy hat, the ever-present cigar in his mouth.

"Howdy, son," he said to me.

I gulped before I answered. "Mr. W-W-Wills, I've always admired you and your music," I said, and told him the story about shelling those peas to his music in the cannery during World War II.

"Would you like to sing a song with me, Mel?"

Me! Recording with Bob Wills?

"I'd love to. How about 'The Rose'?" I asked. I could have sung any one of his songs. I knew them all by heart.

It ended up that I did five songs on that album with Bob Wills. If you've ever had a dream come true, you know what it was like.

I could have sung better, but we did the songs fast and I was awestricken. Some of them I did in a different key from the one I would normally use.

Well, the album did pretty well. The title of it was *Bob Wills, the King of Western Swing, with Special Guest, Mel Tillis*. Lucky Moller booked us to perform together at a big club called Dance Town U.S.A., down in Houston. Of course, I was tickled. I went to the club and listened to him and his band work. I sat there waiting my turn. I waited, and I waited, and I waited. It was almost midnight, and the place closed at one o'clock.

What was going on? When would we play and sing together?

At about a quarter after twelve, he finally introduced me.

"Now I want you to meet the young man who was the vocalist and guest artist on my last album. Here he is, folks, Mel Tillis."

So I got up onstage and started to sing. I was expecting him to chime in with his "a-a-haw," talking behind me as he'd done in that Nashville recording studio. After a bit, I looked around and he wasn't even there.

He'd gone. Vanished out the back door. He had a big ole Lincoln parked out behind. He walked from the dance hall, got into his car, and split.

It disappointed the hell out of me. I couldn't believe it. I felt like an abandoned dog. I told one of his fiddle players how hurt I was. Three years after that night in Houston, after Bob had passed away, I ran into that fiddler, Clyde Brewer.

"I want to tell you something, Mel," he announced. "I mentioned to Bob that he shouldn't have left the stage like that. I told him how hurt you were. And he said, 'You tell that young man that when he came onstage and I heard all that applause, I knew that he didn't need me there. He'll understand.'"

That was his way of complimenting me.

Bob Wills did more than that for me. He gave me some very important advice, which I've followed to this day.

"Mel, when you start your own band," he said that day we recorded together, "hire you a fiddle player. Do it, and you won't ever have to worry about a job. You and your band will always have a place to work."

I took what he said to heart. I've always had at least two fiddle players, and at one time I had four. I have two reasons for that. One is my respect for Bob Wills, a man of great talent and experience who knew how to put a band together. The other is that I just love fiddles.

The fiddle sound is something special—*real country.* People perk up when they hear fiddles. The Canadians, who like traditional country a lot, sure do. I've seen it when we played in England as well. That fiddle music just makes so many people feel so good. I'm one of them.

Fiddle players can be very strong-willed guys. Sometimes that's good, and other times it can be a problem. I've got my rules, what my musicians should and shouldn't do onstage. I spell them out plain and simple to the pickers when they join the band. Two of the things that none of us do onstage are smoking and drinking, although we sometimes slip.

It just doesn't look right, and it's *not* right. Makes us sound and look sloppy, which we're not.

We take our job seriously. We owe the people a good, fast-paced, professional show with everything as close to perfect as we can get it. We rehearse a lot, and we don't just repeat the same routine over and over. We respect our audiences.

One night a while back, when we were in Houston at the same dance hall where Bob had walked offstage on me, I saw that both my fiddle players were breaking the rules flat out. They had a group of admirers passing them drinks of vodka and orange juice. They had several glasses lined up on their amplifiers. They were smoking, too, and laughing. When they stepped forward to play their solos, I eased over and took away those glasses. When they noticed that, they stopped laughing.

They were good fiddlers, Jimmy Belkins and Gene Gassaway. They'd both worked for Bob Wills at one time or another. I don't know why they did that. During the intermission, I laid down the law and I chewed ass. I had to, or the other boys in the band would have tried me. I called Belkins out to the bus. Belkins said Bob's rules weren't as strict as mine. "Well, you don't work for Bob now," I replied. "You know the rules," I told him. "I can't let you get by with this, I'm gonna have to fine you a day's pay."

"Well, if you fine me, I'll just have to quit."

"Well, you just fired yourself. Now go in there and tell Gassaway I want to see him."

"No, Mr. Mel, I don't have to," he answered, "I don't work for you anymore."

I couldn't help it. I nearly died laughing, but he left us. It was too bad, 'cause we all loved ole Belkins and still do.

CHAPTER 17

Folks are always asking me if I'm still writing songs. Well, I've always written songs, from the night I was in that cheap hotel out in Vallejo, California, in 1952.

I was writing songs during those months I drove Harry's cookie truck and the Foremost milk truck in Pahokee. During those early years I didn't handle the business side of my writing that well. Like a lot of other young songwriters, I didn't have the clout to do that. I mean strength in the record industry.

The star singers and artists had clout, and you had to keep them happy to get your songs cut. There were times when I needed money so badly that I sold a song—usually half—to a star outright. That's a foolish thing to do, and is probably done less today, though it's still going on, I'm sure. It wasn't that rare back in the '50s and early '60s. Anyone who'd do that now is making a bad mistake.

I recall selling several songs to Webb Pierce for $100 or $200 each. For that, he got half of the writer's royalties and his name on my song. He'd record them, and Cedarwood, of which he owned 50 percent, would get the publisher's income.

In my earlier days in Nashville I'd once traded Webb a half interest in four different songs for a pair of used cowboy boots and $150. The boots and the songs were good, but the deal wasn't. All four of those songs became hits for Webb, earning him a third set of royalties as the singer. Webb was a better businessman than I was. I don't hold any grudge on that. Other stars and songwriters were making similar deals all over town, and in New York and Los Angeles, too.

After a while the idea of someone else getting the credit for writing even half of one of my songs began to bother me. It just wasn't right, even if it was necessary. I recall Dollie Denny phoning me one afternoon to tell me that Webb had just recorded my newest song, "That's Where My Money Goes." That was good news.

"How do you want the credits to read?" I was asked.

I'd written that song all by myself. "Just Mel Tillis," I said.

But when the record and sheet music came out, there were two names down as writers—Webb's and mine. I told myself that he was a star, with an excellent style and many fans. I decided not to make an issue of it, not then.

Later, when I had other songs recorded by different artists, I thought about it some more. I decided that I had "split" enough. I figured that I'd paid my dues.

Then I wrote another song Webb liked. He told me he didn't want or need any of the money, but putting him on as co-writer would keep his name in front of the public. Well, he'd helped my career, so I agreed. Then when royalties were being paid, I noticed that I only got half of them. He got the BMI award, too.

Well, that's it, I told myself.

When I brought him the next song I'd written, I told him I'd be happy if he recorded it, but I wasn't going to split the credit or the money anymore.

Webb didn't like this challenge. "Well, Stutterin' Boy"—that's where the name came from—"the only reason your songs are hits is that I recorded them for you," he said. Then he told me he wasn't going to cut any more of my songs if that's the way I felt about it.

"That's all right with me, Webb," I answered.

It was time for me to stand up and be my own man. The other hadn't been natural for me at all.

So I didn't take Webb any more of my songs, and he didn't record any, either. He was stubborn as a goat, but I was, too. We were both Leos, with the same birthday, August 8; maybe there's something to that. We weren't enemies or anything like that, but we didn't work together as we had before. It wasn't long before other stars recorded my songs. Ray Price cut "Burning Memories" and "Heart Over Mind," and Bobby Bare recorded "Detroit City" (co-written with Danny Dill). They had major hits with my songs, some even bigger than the ones Webb had had. That made it even easier for me to stay peaceful with Webb, who was still half-owner of the company that published my work.

Cedarwood was my musical home. I couldn't imagine leaving Mr. Denny, who'd done so much for me and other writers. He was a man who understood how to deal with the special kind of people who write songs. He treated each one of us as an individual, and we all loved that man. So did many of the recording stars.

That didn't mean he did all the selling of the songs. The main burden of that was on the songwriter. That was one of the first things I'd learned when I got to Nashville. I wasn't always too successful at it, especially in those early years. My efforts to get songs to Elvis Presley, for example, were a complete failure.

Getting a song recorded by him was every writer's dream. All you heard was Elvis, Elvis, Elvis. Well, I thought I had a way to get to him and pitch him some songs. I had a family connection. It wasn't too close, but it was all I could think of. Elvis's manager, Colonel Tom Parker, was a legend himself. And my daddy was a distant cousin to Marie Parker, who was the Colonel's wife. Everybody called him "the Colonel" and knew just who you meant if you said those two words. I don't know how he got that name—he never was in the military that I know of.

Daddy had mentioned his cousin to me, and said he'd heard that the Colonel was a fish-eating man. Fish was as good a way as any to get a foot in the door, I thought. So Buck Peddy and I went out one day and caught the Colonel a whole mess of speckled trout, right out of Tampa Bay. We had enough to fill a whole ice chest. We bought some dry ice and put it on the fish and drove all the way from Tampa, Florida, to the Colonel's spread in Madison, Tennessee—750 miles.

We followed the driveway around to the back of the house, where the Colonel had set up some temporary offices for Elvis's fan club. It was a big garage with lots of pretty young girls mailing out pictures and answering letters. We knocked on the back door of the main house. The maid came and Buck said, "This is Melvin Tillis, Marie's cousin. We're here to see Mrs. Parker."

"Just a minute," the maid said.

A couple of minutes passed—I timed it—before Mrs. Parker came to the door. She remembered Daddy.

"Oh, you're Lonnie's boy! My goodness!" she said. "I haven't seen Lonnie since we were kids."

"Y-y-yes, ma'am, and I brought the C-C-Colonel some fish, all the way from the Tampa Bay," I stammered.

"Oh, the Colonel just loves fish. We haven't had any good fresh fish in a long time, Melvin."

She called me Melvin, as everybody I knew did before Don Law shortened my name to Mel Tillis to make it easier for me to say. (It's even easier if you say it as one word—Meltillis.)

"But the Colonel's asleep now—it's his afternoon nap—and we don't wake up the Colonel when he's sleeping, now do we?" she asked politely. "You can leave the fish, and I'll tell the Colonel that you were here. You can call back later."

I thought she meant a phone call, but she didn't offer us the number. So we left, wondering if we'd ever get to see the Colonel. It took a while. Would you believe twenty-five years?

A quarter of a century rolled by before I ever got to meet Colonel Tom Parker. I was headlining at the Frontier Hotel in Las Vegas, and Baron Hilton threw a party for some reason. I don't remember why, but I was invited to come. It was a very short meeting.

"Hey, cousin, those were mighty fine fish," the Colonel said.

I didn't know what to say, so I just asked about his wife: "How's Marie?"

The Colonel said she wasn't doing too well, and had to have a nurse with her all the time. We shook hands and the meeting was over. Did you know he charged George Hamilton, the actor, $100 to have his picture taken with Glen Campbell, himself, and me. He has still never heard any of my songs.

I had better luck with a wonderful human being named Burl Ives, the famous actor and singer. He's big in body, talent, and heart. He came to Nashville in 1962 to record an album. The producer was a man from New York City, Milt Gabler, but it looked to me as if Owen Bradley did most of the producing. It was Owen Bradley who sent out word that Burl was coming to town and needed some good songs.

Burl arrived and announced that he didn't want to hear any dubs or tapes. He'd hear the writers singing their songs themselves—live.

Some of us went to his hotel room—Hank Cochran, Harlan Howard, Danny Dill, Mel Tillis, and several other hot writers in town—for what we called "guitar pullings" (demonstrating our songs in person). Burl treated songwriters as artists. He would order up champagne for everyone, and after a few bottles, he'd listen to our new songs. Each writer had his turn.

He was quick with praise, too: "I like that one . . . wonderful . . . it's got a beautiful melody . . . marvelous."

We all loved that man, and I think he liked us. We were part of his breed. He liked Nashville, too. Burl took a good look at the Tennessee countryside and bought himself some property on Old Hickory Lake. Then he bought a twenty-three-foot runabout fishing boat. He said he could use it in the Bahamas. He owned a home and some property on Abaco Island. He wanted somebody to pull the boat down to West Palm Beach, Florida, and put it in the water there.

Jerry Bradley—Owen's son, and only nineteen at the time—and I offered to pull it down there for him. We had to go all the way to Decatur, Georgia, to get a special trailer big enough to carry that boat.

"Pull her on down to Pahokee," Burl said with a big Scottish grin. "You've written so many songs about Florida and that little town that I'd like to see it myself."

There was never a dull moment with Burl Ives around. No, sir.

"Just launch her in Lake Okeechobee if I'm not there when you arrive," he told us. "If you need any help, get somebody down there and I'll pay for it.

We don't need any help, we said to ourselves. And we believed it.

Well, you might know we dropped the boat off the trailer the first thing and bent the damn propeller shaft. We got Billy McKinstry (my sister-in-law Johanna's brother) to fix it up as best he could before Burl got there.

"Don't worry, boys," Burl told us when he arrived. "I've got a man in the Bahamas who'll fix it just like brand new when we get there."

We? What was he talking about? Did he have a rat in his pocket? That was the first time I'd heard I was going to the

Bahamas. It was a surprise to Doris, too. I called her from Marsh Harbor, on Abaco in the Bahamas.

One night before we left Pahokee, Jerry Bradley—now a well-known music publisher and record executive—Burl, the local constable, and I had a few drinks and talked about the trip at the Glades Club. The constable was Benny Sims, a brother of my National Guard friend, James Sims. He decided he wanted to go with us. Hell, you know how you'll sometimes do. We pulled anchor and set our course for the Saint Lucie Canal inlet and over to Riviera Beach, on the east coast of Florida, where we docked the boat behind the Pilot House, a local marina. We started partying again, drinking and a-singing my songs.

"Oh, there's Burl Ives!" some lady said. "Who're those guys with him?"

"Well, they say they're songwriters."

Then Jerry got a phone call from his mother in Nashville. He had to leave and go right home—he'd been drafted into the Army. Benny decided in the cool light of day that he'd better get himself back to Pahokee and his job. I went on to the Bahamas with Burl Ives.

That's when I wrote a whole batch of calypso songs about the Bahama Islands—"Green Turtle," "Curry Road," "My Chicken Run Wild in the Bush," and some others. Burl Ives recorded a lot of those songs over the years—with success for both of us. I'm proud of that, but what's more important is our friendship. I see him whenever I'm near, and hope he'll be in a motion picture I plan to make called *Uphill All the Way*, with Roy Clark.

Burl Ives has never asked for a piece of someone else's song. He understands how hard it is for songwriters. Having been there myself before I got established as a singer, I would never do that, either.

Songwriters aren't any better than other folks, but a lot of them sure are different. I've done all kinds of things for songwriters, including guaranteeing one a job and paying up his back alimony so he wouldn't go to jail.

It takes a special kind of man, or woman, to create a good song. Some of them can be pretty squirrelly, and others are more stable family types. I've told people that I believe we get more good, original songs from the squirrels than the normals. The boys at my publishing companies tell me they agree.

I'm convinced we're right. Whoever is, there's just no way to predict who'll write tomorrow's hit. It could be a doctor or a derelict. That's why we treat each songwriter as an individual. That way you get more out of him or her. Mr. Denny was a master at that, so was Fred Rose. Some of those squirrels can drive you half-crazy. Sometimes it's real hard working with them. Living with them must be even harder. "Right, Judy?"

It used to be somewhat of a fraternity around Nashville. Everybody knew each other, partied together, wrote together, and went out on the road together. Tootsie's was the main place to congregate, probably because it was right next door to the Ryman Auditorium. On any given night you could find Mel Tillis, Marty Robbins, Jim Reeves, Willie Nelson, Harlan Howard, Hank Cochran, Lefty Frizzell, Bobby Sykes, Wayne Walker, Roger Miller, Johnny Paycheck, Ray Price, Darrell McCall, Johnny Darrell, Webb Pierce, Faron Young, Buddy Emmons, Don Winters, Tommy Jackson, Jimmy Day, Waylon Jennings, Cowboy Copus, Ferlin Husky, Hank Garland, Rod Brasfield, and many, many others. Those days are gone now. Time has made Nashville a major music center with thousands of new songwriters and singers coming and going every year. It'll never be the same. I'm glad I was part of that fraternity. Most of those people have done well.

Roger Miller called Tootsie's one time. He was a hot item. He'd just won six Grammy Awards. He asked if I was there, and Tootsie said, "Hell, Bones lives here."

I went to the phone and Roger said, "Melvin, this is Roger. I'm calling from my Lear jet. I'll be coming through Nashville in a couple of hours. See if you can find Willie.

[He was referring to—who else?—Willie Nelson.] I want ya'll to fly down to Tallahassee with me. I'm working the Governor's Ball. I'll bring you back as soon as it's over."

I knew Roger was proud of his success, and that he wanted to share it with a couple of his buddies who were still trying to make it. I told him, "I'll be there even if I can't find Willie."

No sooner had I hung up the phone than in walks Willie. I told him Roger had called, and what was happening. Willie said, "Let's go."

We'd never been on a Lear jet before. Both of us were scared to death. Roger made it easier for us by telling us his crazy stories.

The Governor's Ball was a black-tie affair. Willie and I had on blue jeans and windbreakers. Willie wore sneakers, and I had on cowboy boots. The ballroom was packed. They seated us, at Roger's insistence, out in the audience. It was way in the back, right by the spotlight. Roger was feeling pretty good. He came on stage and did about four of his big hits. Then the governor, who was sitting right down in front, said, "Hey, Roger, how about 'King of the Road'?"

Roger looked at that stately man and said, "Please, sir, let me set my own pace."

A stillness came over that ballroom like the eye of a hurricane. I looked at Willie, and Willie looked at me. We both slid way down in our seats and then out a side door. We waited in the limo for Roger to finish.

He came out of that building madder than hell. He said, "Can you believe the nerve of that guy? He wanted to run my whole show."

Roger calmed down and his Lear jet took us back to Nashville. This happened all in one day. Doris and Martha, Willie's wife, didn't even know we'd been out of town.

Another time, Lefty Frizzell and I had been out roaring. He asked me to go home with him to help break the ice, so I did. When we got there his wife, Alice, threw us both out along with an old buffalo head with one of its horns missing.

He asked me if I wanted it. Well, I'd wanted to be a taxidermist all my life, so I took it home with me. I had good
intentions of getting another horn and fixing the old boy up,
but when I got home, Doris threw me and that one-horned
buffalo right back out again. I took it back and left it in
Lefty's driveway. I roared that night by myself and went
home the next day. I wonder whatever happened to that
buffalo head?

Another time I was over at the Clubhouse, a little watering hole on Sixteenth Avenue South, where pickers and
writers gathered day and night to drink and tell their
stories. It was midday and I had slipped across the street
from Cedarwood to have a cool brew. Well, a friend of mine
needed some money and he sold me a .25-caliber pistol for
$20. I checked to see if it was empty. It wasn't. I emptied it
and put that pistol in my pocket. As I walked back across
the street to Cedarwood, I met Noro Wilson, a good writer
and producer, who does independent work. He said mock-
ingly, "Why, hello, M-M-M-M-M-M-" (I thought he would
never get it out) "M-Melvin." I pulled that pistol out and
pointed it right at his head and angrily said, "You son-of-a-
bitch, you don't know me that well."

He fainted right there in the middle of Sixteenth Avenue.

I felt bad about it. I didn't mean to scare him that bad.
We're still big friends today. He's told that story to
everybody.

CHAPTER

18

Things were looking good in the months after I came back from the Bahamas with Burl. I was writing some good songs, and our family income was growing. Our family was growing, too. We had a third arrival, another cute little daughter we named Cindy. (Whew, what does it take to get a boy? I thought.) I'm very proud of her. She's in her last year at American University in Washington, D.C. She's into communications and anthropology. I told her we have some Indian campsites on the farm, whenever she wants to start digging up bones.

I've never tried to tell our kids what profession they should seek. That seems to come naturally. It did with me. I do want them to get as much education as they can, though, because it prepares people to face life with a little sense. I believe Cindy took my message to heart. She's studying hard in school and I don't worry about her future at all.

It's hard for a father or mother not to worry. But, like everyone else, I'm trying to cope with the new generation, and sometimes I wonder what in the name of good sense is going on, especially in their music. It doesn't matter how

big you may think you are, you can't live your children's
lives for them. I've learned that. I've tried to share the
lessons I've learned . . . to love them . . . and hope for the
best. But as they grow up, they become their own people.
Just as I did. The Good Lord meant it to be that way.

Two years after Cindy was born, we had a son. I thought
he'd never get here. We named him Lonnie Melvin Tillis,
Jr. Everybody who knows him calls him Sonny Boy. He
likes it—I think!

He looked a lot like me when he was born. I think the
resemblance is still there. He loves hunting, fishing, camp-
ing, and music, as I do. A sophomore at the University of
Florida, he's six feet two inches tall, slim, good-looking,
with blond hair and full of ambition. Would you believe he
wants to be in the music business? He's got a guitar, a tape
recorder, a set of drums he plays, and some good ideas of
his own. Having grown up in the home of a singer-
songwriter-publisher whose family lived well, it's not surprising that he's thinking along those lines.

Now, I don't mean for you to think that we were rich
when he was a little boy, but we were fairly comfortable.
Doris was busy raising our children, and she was doing a
good job. She'd got over her homesickness. She had her
own home now. We were settled in Tennessee, living in a
nice house. The family car was quite an improvement over
that tired old '49 Mercury with the hole in the windshield.

One time we planned to go home for Christmas. Doris did
her shopping early and got all the kids ready. They were
stairsteps full of energy and ready to go. I'd planned to
take my bird dog, Goldie, and her four pups with us. Birds
were plentiful in Florida. I was gonna train those puppies
to hunt. We took ole Spider, too. He was a male Irish setter
with not a whole lot of sense. I rented a U-Haul trailer,
bought me a sheet of 4′ × 8′ × ¾″ plywood, and made me an
upstairs compartment, where we put the toys and luggage.
Underneath that plywood I put all those future champion
field trial dogs. I fed and watered them real good before I

put them in there. I even left them a little three-inch space between the plywood and the door of the trailer, "so the air can circulate," I told Sonny Boy.

Goldie was the only one with road experience, and I knew the others would get road sick about three miles out of town, but I assured Doris they couldn't get into the top compartment, where our Christmas was. Doris never did care too much for my dogs. They got on her nerves, she said.

I had to do a show over in North Carolina, and we figured to spend the night there and go on down to Florida the next morning.

I didn't let those dogs out until we got to where I was going to sing. I didn't mean to let them out then. I opened the door just a little bit and peeped in at them. When I did, every one of them canines made a huge lunge for the door. They wanted air. And not that foul, putrid air inside the trailer. They knocked me down and took off in every direction. "Oh, Lord God, I've done it this time, I'll never round them all up," I said.

The kids were laughing their heads off, and Doris was just a-fussing. She really fussed when she took a look inside the trailer. Those dogs had chewed into the area where our Christmas gifts were stored, brought them down onto the bottom compartment floor, and crapped all over everything in sight. The scene was a disaster.

I still haven't heard the end of that one. I didn't have a band then, so a few of the local pickers helped Sonny Boy and me round up the dogs. I worked the show, and the next morning we went on to Florida. When we got to Mama's house, Sonny Boy and I had to wash that dog doo-doo off what toys we could save. Some we threw away, and then Doris had to go Christmas shopping again in Plant City.

I gave those dogs away in Florida. I had to. Doris wouldn't ride back with us to Tennessee if they did. She told me so several times.

By now, we had lots of friends, most of them successful

folks in the music world. Some were performers who were a lot more famous than I was. Performing is where the really big money was, and still is. I was spending most of my time writing, but went out for an occasional one-nighter now and then to sing and tell a few stories. People wanted to hear me talk just as much as they wanted to hear me sing, maybe more. I was slowly building a reputation in the business as a good performer who pleased the audience—but I was far from being a star.

I wasn't known to the public around the country as a performer or well-established singer. Until the late 1960s that was something a country artist could accomplish only by lots of touring and making big-selling hit records. That was the old way, and it took years.

Then along came television.

It hadn't paid much attention to country entertainers and their music. TV zeroed in on country slowly, long after it had presented other kinds of popular music. But even on a reduced scale, the exposure it gave to our music—and the talents—made country music a whole new ball game. It was a giant step forward.

Television was an exciting thing for me—now I could be introduced to millions of people all at once. I recall the first time I was on a national television show. It was a one-time shot. My friend the singer Jimmy Dean was co-hosting Mike Douglas's show for a week. He wanted me to appear as a guest on one of those shows up in Philadelphia, but he had a hard time getting Mike to accept me. No talk show had ever had a stutterer on—a real stutterer. "You'll love Mel, believe me," Dean promised.

Well, they decided to take a chance.

I was so excited that I bought me a new Martin guitar. When I got to Philadelphia, I went to the studio to rehearse with Mike's band. When I opened the guitar case, I found it didn't have any strings on it, so I couldn't play it. I had forgotten to tell the clerk to put strings on it when I was buying it.

Well, I went ahead and rehearsed with the piano. I think Jimmy played his accordian. Now, that's a treat, if you've never heard him play. Since I couldn't play my guitar, I sang a duet, "Detroit City," with Jimmy, told a few anecdotes, and did one song with Mike's band.

In 1963 the song "Detroit City," which I'd co-written with Danny Dill, had become a big, big hit, and I still close my concerts with it. It was inspired by people I'd met while touring—men and women from the South who'd gone up to Detroit to work in the automobile factories. They missed the southern ways of life, their homes, the loved ones they'd left behind.

> *Home folks think I'm big in Detroit City,*
> *From the letters that I write, they think I'm doing fine.*
> *By day I make the cars, but by night I make the bars.*
> *If only they could read between the lines.*
> *I wanna go home . . . I wanna go home,*
> *Oh, Lord, I wanna go home.**

That's the heart of it, and it touched a lot of homesick hearts everywhere, especially the soldiers overseas.

My first break on a weekly television series came with Porter Wagoner. He was hot, with a lot of hit records and big audiences wherever he toured. He had just hired Dolly Parton to be his girl singer, and his syndicated television show was doing well. It was in a lot of markets. Porter and I were good buddies. We fished a lot together. I taught him how to fish, as a matter of fact.

One evening we were fishing up on Center Hill Lake, near Smithville (the night was quiet and the fish weren't cooperating at all), when he suddenly said, "Tillie my boy, I'm gonna make you a star."

"You're gonna what?"

---

*"Detroit City" copyright © 1962 and 1977 by Cedarwood Publishing Company (A Division of Musiplex, Inc.).

"Television is really, really powerful," he told me, "and I'm gonna make you a member of my show."

And he did.

I joined as singer, and did a little comedy, too, but from the first day I went to work for him, our friendship seemed to change. He made it clear that I was working for him, which was okay. I knew who the boss was. I did whatever he said as long as it pertained to the job. But I had a mind of my own on other things.

It just didn't work out. He *was* right about TV, though. That exposure really did change my career for the better. Porter introduced me to the whole country audience, and later, Glen Campbell, with his "Good Time Hour," introduced me to the world.

Why did it go wrong between Porter and me? He was a star, and somehow had to be the boss at everything, even offstage. We'd make a bet on a football game and I'd win. He didn't like that. I won bets week after week, and he got madder and madder. He didn't know that I was well informed on football, that I'd played it, studied it, and loved it. Football's my favorite sport. Just ask my wife, Judy. She knows.

Those days I was doing a lot of writing. When I'd pitch him a song, he'd brush it off, saying Dolly's songs were better. Maybe they were—she's a fine writer—but he could have at least *listened* to mine. I had a track record of my own.

I was doing well on his show. People liked me. My songs weren't doing so badly, either. That included ones he'd refused even to hear. He just wouldn't admit he could be wrong. I believe all that troubled him.

Well, one Friday night I was with a friend—Earl Richards—at Linebaugh's Restaurant having some of the world's best chili. We'd put down a few beers earlier, across the street at Tootsie's. It was a peaceful Friday night.

Until somebody started a fight.

I got hit immediately. Somebody sucker-punched me right in the throat, which is bad for a singer—hell, bad for anybody. I couldn't talk above a whisper for three days. I wasn't even in the brawl and didn't have the slightest idea what they were fighting about, but I caught that punch. The police came and arrested everybody but Earl and me. We were hiding underneath a table, so they missed us. Still, the damage was done. Porter heard about it pretty fast.

I phoned him myself the next morning. "Porter, I can't do the Opry tonight," I whispered. "I've got a sore throat." Which was the truth.

"I've already heard," he said. "I want you to meet me at my apartment Sunday morning."

I knew what was coming.

I guess I was agitating him. When I started to realize that TV was telling me that I was somebody myself, I really began to get in his way, which I shouldn't have done. But he shouldn't have treated me the way he was doing, either. I hadn't done anything but try to make his show a little bit better.

I worried about it all night. Here I had had a chance, and I blew it. I dragged my guilty ass over to see him the next morning.

He was sitting there in his housecoat, eating crackers and milk. That was his favorite snack.

"I just want you to know that you're not the kind of image I want to project on my show and for my fans," he announced, "so I'm going to have to let you go."

I kept my cool. "Well, Porter, I hate for you to feel like this, and I'm sorry all this has happened," I answered. I had my temper in hand. "And I want to thank you for trying to help me. Maybe I'm not ready for the big time."

Then the question of the next tour came up. The Porter Wagoner Show was about to go on the road.

"What are you going to do about me on the tour?" I asked. "My name's on the posters and the advertising. The promoters are expecting me to be there."

"You can go on the tour," he broke in, "but you're not gonna use my band."

He still had to pay me $300 a night, and I had a little money from my songwriting. "Well, I'll just start my own band," I said.

So I hired me three guys. That's another thing I owe my friend, Porter—he pushed me into starting my own band. Porter and I have been friends again for years—and we laugh at our childishness. I suppose I was as guilty as he was. Both of us were headstrong at the time.

First stop on the tour was Kingsport, Tennessee. I got a standing ovation. Porter was still in his bus, but he heard about it—I told him. And then a new singer named Charlie Pride came on. He's a superstar today. Well, Charlie was just great that night. He was really on, and the same thing happened. Porter had to follow him.

And this went on night after night. I was getting tight with my new band—which added to Porter's aggravation. Finally, in Oklahoma City, Porter announced that he'd open from here on out. He said we stayed on too long, and he got tired of waiting, but we knew the real reason.

Charlie and I kept getting standing ovations anyway. Porter, who's a very talented guy himself, couldn't wait for that tour to end. When it did, I began getting some bookings on my own for my little band and me. There's no doubt that the exposure on Porter's TV show helped a lot—and so did my success on that tour.

After Porter Wagoner fired me, I didn't want to see another rhinestone cowboy suit for the rest of my life. They were going out of style, anyway. David Allen Coe had hit town and he was hanging around my office, singing me new songs every day. I liked him. He was different. I asked him if he wanted my rhinestone suits. He said, "Hell, yeah, I'll take 'em." He could barely squeeze into them, but he made it. In exchange, I made him take my picture out of the back window of an old hearse he used as his band bus. He liked the trade.

He became known as the Mysterious Rhinestone Cowboy. He's a pretty big act today.

It wasn't long before I got another major boost. I was invited to appear on NBC's "Tonight Show" with Johnny Carson. That man and his producer are both great guys who've been so friendly and helpful—and they're masters at what they do. Johnny's TV show is the best, the tops, and it draws millions of people every weekday night.

But before I got to Johnny Carson, who has helped make so many singers' and comics' careers, I was invited to go on another television series—the day after Porter had fired me. Fate? It was the "Glen Campbell Good Time Hour," a huge success between 1969 and 1971. Glen isn't just a good ole boy from Arkansas. He's a *great* ole boy—and a super singer, actor, TV personality, and friend. He's one of our closest friends. When he comes to Nashville to record a new album, he and his wife, Kim, and new baby, Caledonia, stay with us at our farm.

I went on his show seventeen times, doing more comedy than I'd ever tried before. Glen, who has a gift for being funny himself, encouraged me to do comedy. Others, such as Minnie Pearl, Jimmie Dean, Webb Pierce, and Porter Wagoner, had also told me I should try and talk a little onstage. They kept saying I could and should do it. But it took me a lot of years to get up the confidence.

When I'd gone out with the Duke of Paducah, I hadn't said *one word* onstage the whole tour. I didn't think that I could. If I just stood there choking, stuttering, and failing, I'd really have been embarrassed, so I didn't risk it. At the end of the tour, when the Duke dropped me off at our little apartment on Peachtree Street, I joked about it.

"N-n-n-next time you n-n-need a good MC, just gimme a call," I told him.

Having a sense of humor about yourself, even if you don't have any big problems, is always the best way to go, I've found out. It helped me through a whole lot of difficult times. Being a good-natured person, I'd begun to kid a little about the way I spoke. I couldn't exactly ignore it, could I?

If I wanted to be more than just a singer in somebody else's band or show, I would have to talk. Since I spoke differently, I might as well make an asset of it. A major performer must share his personality with the audiences. The easiest thing for me was to show my sense of humor. And people liked it.

While I was doing those Campbell shows, I was flying out a couple of days every week to meet my new band. We worked all over the place. It was hard work doing both, and I hardly ever got home. I didn't think much about what that could do in the long run. My mind was on today. I finally had my own band and I was my own boss. We were moving up the way every country band has to. We were on the road.

CHAPTER
19

A lot of people think that a musician's life on the road is one big good time—a traveling party.

It sure sounds that way from what you read in the *National Enquirer* and other newspapers. Going from city to city with hardly a care. Seeing the world from one end to the other. Traveling first-class in sleek jets and staying in the best hotels.

Meeting scores of pretty girls—*all friendly*. Eating in the best restaurants, staying up as late as you want, and drinking as much as your body can hold. Meeting eager fans who flatter you and beg for your autograph. Doing exactly what you enjoy doing, with big money to spend, and no nagging boss or dreary nine-to-five schedule. Every day filled with total pleasure—each a new adventure. Never a dull moment or a wasted hour, just nonstop fun with exciting, talented, and famous people who're all rich, good-looking, and horny.

Well, it may be like that for the Rolling Stones or other top rock groups who move from major city to major city by jet—often in planes they own or charter. But that isn't the working life of country acts on tour, at least not mine.

Country acts don't play in big cities with the luxury hotels nearly as much, though that's starting to change. We find at least half our fans, maybe more, in smaller towns, where the best place to stay can be a Howard Johnson's or a Holiday Inn.

Now, a country star may fly to most of his show dates by plane, and he may even own the plane, but the musicians in his band do most of their traveling by bus.

Night after night—after each show—they hear, "Pack 'em up, boys, we got a long way to go and a short time to get there."

Thousands and thousands of miles each year on the same highways, in rain and snow, across mountain passes, deserts, and beautiful farmlands that stretch on forever. Trying to get some sleep on bunks in the back of the bus. Somehow it's always either too hot or too cold! But musicians do get so used to the swaying and rolling that they have trouble sleeping when they get home to their regular fixed beds.

Drinking light beer after light beer to kill the time—and maybe relax enough so you can get some sleep. Sometimes it's vodka, but not for me. No hard liquor until after the show. The audiences always come first.

Drinking all you want? You'd better not want too much if you mean to keep your job. I have a rule that covers both liquor and other stuff. Get stoned—stay home. Get high—bye-bye. I'll fire you. I've done it. I'm talking about band members who come onstage stoned.

I had one fall asleep onstage at the Riviera in Las Vegas. I lost my temper that time. It wasn't just that he was stoned. He had the audacity to fall asleep standing up in the middle of one of my stories. I told him to get his ass off the stage.

No interviews for the band—only for the star. It's almost always questions you've heard a thousand times or more. But you've got to sound fresh and interested, and usually you are because you take the press seriously.

Musicians rarely eat in anything close to fancy restaurants. Generally it's lunch on the road—some truck stop or fast-food restaurant. The boys and I know every hamburger spot from Anchorage to Miami, including the southwestern chain Whataburger, whose commercials I've been doing for quite a while now. I wish the others came up to their creed: "It's not just a hamburger, friends, it's a WHATABURGER."

To pass the time, you also eat all kinds of jungle food—jungle is the slang word we use for snack foods like potato chips, pretzels, cheese, sardines, and just munching food in general.

As for breakfast, Radio Red usually gets the bus to where we're supposed to stay around eleven in the morning, or else we get "clean-up" rooms about that time. After a bumpy all-night ride, the boys are hungry when they pile into the dining room for some ham and eggs. All too often the dining room has just closed for breakfast, since most people finish their breakfasts earlier. So it can be just a cup of coffee and a honey bun or a patty melt. But when we play casino hotels in Las Vegas, Reno, Tahoe, or Atlantic City, we don't have that problem. Their dining rooms are open twenty-four hours a day, and their food is much better, especially John Ascuaga's Nugget Hotel-Casino in Sparks, Nevada. John, the owner, is a former chef. The food there is Number One, and so is what we eat at Harrah's Hotel. But that's not what we find at most places.

For the record, there are states where we all agree on the food. Two that come to mind immediately are Texas and Louisiana—lots of good places, big and small. And to be fair to that huge city they call the Big Apple, New York's a great place to eat any ethnic dish you want. I like great variety—including plenty of Cajun seafood and Japanese, which I find best because it's light, tasty, and not too fattening. I guess I'm just naturally slim. I'm sure thankful for that. I don't watch my weight like most folks do today.

My band members are country boys and they're always

STUTTERIN' BOY 147

looking for some home-style cooking—the southern dishes they know best. We do have a Westerner from Cheyenne, Wyoming, and a Northerner from Bennington, Vermont, but most of the band is Dixie. After a show they're most likely to be found out looking for barbecue ribs and a chili joint. Country bands tip each other off about places with down-home cooking, and we get the "Smokey" reports on the road.

There was one day in Texas I recall (we were going from Fort Worth to Austin) because of Irving Cain. He's right out of Philadelphia and he comes from a good Jewish family. He's a fat little guy (he looked like Porky Pig with those cowboy boots that I made him wear onstage), with a good sense of humor. A good sense of humor is a very important asset for a touring musician. We're together on the bus, or elsewhere, for such long periods of time that fun and jokes are essential. Irving worked with us for a couple of years and played a mean trombone. That day the band was dead set on some Texas barbecue. We knew of this little barbecue shack, called Cooper's, in Mason, Texas. Sometimes we go out of our way for miles to stop there because it's really good Q.

"Irving, I think we may have a problem," Jerry Reid told him. "We're gonna stop for some Texas Q. You being Jewish, do you eat pork?"

He said, "Pork, pork. Why, you f---ing Gentiles, I mainline lard!"

Usually we're not in any place long enough to "dine" well. The bus pulls into wherever we're working during the afternoon, and the musicians set up their instruments. They do a sound check, and some look around for female companions. Often there are women who are looking themselves, out to meet musicians. Some ladies are pretty and some are lonely and others are just curious. Some are all three.

There isn't an awful lot of time for the touring musicians to find out, but they usually manage. There's only a few hours for that. We don't stay overnight in too many places. When we do, two musicians will share a room to cut down on expenses. They like Vegas and other similar resorts because we get to stay for a week or more, and the casino hotels furnish them individual rooms free. When we're doing one-nighters, the musicians in most bands pay for the room themselves. That's because a lot of them are paid on a nightly basis. Mine are.

And what about staying up late? The traveling musicians' problem is just the opposite—it's getting to sleep after a rousing performance in a bus that's traveling a bumpy highway.

Autographs? Usually nobody asks the musicians in the band to sign anything (unless they're Chet Atkins or Floyd Cramer), except the hotel clerk when they check in somewhere. Being asked for an autograph isn't all that wonderful an experience for the one whose name is on the posters or marquee—the one they call the headliner. I don't mean to rain on your fantasy, but years of experience tell me that perhaps half the people who get your signature "for my sister" will lose it before they get home. Finding that out should shrink a lot of swelled heads, but it doesn't.

What about the pay? Well, most touring country musicians get $500 or $600 a week. I pay my band members $250 to $300 a night, and sometimes more. It depends on what the job pays me. They earn some more from recording sessions and television appearances, and they share in the money made from sales of pictures, albums, and T-shirts after the shows. I've always wanted a first-class band, and I've got one. I believe I owe that much to the people who pay good money to come and see us and hear us pick. Without those people, I might still be picking strawberries, glazing doughnuts, or driving Harry's cookie truck.

As for a road musician's schedule, true, it isn't nine to five, but in some ways, it's worse. Natural habits changing as the tour requires, meals are eaten when the schedule permits. You are not your own boss. The schedule's in charge.

Is the life really full of excitement? Sometimes it is, but the biggest and most frequent problem on the road is boredom. Monotony and idle time . . . hours of lonesome highways . . . being cooped up in the bus like sardines with the same bunch of guys, who've already told you all their family problems and jokes eighty-nine times . . . rarely having time enough anywhere to take in a movie, go to a ballgame, go fishing, or do just about anything else.

CHAPTER

20

I've always found that life on the road is actually like being in the Air Force. You're far from home, living with a bunch of men who also work with you, trying to do your job right and to beat off the empty hours.

You share the gossip about other bands—which ones are selling records, drawing big or small audiences, drinking too much or using drugs, or getting into various other kinds of predicaments.

You argue about sports—defending favorite teams and confidently predicting the defeat of rivals. You can get fired for that. I know.

You tell jokes—clean and not so clean. You discuss television shows you've seen.

You tell stories, some pretty funny, about crazy things that happened last night or two years ago. Humor is a very precious commodity on the road—as necessary as water.

You play video games in motels, hotels, truck stops, or anywhere else you can find them. I guess they're a challenge and a distraction, a way to pass the time.

You flirt with waitresses . . . maids . . . other women. A

lot of times they flirt first. Half the time they're just kidding. Three quarters of the time your fellow musicians will kid you about those ladies—their beauty and intelligence, or lack of either. The joking rarely gets serious. The road would be even worse if anyone was too serious.

Keep it light.

Keep it funny.

We're moving on in an hour—five hundred miles to the next show.

You talk about the food at the place you just left, and whether you can get your laundry done at the next.

You take catnaps in the bunks—rolling and swaying in that special half-sleep. You smoke too much—if you're not careful. I've given it up myself. And if you're off smoking, you may chew tobacco or gum or snuff. I've given up snuff several times.

And some guys will even raise questions of religion. Breadman—that's what everybody but me called my brother—was the best at that. Like our two grandmothers, Richard had read the Bible many times and studied lots of books on the subject.

We talk about nature, too. Yes, the conversation does turn to beauty and scenic wonders. We recall great mountains and forests, lakes and waterfalls and sunsets. Dawn breaking over the desert . . . the majestic marvels of Alaska and the crisp, clean air of Canada . . . that flight of geese . . . the swaying golden fields of wheat . . . forests that looked on fire as the leaves turned in autumn . . . the deer by the side of the road.

Musicians do a lot of crazy things to break the boredom. They have to or they'd go nuts. I've sure as hell done my share. It helps.

One summer we were in Williamsburg, Virginia, and it was hot as Hades. We were finishing up our last performance at the beautiful Busch Gardens. It's a great place to take your family. It has lots of joyrides, all kinds of animals, good hamburgers, and no alcoholic beverages. We played our music in the amphitheater. It really is a beautiful place. There's a moat about six feet wide and maybe five feet deep that separates the audience from the stage. The crowd was very enthusiastic, even in that July heat. We tried hard to please. Little did they know that we were bored and tired. We'd been out on the road for quite some time and all of us wanted to go home. I could tell the boys needed a good laugh. I introduced Paul Franklin, our steel guitar player, to do a solo number. While he was playing a very beautiful "Harbor Lights," I leaned over and whispered to Buchanan, "When Paul stands up to take a bow, push him in the water and I'll give you fifty dollars."

"You got it, chief," he said.

Paul finished his solo and then stood up to take a bow, as the audience applauded. Ole Bukes just walked right over and pushed him off the stage, into the moat below. When Paul hit the water, he was pale as a ghost. He went down and came up kicking and hollering, "I can't swim, I can't swim!"

That scared the hell out of us. We all jumped in to save Paul. Nobody wanted a drowning on their conscience. My feet hit the bottom of that concrete moat and jarred me goofy for a second or two. That water wasn't but three feet deep. The crowd just went crazy. I think several of them jumped in, too. Finally I said, "Boys, I was getting tired of these old blue uniforms, anyway."

We got a standing ovation. They wanted us to go back onstage and play some more music. I begged off and told them we couldn't play our electrified instruments with those wet clothes on. They understood. They must have, because they invited us back the next year. I paid Buchanan his $50, got on the bus, and said, "Let's go home, Red."

I heard the Oak Ridge Boys did the same thing a few weeks later. I'm glad we were first. I think the band was, too.

One time we were working a fair-rodeo in Billings, Montana. We had an off day before we moved on to the next town, so I asked the boys if they'd like to go somewhere and do a little fishing. "We could buy a few staples and cook our catch right on the creek bank," I told them. They were all for that.

I announced onstage that night we had a day off and wanted to do a little fishing. Was there anybody there kind enough to tell us where to go, or take us and we'd follow them in the bus? Well, four hundred people showed up after the show, and each one of them was an expert in the art of angling. They knew just where to go. We quickly chose one at random, then apologized and thanked the rest. That ole boy said, "I'll meet you at your motel 'bout seven in the morning."

We were up and at 'em, sitting and waiting on the bus when he got there. He was about an hour late, and looked like death eating a cracker. He mumbled something about too much beer last night. Breadman told our new fishing friend that we had to stop somewhere and get some groceries and a couple more cheap fishing rods. He said, "We already have four or five on the bus from one of Mebin's last safaris." We needed a skillet and a coffeepot, too. I think I spent more than $600 for that stuff. We bought enough for three weeks. Finally we took off for the mountains, following our fishing friend in his pickup truck. He rode by himself, because nobody wanted to ride with him in his condition.

Every one of us had envisioned a beautiful silver mountain stream winding through virgin evergreen timber. Boy, we couldn't wait to get there. Then he made a left turn and Radio Red followed with the bus. After a while somebody noticed the mountains had become hills, then it was flat sagebrush land. "His damn compass must be broke, we're headed away from the mountains," Larry Lee said.

"That ole boy knows where he's going, leave him alone," Buchanan said. After what seemed like hours, we began to wonder.

Finally the pickup truck pulled up to an old farmhouse in the middle of nowhere and stopped. Alvin Angler (we'd named him by then) got out of his pickup and hollered, "Okay, boys, this is it. Get your poles ready."

"You gotta be kidding us," I said. "There's not a fish within a hundred miles of this place."

"Oh, yes, there is," he said defensively. "Right over there behind that big old barn."

We all walked over behind the barn to take a look. I couldn't believe it. There was a little stream about five foot wide flowing through that flat land, and it was running about a hundred miles an hour.

We eagerly started tying on plastic worms and spinners; some were even gonna use corks.

"You'll need a forty-pound sinker to fish like that," Alvin Angler said, chuckling. "You gotta use grasshoppers to catch 'em here. Live grasshoppers!"

"Well, we ain't got no grasshoppers, sir," I argued.

"You gotta catch 'em," he told us. "There's millions in the fields around here."

You've never seen the like in your life. The band was jumping around mor'n the grasshoppers. "I got one, Melvin," Whipple, our piano player, hollered.

"I got two," said Bukes.

"They're too damn quick for me," Larry said angrily.

We finally got to fishing. Man, oh, man, we caught brook trout and rainbow just as soon as those poor little grasshoppers hit that cold, swift water. This went on for maybe an hour. We had plenty enough to eat. "Let's get to cooking 'em," I said.

Larry Lee and Ronnie Mac (Whipple) were always going on diets. Larry weighed about 240 pounds and Whipple was a large 350 pounds. It just so happened that they were on one of their off-and-on diets that day. I think they had a $50 bet on, and the first one to fall off had to pay off.

Mother Nature put on quite a display that evening in Montana. Her old sun slowly sank into the west, and then it was gone. But the campfire was going by then, popping and crackling. It felt good! Pretty soon the coffee was boiling, and it had the best aroma you ever smelled in your life. Coffee always does smell better to me in the woods. That skillet we bought at the grocery store in Billings was big enough to cook all our trout at one time—they were about eight to ten inches long. Reid peeled the onions and cried and bitched the whole time, asking what he'd done to deserve this. I laid several cans of pork and beans up against the fire, while Radio peeled the taters. Everything was pretty close to perfect, I'd say.

Buchanan finished the chores that I'd assigned to him, and I told him to go and get his fiddle. "It seems right for a little campfire music," I said. Someone else got a guitar and Reid continued to bitch.

Well, with the music going, the fish frying, the coffee boiling, the pork and beans simmering, and Jerry Reid crying, Whipple allowed he'd better go to the bus, get in his bunk, and finish reading a new Louis L'Amour paperback. He said he just couldn't stand around very long and smell all that good food cooking and not eat any of it. He reminded us that he had this bet with Larry about their diet, and that he certainly wouldn't be the one who fell off first. "I haven't got fifty dollars to give away," he said. Then he waddled to the bus.

Larry waited around for a few minutes, then he said, with a puzzled look, "I'd better go and check on him. He's probably got about six of those rainbow trout in one pocket and a can of pork and beans in the other."

We all laughed at his comment. Larry was funny, and just as hungry as Whipple. He departed for the bus and a few minutes later came back to the cookout and told us this story. He said that when he got to the bus he felt the whole darn thing shaking up and down. He told us he looked up the aisle to Whipple's bunk, which was on the floor, and for a reason. When the bus was new, the others had made Whipple take a bottom bunk. "Nobody wants to sleep with

three hundred and fifty pounds of live weight above them,"
Mouse, one of the fiddle players, had said.

Larry told us, "I crawled as quiet as I could, on my hands
and knees, to that gadget-ridden bunk. His curtain"—each
bunk has its own—"was going in and out, like someone was
punching it with their fist from the inside. I yanked his
curtain back and said, 'Ah-hah, I've caught you—' 'You
wanna bite?' Whipple said, with a grin."

"What was he doing, Larry?" someone asked.

"He was salting a big ole low-calorie red tomato," Larry
disappointedly told us.

Larry went on to become Lee Greenwood's manager.
Lee's doing great these days, and so is Larry. I'm really
proud for the both of them.

Whipple couldn't take the road anymore, so he moved
back to Texas. I think an awful lot of that ole boy. He wrote
a lot of hit songs for me. He sure has the talent, but he
hasn't written any for me lately.

The first time my brother, Breadman, went out on the
road with the band and me, I didn't have a bus, couldn't
afford one. We traveled in a car and a station wagon and
pulled a trailer behind it.

The day we left, Richard loaded my guitar and our
clothes from the house in Brentwood into the trunk of the
Cadillac. He'd yet to learn the lingo of the road. After we
arrived at our destination, and as I was checking out my
dressing room backstage, I told him to go out and get me
my axe.

"Okay," was his answer, as only he can say it.

It was forty-five minutes before he returned, looking
worried. "Mebin," he said, "I looked all over that car for an
axe and I ain't found it yet."

"Richard," I translated, "my *guitar!*"

"Oh, hell"—he hardly ever cussed—"why didn't you say
so? I was wondering what you were gonna chop."

He learned fast after that.

Sometimes touring isn't the least bit funny. It can be dangerous. Our bus spun off an icy highway in the Rockies, hurting one band member enough for us to take him to the hospital for an examination. Luckily nothing serious was wrong with him, he was just very shook up.

But nature isn't the only threat.

One night, after we got our first bus, we were playing at a little club out in some scrub oak woods near Skidmore, Texas. I had a real good band—Tommy Jackson was on fiddle—but only about two hundred people came to see us. The rest of the town went up the road to see another entertainer named Al Dean, and his band. They were currently a "hot" act in those parts.

Well, the owner of the place where we were playing wasn't too happy at all. To him he was paying us plenty for that night, and he could see he wouldn't take in that much. So he got drunk and questioned our worth.

He asked me to come over to a little annex, where he got drunker and drunker.

"You ain't worth that kind of money," he said. "You ain't never had to go out in a hot Texas morning and treat a sick calf dying from screw worms in its navel."

I was drinking a little, too. "Well, you didn't have to drive two thousand miles round-trip from Nashville to do it either," I answered. "Mister, if you don't have the cash to pay us, that's fine, I'll take a check."

"I got the damn money," he roared.

"Then pay me."

He called to the main building and told his wife to cut my check. Then he staggered out the door. There was a girl sitting there, who'd been watching what was going on, and she told me I'd better get myself over and pick up my check before he got back.

"I know this cowboy, and he's gone to get his *gun*," she warned.

So I told the boys to get on our new bus (it was a '49 Flex, but new to us) because we'd probably be leaving in a hurry.

There was no way I was going into that main building to pick up that check alone.

"J.R.," I said to my drummer, "let's go in there and get our money. You cover my rear and don't let anybody jump on me."

We went over to the main building, where we found that drunk owner's wife and eight mean-looking Mexicans, who worked there waiting for us.

"Here's your money," the lady said.

As I reached for it, she dropped the check on the floor. It wasn't any accident. I guess she was trying to delay us. She knew her husband was going for his gun.

I eased down and picked up the check, then we backed out of there real carefully, just like in those old Western movies. We got on the bus. Would you believe it wouldn't start? It was an old bus, one I'd bought third-hand. I'd named it *Old Faithful*, after one of my earlier hits. It had a lot of miles on it, but it was all I could afford then. I traded up to a Silver Eagle later, when we were doing better. (I sold the old bus to the New Haven Blades ice hockey team. I hope they didn't have any trouble with it.)

Knowing that numb nuts was coming with a gun, we piled out of the bus and pushed it off. We put a lot of spirit into that pushing, and it began to roll. Just after it started, we all jumped on, and I turned to look back. I saw that man coming about forty yards away, with a shotgun under his arm. We split, and that was the end of that. I couldn't believe the check was good, but we cashed it—fast—and it was.

Well, I haven't been back to that club since, and I'm glad!

Another time we were headed for the Oklahoma State Fairgrounds in Tulsa. Some promoter had rented the place for our show. We were hot as a group, "Mel Tillis and his

Statesiders," and had filled that spot several times before. The Oklahoma State Police stopped us at the first toll gate and told us someone had phoned that they'd bomb the fairgrounds if I played.

A gang of security men went through the building from top to bottom, searching for the bomb. I needed the money badly and I didn't want to disappoint the people who'd bought tickets, so we went ahead and played, anyway. But I sure was plenty scared.

Sometimes one of our own musicians gets out of line. This one time I recall, they were having a bass tournament down at our favorite fishing camp near Moore Haven, Florida, with professional fishermen from all over the nation competing for money prizes. There was serious prize money at stake. The camp was located on the west shore of Lake Okeechobee. It's gone now, torn down when the Corps of Engineers decided to raise the lake. It was an old camp with cabins, which you could say were slightly run down. Naturally, anytime we were in southern Florida and had some time off, I'd want to go fishing. I may be only a fair poker player, but anyone who's fished with me can tell you that's one thing that I do very well. I take my fishing seriously. I just love it.

And I've known that lake for a long time. It's still one of my favorite places. Great large-mouth bass and boyhood memories to match. The place was Howdy Bateman's Sportsman's Village.

When we finished a show somewhere near, we'd pile into the bus and drive straight there. We'd check in by one in the morning, drink a few beers, and go to bed. We'd get up the next morning and fish out of airboats until about noon. The fish usually quit biting after that. Then we'd bring in the fish we caught.

The ladies who worked at the fishing camp would always tell us, "We gonna cook ya'll a bucket tonight, hon." We'd have the fish we caught with turnip greens, hush puppies, iced tea, grits, and everything traditional that a meal like that calls for. In the evening we'd have a big time, with plenty of good food, cold beer, and high spirits. For some, high spirits meant joking, but for other guys it was the kind of spirits that run 90 proof.

"Break out the instruments, boys," I'd tell the band, and after the normal complaints they'd get their instruments from the bus, set up in the lodge, and we'd play a free concert for everyone. We'd all enjoy it, singing songs, playing music, eating some more fish, and dancing all night. I didn't mind if the boys drank, since this was an informal gathering, a labor of love—our way of letting our hair down for a night or two. It was a bonafide redneck party.

This night during the bass tournament, one of my band members Odell Martin, from Allegre, Kentucky, had about three drinks too many. Or maybe it was five, which was unusual for him. He hardly ever drank. Anyway, he was roaring.

The pros had come in earlier and weighed in their catches. One had come up with an obvious winner—a twelve-pound large-mouth bass. It was tagged and placed—alive—in a holding tank by the docks for the judging later. Somebody bet Odell that he couldn't catch one of those big prize bass—there were several in the tank—with his bare hands. Now, that's a powerful challenge to a Kentuckian. Well, that drunken guitar picker climbed right into the tank and, laughing his head off, caught that twelve-pounder, threw it out on the dock, and was stomping the life out of the frightened fish when the rest of us were alerted by the noise.

He was usually a peaceful guy—as musicians go. I've had wilder ones with us, and guys who did much stranger things when they were cold sober. We had a piano player who never liked the lighting fixtures in any of the hotels and motels we stayed in. So as soon as he checked into his room, he'd disconnect the switches and install his own dim-

Mel receiving the Entertainer of the Year
award, 1976 (The Nashville Banner)

Mel with Glen Campbell on TV's "Hee Haw"

Mel with Burt Reynolds and Dottie West

On the "Tonight" show with Johnny Carson

Mel addresses the guests at Frank Sinatra's sixty-fifth birthday party in Palm Springs on December 12, 1980.

Mel with Willie Nelson *(Bob Younts)*

Mel with Clint Eastwood during the filming of *Every Which Way But Loose*

Mel with Roy Acuff at the Grand Ole Opry

Pahokee, Florida and Okeechobee Lake *(Dunn's Aerial Photography, Inc.)*

Carrie April (Mel's youngest daughter) singing onstage in Las Vegas at the Frontier Hotel

mers. He'd take them out before he left, and fix the room up the way he'd found it.

Going back to the guitar picker who was in the fish tank, I heard all that commotion going on, so I ran over to see what was happening. I could hardly believe my eyes.

"If the pro who caught that prize-winning fish comes by," I said to him, "he'll kill your Kentucky ass right here."

So I got several of the boys and we dragged him out of that tank—a-fightin' and a-kickin' all the way. He passed out a few seconds after we put him to bed. I believe that I saved two lives that night—Odell's and that twelve-pound bass.

We've also had problems with other people's roaring. There have been plenty of times when we'd catch it as soon as we reached some town to check into the motel. Another band, and not necessarily country, had just been through—and they'd raised all kinds of hell. They'd broken up furniture, started fights, or made trouble with a hotel owner's wife or a policeman's pretty sixteen-year-old daughter.

There are at least two kinds of trouble that road bands can get into with some local man's little precious. I've warned my boys about that a million times. One happens when the lady is annoyed by the flirting, and the other when she isn't. If she doesn't mind, it could agitate a husband or father who doesn't think too highly of traveling musicians and their loud electric amplified instruments. A lot of bands don't take that advice to heart, which can lead to a real unfriendly reception for the next group of pickers to hit town.

But on the whole, we're a group that's easy to get along with and that trusts one another—very important, if you're cooped up together the way we are for so many months a year, living and working side by side day and night.

Much of our talk together is about people we've met. It could be a policeman who was friendly in some town—who told a joke as he let Radio Red park the bus where he wasn't supposed to. It could be a motel clerk who was confused, or a huge security guard on duty backstage somewhere. It could be that wonderful widow in Texas who bakes us cakes and cookies—one of the nicest people we've ever come across.

We're just crazy about that sweet lady, and she feels the same about us. Her husband died some years ago, and she took it very hard. She missed him so much that she went into a terrible depression. Feeling that there wasn't much left for her, she just holed up in her house, hurting.

One night a friend of hers talked her into coming to see one of our shows. That was in Victoria, Texas. It was her first time out of the house in months. We're a happy group and we play happy. Somehow she caught the spirit. She had a ball. She broke out of that depression and went back to living again, as much as she could. I guess it was a small miracle—or maybe it was the magic and positive energy of country music. It's hard to tell what will heal the human spirit.

Well, she was so grateful that she became the number-one fan of Mel Tillis and the Statesiders. Why the Lord chose us to help her is a mystery, but that's what we did that night in Victoria, Texas. My band talks about the amazing number of beautiful young women in Texas, but that gray-haired widow lady is our favorite.

My band does plenty more with their spare time than talk about women, eat, play games, and watch television or taped movies. Quite a few of the boys read—whatever they can get their hands on. If you have an image of these guys as simple redneck pickers, forget it. They read a variety of books, and they discuss and debate them. Breadman was the champ at that. They often talk about serious things.

Yes, there's conversation about women—Brown Eye, the Pennsylvania Queens, Lottie Applecrumbie, just to name a few—and beer and sports, but they discuss religion, family things, music, and how to save for their children's future. They're not scholars, but they're better educated than most musicians were when I started out. Seven of my band members have completed college.

Some might ask, Then what are those guys doing in country music?

I think the answer sticks out all over. They're the lucky ones. This is what they want to do. Country is the music they want to play. I'm proud to say they're real good at it. I wouldn't settle for a second-class band. Mama raised me to try to do the best . . . to be the best.

Well, Mama, I'm still trying.

CHAPTER

21

As we began to get more jobs and better money, I found I was on the road more and more. We cruised the highways from one end of the country to the other—building a name and a following.

But I still kept writing songs. It isn't hard for me to do that on a moving bus or in some hotel room. When the urge comes, I can write anywhere, anytime. It doesn't matter whether it is high noon or one in the morning, a moonlit night or a winter storm. I didn't use to have to write down the words of new songs as I thought of them. I did them in my head. But I need a pencil and paper now. I guess that comes with age.

What I do need to write a song is an idea with a feeling.

I think that most other men and women who write songs (there are plenty of good lady songwriters) also work from stories they hear or read in the papers, or heavy feelings about something. Lots of times the story is a true one—something that gets into a writer's heart. It could be something that's happened to them or a friend or relative. It might be a happy experience or a sad one that touched a neighbor.

Not all the stories in songs are true, of course. But most of the best ones are.

Real life touches on people and their ways, which means basic feelings. A song that deals with those feelings—which we all know so well—can find a very big audience fast. My most successful song was the result of a tragedy that took place less than thirty yards from where we lived on Cypress Avenue in Pahokee, Florida. Kenny Rogers's recording of it sold millions of copies (over fifteen million by the last account), and other artists have done it. I sing it in every show I do. I tell the people that song paid my grocery bills for fifteen years, and that's the truth. It was a tremendous hit, a songwriter's dream.

The song was "Ruby, Don't Take Your Love to Town." I wrote it driving home from Cedarwood to Donelson, where we lived at the time on Cabin Hill Road. I didn't have to write that song down because that story had been working inside me somewhere for years. Both the words and the music came to me at the same time, as they often do.

It's a song full of hurt. Many of the best country songs are. Doris said it was the most morbid song she'd ever heard. It goes:

You've painted up your lips and rolled and curled your
 tinted hair,
Ruby, are you contemplating going out somewhere?
The shadows on the wall tell me the sun is going down,
Ruby—don't take your love to town.

It wasn't me that started that old crazy Asian war
But I was proud to go and do my patriotic chores,
And yes, it's true that I'm not the man I used to be,
But, Ruby, I still need some company.

It's hard to love a man whose legs are bent and paralyzed,
And the wants and needs of a woman your age, Ruby, I
 realize,

*But it won't be long I've heard them say until I'm not
    around,
Oh, Ruby, don't take your love to town.*

*She's leaving now 'cause I just heard the slamming of the
    door
The way I know I've heard it slam one hundred times before,
And if I could move I'd get my gun and put her in the
    ground.
Ruby, don't take your love to town.**

There really was a man, wounded in battle, who lived
with his wife right behind our house. I guess his war in-
juries played hell with their love life, and she was too
young for that. Anyway, she'd get all dolled up and go out
at night to find strong and healthy lovers—leaving him
alone to think about it. She had a woman's needs for physical affection, and he had guilt, loneliness, and pain.

He had treated her real bad, beat her up all the time
when he could get his hands on her. He'd accused her of
doing things she hadn't done, and finally she did those
things. I guess she figured if he was gonna beat her up, she
might as well. He later divorced her and found another
wife, and then another after that. I heard he went berserk
and killed that one. The hurt in that man must have burned
like fire. I guess he felt that he wasn't a whole man, and he
couldn't live with that. Trapped in his crippled body, he
finally killed himself.

When that song became a blockbuster hit, some people
read a political meaning into it. They thought I'd written a
protest song attacking the Vietnam War. Well, I've never
written any kind of political or protest song in my life,
intentionally. I've got my views on politics—being a man
who cares about what happens in the world he lives in—but
I've never put them into my songs.

*"Ruby, Don't Take Your Love to Town" copyright © 1966 and 1977 by Cedar-
wood Publishing Company (A Division of Musiplex, Inc.).

The people who were so sure I had were wrong. That song had nothing to do with Vietnam or the antiwar demonstrators in the 1970s. The real-life tragedy—and the Lord knows it was truly that—involved a man who'd been wounded in Germany years earlier in World War II.

It was another war, another place. I just updated it by using the current war in Vietnam. The cause I wrote about really was people cut off from each other's needs and feelings, something that goes beyond any individual war or disaster. A ruined love . . . a broken marriage . . . the hurt of watching the one you care for desperately go off to another when you can't do a damn thing about it.

Even people who've had no personal loss from a war know about it. It's the kind of human situation so many have suffered. Rich and poor, young and old, sick and healthy, millions of people have felt that hurt. That's why the song "Ruby" could reach so many folks, and Kenny Rogers sang it with all his heart.

Those powerful emotions are a basic part of so many country songs. I think that's why country songs reach all kinds of people, in big cities and small towns, in many faraway lands. As an example, "Ruby" was recorded by a group in Ireland years later, and they used the Irish War instead of Vietnam.

Some sophisticated critics put down country lyrics as shallow, crudely written stuff for simple-minded rednecks. They say our songs are all about broken hearts, triangle love affairs, and homesick truckers. That's far from true. We have plenty of upbeat songs, happy ones, even funny ones. There are a lot more funny country songs than you'll find on pop and rock records.

And we're not the least bit ashamed of writing about the hurt and loneliness as well as the joys of love, 'cause that's what's happening. Sometimes I think women understand and feel songs better than men do. That could be because women are more in touch with their emotions and less guarded about showing them. I believe that emotional freedom and openness help women write songs with a different view—they write songs that I couldn't. We all try to write songs that people can identify with, of course. And a really good song will do that.

I think the songs country writers create do something else that's important. Since we deal with the basic things of life, and aren't ashamed to do so, our audiences feel especially close to us. That's an honor for us. We're grateful that they think of us country writers and performers as flesh-and-blood men and women, just as they are.

People come thousands of miles to visit Nashville every year—some two or three times—hoping to get closer to favorite singers like Conway Twitty, Loretta Lynn, Bill Anderson, Johnny Cash, and to the home of country music. There are no pretensions in the community that the hard-working Nashville Chamber of Commerce calls Music City, U.S.A. Everybody knows that today's big success was once maybe just a hopeful picker or farm girl not too long ago, sitting out on a stump, practicing, waiting for his or her star to shine. We've got a lot less psychiatrists, managers, and investment advisers than, say, New York or Hollywood. We take care of that kind of business ourselves.

Even when I was first building a name on the road with the Statesiders, there wasn't much patience for musicians who weren't willing to work long and hard. Success doesn't come overnight in any field—and that's especially true in country music. That's because nobody really gets that good overnight. There are exceptions, of course. You can get a hit song the first time out, but still, that doesn't make you a seasoned stage veteran. You may say, "Well, how about Lee Greenwood and Alabama?" Well, let me tell you they spent many years on the road before things happened for them. Alabama in Myrtle Beach, South Carolina, and Tallahassee, Florida, and Greenwood polished his great style in the lounges and piano bars in Vegas. Somebody may have plenty of raw talent, but that's not enough to make a first-class writer or entertainer.

That's not just my opinion. Ask the biggest names—the most successful stars. They all worked hard for a lot of years, learning, getting better, and slowly earning national attention.

A good part of the country music tradition is for established artists to encourage the younger people who're getting started. I make a point of encouraging the boys in my band to write songs—to keep at it until they come up with something good enough to record. I don't expect talented people—and my boys are certainly that—to stay working in my band forever. Many have gone on to success on their own.

I give my boys regular chances to sing in our show, to put down a foundation for going beyond being backup musicians. I encourage them to present their songs and demo tapes to other music publishing companies, not just the ones I own.

I'm a "go after it" person, always have been, and I'm not a bit ashamed to say so. Mama taught me that. Hard work and dreams are what made America the great nation it is today. If I'm not a workaholic, I'm not too far from it. I love to be with my family and I enjoy a social life, but I also find work very satisfying. On a stage, in a recording studio, on our farm, in my music room at home, writing—I don't waste any time. Well, not much, anyway.

When I was a youngster, Mama always told me, "Nobody's going to put the dime in the phone for you, Melvin. You've got to do it yourself." I still work on that principle.

Some young people who show up in Nashville these days seem to expect overnight success. That ain't gonna happen, folks. There are no instant stars—or ways to become one. Still, some inexperienced folks come to Nashville with a guitar and a ton of confidence, looking for a recording contract or publishing deal the first week. Many of them don't want to listen to anyone who won't promise that—even professionals who tell them that they have real promise. Encouragement isn't enough for some amateur writers and singers.

"Get a regular job, or at least a part-time one, to support yourself, a day job," I tell them, "and work on your music at night. Or go for a job doing anything at a record company or a music publisher. Sweep the floors if necessary. It's going to take a while and some good songs to get noticed. But never be a burden to anyone."

Some are lazy, and others are too damned proud to work at a regular job. Some of them wouldn't hit a lick at a cottonmouth snake even if it were coiled and ready to strike. And most of the time, a lot of licks are necessary.

That's been my experience. Take the case of my song "Ruby." I recorded it myself first, on an album in 1967. I didn't put it out as a single, not after Doris told me that it was the most morbid song she'd ever heard.

Anybody can be wrong about a song. They say that Gene Autry only recorded "Rudolph, the Red-Nosed Reindeer" because his wife liked it; he didn't think it would work. Well, my album did well, but "Ruby" was a timely song and that wasn't the time for it to step out. It looked as if Doris might have been right.

Then Waylon Jennings took a lick at it on an album, and my old buddy Roger Miller covered it, too, in his album. And although they're outstanding artists, nothing much happened with the song.

Later that year Johnny Darrell took another lick at it. His record made it to the top ten on the country charts— which was good, but no blockbuster.

Then Kenny Rogers and the First Edition—a group that wasn't even country—cut it for their *Something's Burning* album, and the record label had to pull it for a single by popular demand. It flew like the great speckled bird, all the way up the charts. Kenny Rogers has put it on several of his albums, pop and country, and a bunch of other artists have cut it, too. Faron Young, George Jones, Carl Perkins, Flatt and Scruggs, Danny Davis and the Nashville Brass, and even Mel Tillis. Yes, I did it again in 1975.

Now, that's a lot of licks—and by top artists. Of course, they couldn't have done it if the song wasn't there and the timing wasn't right.

A song has a life of its own; the timing has to be right. There are a thousand examples of this, including the huge success that my friends Willie Nelson and Linda Ronstadt have had in recent years with some great American standards—evergreens of the '30s and '40s. Willie is Mr. Country and a great songwriter. Linda is considered to be the country rock queen. But they're both as smart as they are talented, so they recognized the strengths and values in the supposedly out-of-fashion standards of Tin Pan Alley, and created a new trend out of them.

Around the time that Kenny Rogers and the First Edition decided to make their wonderful recording of "Ruby," I made an important decision of my own. My work on the road with the Statesiders was going well, and my future looked promising. However, like a lot of other guys on the road, I was drinking.

I don't mean that I was a drunk. I was far from that, but I still had the habits of my early days in Nashville when we all wanted to be like the legend who'd just died a few years before—Hank Williams. I'm not blaming him for what we did. We were grown men, making our own choices and mistakes.

But drinking a lot of hard liquor was the custom for many of us, especially out on those long trips. Some guys were hitting the bottle in Nashville as well. Being the father of four and having fairly good common sense, I didn't drink much when I was home, though there was always some

partying going on when songwriters and artists got together in Nashville. A lot of them kept little apartments in
Nashville just for that. We had a hangout called the Bores
Nest. A dear lady named Sue Brewer paid the rent. We
used to help her pay her bills, although she never asked.
You could go there anytime and find four or five pickers and
singers drinking, writing songs, or telling Sue their problems. She befriended all of us at one time or another. She
died of cancer a few years ago.

But there was always more drinking on the road. One of
my best friends was a star who'd throw a party almost
every night on the road, filling his suite with loads of pretty
women and plenty of firewater. He'd tell those happy ladies
that it was his birthday. By that reckoning, I'd guess he's
about ten thousand years old.

Well, I went out for two one-nighters in Texas in 1969. I
woke up eleven days later in Butler, Georgia—and I didn't
have the foggiest idea what had happened to the other nine
days. It didn't take a mental giant to figure it out, though.
I'd been on a nine-day roar. As Webb Pierce would say,
"The old firewater got me, Tillie my boy, and I just stam-
peded." The fact that I'd lost nine days worried me.

Not long ago a Nashville magazine quoted what some
unknowing person claimed was the "hillbilly creed." It was
supposed to explain the extravagant taste in cars, houses,
swimming pools, clothes, and other items of certain well-to-
do country artists. "Whatever is worth doing is worth over-
doing," it read.

Now, I don't think so. I certainly didn't when I came out
of that alcoholic fog in Georgia. Maryjohn Wilkin, another
great songwriter and dear friend, was kind enough to come
down to Butler and bring me home. On the way back to
Nashville, I thought about the time Daddy came home
drunk and I went up the grapefruit tree. I had seen a good
deal of the damage that drinking too much could do. It had
ruined marriages and careers, disappointed little children,
and even killed people. I faced up to that.

So I stopped drinking hard liquor right then and there. Cold turkey.

Since I was not an alcoholic, that was the easy part. The hard part was turning down my friends when they wanted to party. But I've never had another glass of whisky or vodka since. It's not that I feel I'm better than the others, and I sure don't preach. But I saw the danger. Since I wasn't sure that I'd be able to limit myself to just a couple, I chose to give up liquor altogether.

Now, none of us are saints and most of us don't claim to be. There are some teetotalers in country music—maybe one or two—and some give up drinking for a month or so. What I drink now is light beer, usually Stroh's or Miller's, and we carry that and soft drinks in the cooler on the bus. When we are working a Vegas hotel, there's always an assortment of food and drink provided by the promoter in my dressing room. It includes wine and hard liquor. There's a sort of standard clause in booking contracts that allows each headline act to specify what he or she expects to be provided. I drink only the beer and leave the rest for guests, friends, my band, disc jockeys, journalists, and other performers who come by to shake hands and say howdy.

There are some stars who don't socialize with their musicians, feeling that it's bad for discipline. Their idea is to keep some distance between boss and employees. I'm aware that I'm in charge, but I'm more comfortable being closer with my band members. They like it, too. There's no confusion about who is the boss, but we can be friendly. We are all in this trip together.

Over the years, we've learned that life on the road can be hard or easy. Well, *easier*. We know there will be blown-out tires, bus breakdowns, terrible snow and ice storms, and lots of pressure, so we don't need any other problems. Of course, I understand that men on long, tough tours may need to let off some steam once in a while. So long as there's no harm done, I'm not the kind to stop people.

CHAPTER

22

There seem to be all kinds of wild—and wrong—ideas about how musicians behave on the road. Most of the country musicians I know, at least my boys, don't go around much bothering ladies who don't want their company. Sober or otherwise, they find women who like the notion of spending some time with them. Or the ladies find them.

It's surprising how many different kinds of women come looking. Country boys attract an outstanding assortment—not just those squirrelly teenage girls who pursue rock stars. There are fewer of those girls in the '80s, anyway, and I hear they're not nearly as aggressive as before.

They're not exactly new, either. Long before the rock explosion of the 1950s or those screaming kids at Sinatra concerts in the 1940s, young females—and some a bit older—found musicians attractive. Music and dancing, which often go together, seem to unlock female emotions. That was happening centuries before the stormy '60s or the "sexual revolution" people talk about.

Music appears to let folks put aside their inhibitions—at least for a while. I'm no mental expert, but I suspect there's a sexual element in many kinds of popular music. The sort of dancing a great deal of today's music generates points that way. It's much more out in the open.

And women are much more out in the open about what they want—after a lot of centuries. A lonely lady doesn't feel she has to sit at home caring for babies and waiting for her husband or some man to call her. Since musicians have seemed like perfect prey for a long time, more women are coming to meet them. Women of different ages and backgrounds, education and class, want to be with sexy traveling musicians nowadays. Some of them even feel they've a right to grab a musician *anywhere* on his body. Hell, it feels good, but that's embarrassing.

There are a lot of divorced women with romantic fantasies and notions about traveling musicians—some married ones, too, and they can be dangerous. They often take off their rings and pretend to be unattached. The trouble comes when their husbands show up. One singer I know was having a drink with such a lady in Amarillo one night when her cowboy appeared. Highly aggravated, this ole boy meant to hurt the big star for wanting to tamper with his wife. Four of his buddies pulled him away, and said that if he whipped anyone's ass, it should be his cheating lady's. I'm told that he finally calmed down and agreed with them. He apologized to the star before he left with her. Scared the hell out of me!

Now and then, even a female journalist doing an interview with a well-known entertainer may want to have a brief fling. You'd think that a smart professional reporter wouldn't be impressed by all that "star" stuff, but a few are. Some women will track a band or its leader for weeks, phoning long distance to find out when the act will reach their town. They'll take days off from work to try to get to those men when they arrive.

They build up these huge fantasies, thinking the entertainer is nine feet tall with a twelve-inch dong. They go through some crazy things to get at him. One friend of mine—who doesn't lie to me—told about a woman with two or three kids who was absolutely determined to be his lover, even if only for a night. She left her children with an aunt or something, drove hundreds of miles, and was waiting for him when his band arrived.

She had a plan. She knew it would be difficult for a total stranger to get to the star, so she began by seducing his bus driver. That way she met his boss. She followed the band on to the next city where they were working, and there she managed to get the star alone an hour before he had to catch a plane. She got what she wanted, but I'm not sure that he remembers her name. He does recall her wedding band, though.

There are a lot of lonely or unsettled, discontented women across these United States—that's pure fact. Usually it's of their own doing. Traveling musicians didn't cause it. My brother, Richard, says that the idea that a musician will be here today and gone tomorrow appeals to some of those ladies. They won't have to deal with him but for a night or two, so they don't have to think that hard about what they're doing. It used to be only male philanderers who figured things that way, but times have changed. Touring musicians were among the first to find out about that.

Some people figure that men on tour are likely to fool around with female entertainers—which is rarely true. If you rode together, like in the old days, you couldn't stand each other when you got to where you were playing. Today a male band on the road hardly meets such women, and if they do, the ladies are often involved with their boyfriends or husbands or hairdressing appointments. And, being entertainers themselves, they're not impressed by the rhinestone glamour of a fellow entertainer. Frankly, musicians aren't considered to be the most reliable of men, and women in show business know that. The great majority of them are as smart as they are pretty and talented. Sometimes a woman star will marry a member of her band or her manager. They can then travel together as a family unit, which sometimes works fine.

Musicians usually don't think of themselves as romantic or sexy figures. Well, not all of them. Sometimes when they're red-eyed and weary on a bus rolling through the dark night, they wonder why so many women do. Not all women, of course—but a surprising number. They don't know or care that a musician's usually just a lonely man a long way from home.

What about the musicians' wives and girlfriends back home? Most of them aren't exactly content about how much time their men are away. It just isn't natural to be apart 200 to 250 days a year. That puts a strain on any relationship. It's even harder on children, who only get to see their fathers when they come in from the road for three or four days. Half the time the kids don't even know where their daddies are, they only know Daddy's making music.

A traveling musician's wife carries a double load. She's got to be both mother and father most of the time—and that's not the natural way. She misses her man, emotionally and physically, and that's not good, either. And when her man comes home—tired from the bus rides, the poor sleep, the bad hours, and other wearisome things that go with life on the road—the woman wants to go somewhere just to get out of the house. She wants loving and celebrating—a little vacation or sort of honeymoon. She wants to go out for dinner, since she's been cooking a hundred meals without a break. She feels she's entitled to that—and she's right. She's done two jobs.

But that's the last thing the man wants to do. He wants the peacefulness of home, to be with his loved ones alone. He's had nothing but eating out, and he's been dreaming of good home-cooked meals, eaten in a happy family atmosphere instead of some jungle food stop. And he wants to sleep fourteen hours in a bed that doesn't swing and rock like those bunks on the bus, a confined space as small as that in which sailors sleep in submarines.

While he's been away, she may have been wondering what he's been doing. When he comes home worn out and exhausted, she might wonder about it even more. It can really eat at her.

Singers and pickers do different things to relax when they come in from the road. I work on our farm, doing physical chores that have long needed doing. I love that. And I go to my office in Nashville, about twenty-five miles away, to check on projects, tour schedules, and just business in general. I listen to the new songs that have come in the mail, the ones that have passed a careful screening by the Steve Nobles, the Buddy Cannons, and the Jimmy Darrells—the people who work in the music publishing operations. I read a lot, too—newspapers, *The Wall Street Journal*, magazines, and some books. Of course, all that comes a distant second to being with my wife, seeing my kids and the grandbabies. In between, I'm in a recording studio several times a year, trying to get the next album ready.

Just as we deal with our situations in different ways, so do our wives and girlfriends. Some of them are able to accept the hard realities of how their men earn their livings and how much they love their work—and those women manage to get the most out of their man's little time at home. Even if they wonder if he was one of those who mess around with other women on the road, they tell themselves that he wouldn't, or that such passing things aren't important. They say those are just minor incidents that don't threaten the marriage.

The great majority of us troubadors would say they're right. I've been on the road for a lot of years, and I don't recall but a handful of marriages being broken up by some girl that a man went bananas over on the road. If anybody wants the truth, most musicians are pretty honest with the women they meet out there. I mean, they don't say they're not married if they are, and they don't lie about the future. In other words, we may not be saints, but we're not total sinners, either. And some aren't sinners at all.

Other wives can't cope with the what's-he-doing syndrome and the separation. They try, I suppose, but it's rough. For some women, it's impossible. They don't sleep well, or maybe hardly at all, while he's gone. They start to think that it's unfair, imagining that he's on a nonstop party while they're washing shitty diapers or trying to handle a hundred other problems at home. Why isn't he here to help fix a leaky faucet or discipline a restless child, instead of living it up in high style with those hard-drinking buddies of his?

Or is he fooling around with other women?

Young ones, younger than me?

Pretty ones, prettier than me?

A man rarely tells his wife much about any partying he's done on the road, and he damn sure doesn't talk about what others have done. Entertainers know that their wives aren't stupid; if they were, they wouldn't have married them in the first place. If a woman hears that some other guys had a big night with a couple of ladies in Rifle, Colorado, or Lubbock, Texas, or Owens Sound, Ontario, she might get to wondering what her man was doing at the time. Just standing there whistling?

But if the talk about the road is general at home, it comes out freely and more detailed when musicians gather in Nashville's hangouts, studios, restaurants, publishing offices, and bars. It can be damaging, especially if beer is flowing and memories are fresh and the events were funny. So the word starts to seep around, a leak here and a leak there. With the help of a blabbermouth or a torked-off ex-girlfriend, it could get back home, your home.

Even if the poor bastard's been celibate on the road, his wife might think he wasn't. To get even for her hurt, or just because she's hungry for affection and hasn't had enough with her man away so much, she might have an affair with some jerk in Nashville or wherever she lives. Most wives don't do that, most are pretty decent. Most stay busy and don't let themselves think about it.

But there are a lot of divorces, though I don't think that country entertainers divorce more than the rest of the population—which isn't saying much. It's hard to predict what the effects of a divorce can be. I had a first-class steel guitar player with the Statesiders for a few years, and his marriage ended with a divorce. Even though things hadn't worked out with his wife, he loved and was very concerned about his young son. So he quit his good-paying road job to spend all his time in Nashville . . . to be near his little boy and raise him right. I respect him for that. Being one of the best steel guitar men in America—maybe the world—he's getting plenty of recording work in the studios.

But most musicians aren't that confident about earning the same amount of money if they stay home. They want to be good fathers, real daddies with normal home lives, but the money on the road is so much better for them. So they crisscross America on those endless bus rides, hoping and praying that their wives and children are okay. And they consider themselves lucky to have a regular job, what with ten thousand pickers in Nashville. Just as the women tell themselves that their men aren't getting into mischief on the road, the wandering husband tells himself that everything's all right with the family he sees only a third of the year.

Yes, the men hurt, too. I do.

They don't admit it too often to the other guys on the bus, but they feel it and they try to live with it. Sometimes they break down and have to talk about it with someone.

I recall one night in my dressing room at the Nugget Hotel-Casino in Sparks, Nevada, right next to Reno. Another country band was laying over for three days between show dates and I invited them to come by for a visit backstage and to have a few beers. They'd been on the road more than a hundred days, and they sure as hell looked it. You could say they were just about burned out—and they knew it. We'd played a charity show with them that afternoon to raise funds for the U.S. Olympic ski team.

My boys looked a lot more rested, which they were. We try to take good care of ourselves on the road. We get sleep, such as it is, and we have the benefit of "sitdown" bookings, where you're at a place for more than a week. We do that a lot these days.

After we'd finished our second show, some of those other band members were hanging out with my boys in my dressing room. One of those guys just couldn't keep it in anymore. It was after 2:00 A.M. I don't know if he'd been drinking or taking some pills to stay awake or what. He looked as if he needed to when it all poured out.

"I can't take this damn road anymore," he said. "It's not that I'm burnt out. It's my little girl. She's twelve years old now, and I hardly know her. I haven't even seen her grow up. A little girl needs her daddy."

There was an immediate silence in the room.

"I'm practically a stranger to that little girl," he continued. "That's terrible. She's got a right to a full-time father. I owe her that, damnit!"

We all nodded in sympathy.

"After this tour I'm getting off the road," he swore.

Everyone in the room sighed.

None of us really believed that he would leave the road, but that wasn't what mattered. We understood what he was feeling. Some guilt . . . some frustration . . . a lot of fatigue. We'd all been there too.

For a long moment I suspect each of us thought about our own families and hoped that these long separations wouldn't hurt our wives and children. Quickly things cheered up . . . they had to, you can't dwell on that stuff too long. If you can't enjoy the positive side of touring—the new places and new people . . . the wonders of our beautiful America . . . the jokes and sense of fellowship—the road *can* burn you out in a few years. It's easier if you take it as a great adventure, and figure that *your* family will be strong enough to cope.

I know all about that. That's what I did myself.

I paid for it, too. And the price was bigger than I expected.

CHAPTER

23

I thought everything was all right at my home.

We had a nice house in a good neighborhood, close to the schools, a rising income, and that special pleasure of another baby. Eight years after our fourth child, Sonny Boy, was born, Doris gave birth to another daughter. A baby is truly God's greatest gift to all of us. Carrie April was to be the last child I would father. I'll tell why later. She was born in January of 1972. She's a little blonde, pretty (like the others), bright, and sings well. I've had her up on stage with me in Las Vegas twice. She made me mighty proud. I'm not encouraging her to be or not to be a performer. She'll make up her own mind when she's ready.

Even though she was a good baby, her mother had her hands full raising five children. And running the house was a job, even with the help I could now afford to pay for. Since I was getting more successful as a performer, that affected our social life some. We were invited to more parties and music business events. Doris loved that sort of thing. It meant a new dress—which I could now afford—so we went to those functions when I was in town.

In the earlier days I hadn't been too interested in going

to those big blowouts. I didn't think of music as an industry, and those banquets seemed stuffy and a waste of time
to a young songwriter. I wasn't a businessman or a star,
just a free spirit who wrote songs about life and drank with
his cohorts.

When the songs I was writing with Wayne Walker began
to hit and the records were climbing up the charts, including the album charts (I had seventeen in the top fifty at one
time), we started to get invited to the annual country music
awards dinner. That was given by BMI each October.
Frances Preston, the BMI lady in Nashville and certainly
our friend, started to lean on me and Wayne—nicely but
firmly—to come to those affairs and pick up our awards.
Jim Denny had accepted them for us in past years, and now
he also was on us to attend. They were formal-dress
events. The thought of wearing tuxedos didn't appeal to
many of the good ole boys of country music then. Two of
those who didn't like the idea of getting into such outfits
were Wayne Walker and Mel Tillis. We didn't even own
them.

But Frances Preston is a charming woman who has a
wonderful way with songwriters. I expect that's because
she likes most of them and their songs about life, and because she's a classy lady who loves her work. So after staying away from those awards banquets for three years,
Wayne and I started to go and accept our own awards.
When your song is a top-ten single, you get to go up front of
your friends and competitors to receive an award. BMI
gives them to both the writers and the publishers.

Now, getting an award can be almost contagious, and it's
hard to resist. Once you start getting such honors, you
come back again if your songs have earned them. Since I
wrote or co-wrote a lot of songs that did well on the music
weekly trades country charts, I was invited to BMI awards
banquets often (I've got about twenty-five awards hanging
on my walls). After attending a few of those dinners, I
found myself enjoying them as much as Doris did.

You've probably noticed that people in the entertainment business love awards. That's hardly surprising—it isn't a line of work for shy folks with tiny egos. Since performers tend to get most of them, songwriters are especially happy when they're recognized. My friends in New York and Los Angeles argue that Nashville is an awards-crazy town—that the country community gives more awards to its writers and artists than any other branch of music. I don't think they're right, but there's nothing wrong if they are. For a heck of a long time country talent got hardly any recognition at all.

Before I got to the point of really enjoying these banquets, there were times when I'd come in from the road after a long run of one-nighters and be so wrung out that I didn't feel like going to any Nashville social event. These events were multiplying as Nashville and country music grew, and I always tried to make the BMI awards dinner and the CMA show, but I'd rather go fishing at Center Hill with Shorty Lavender than put on a tuxedo for most of the others. But since I knew that Doris had been alone with the kids for weeks, I'd agree and we'd go.

She loved to dress up, and I was starting to earn enough to buy her better clothes. The quality of clothes she bought were not found in discount stores. Neither were the prices. I didn't argue about that. She worked hard raising our five children, so she was entitled to her rewards, too.

While this is hot on my mind, I'd like to ask why—without it sounding like sour grapes, which it's not, since my career is pretty well set, thank the Lord—the Country Music Association, of which I'm a long-standing member, is hell bent on inviting the whole pop and rock performing world into the country music business? I know country greats who aren't even on labels these days, but some years back, a well-known movie actor was made MC of the Country Music Awards Show, even though he couldn't pronounce the artists' names right. Jimmy Dickens or Roy

Acuff—either one could have done a better job and known what they were talking about.

I met this fine actor in Hollywood not too long after that. I was out there doing the "Merv Griffin Show." I walked up to the bar where he was sitting and said: "Hi, I'm Mel Tillis." He turned and looked at me, and then, without saying a word, he went back to his drink. Now, he may have thought I was a squirrel or something, or maybe he had something heavy on his mind. I don't know. But that ain't country. I believe in progress and some of the good things it brings with it, but let it come on its own. Don't put the old road warriors out to pasture. Don't slap them in their road-weary faces, 'cause that ain't country.

Anyway back to Doris and me. Being stubborn, as the both of us were, isn't all that bad, but for married folks not to speak out what's on their minds isn't that good, either. How can they ever work out their differences if they don't level with each other? If a husband or wife has something troubling them, the best and most practical thing to do is lay it on the table. It isn't going to help a family for one to try to manipulate the other.

And it doesn't settle anything. It only works for so long. My mama tells how she coped with my daddy's endless contrariness. Being a woman of good judgment, she figured that she'd say the opposite of what she wanted him to do. If she pretended to be against it, then her contrary husband would favor it. That worked for a while—but Daddy finally caught on to the game she was playing. Daddy was stubborn, but no dummy.

Then Mama recognized how he favored my sisters over Richard and me. He was close to spoiling them—not so unusual for a father with his daughters. So Mama would get Linda or Imogene to ask him to do things, and he would. He did for years. But then he saw through that, and the problem was still there—aggravating her.

Well, Doris's feelings against my being away on the road

didn't go away, either. It was getting so that she felt the road was her enemy. That's not hard to understand. But it's hard to live with—for both the woman and her man. The wife of anyone who supports his family by working away a lot has a hard row to hoe. If she can't accept and learn to live with those frequent separations, she's likely to turn more and more discontented.

There are a thousand ways that the frustration and discontent can affect what a woman does—how she talks and the ways she deals with ordinary things. She'll insist on having her way in lots of little things that don't matter much, which doesn't do anything about the big problem that's burning inside her. Under most circumstances, a reasonably intelligent husband is supposed to notice, then try to find out what's bothering his wife. Well, I sensed that something wasn't exactly right, but I told myself it was just her being stubborn. Or maybe she was bored and annoyed by the chores of running the house alone, so she wanted some extra rewards.

I'm afraid that I had my attention fixed mostly on my career and thought that our marriage would take care of itself. I took everything for granted. It wasn't only touring as a performer and writing songs that I was involved in by the early 1970s. Now, either of those two can be a full-time job for anyone; the competition is terrific in both of those fields. But I had a third interest—a regular business. Well, some folks might think that music publishing isn't exactly as "regular" as other businesses. But if it is run right by people who know the field and really care, it can be a good business.

The inventory is songs. And you don't sell your inventory. You just collect royalties from other folks who use the songs. If records of your song are sold, if the song is broadcast on radio or television, if it is played in clubs or Muzak systems or in public places such as airplanes, if it is used in a regular or TV movie, if sheet music is sold, the songwri-

ter and music publisher collect royalties. Thanks to copyright laws, that income comes in for many years.

During the years that I had worked as a songwriter at
the Cedarwood offices, I got to see how this business
worked. I admired Jim Denny and the way he ran his business. He treated me and other songwriters well, and we
appreciated him as our partner. We weren't partners *in*
Cedarwood, but Cedarwood was our business partner in
promoting the songs and collecting the money from users.

Well, Jim Denny got sick. He was as brave as he was
good. He fought that old cancer with all the fight he had,
and with a lot of courage and dignity, but it beat him. He
died in 1963. That was a real loss to the country music
industry of Nashville, and especially to Wayne and me.

His wife, Dollie, was a fine woman—someone we all
loved and still do. The Denny family—Bill, John, and Dollie—and the Cedarwood staff, headed by the very capable
Mary Claire Rhodes, kept the company going, but it wasn't
quite the same. Bill brought in a new writer, Jan
Crutchfield, to screen Wayne Walker's, Maryjohn Wilkin's,
Danny Dill's, and my songs before we demo'd them.

Hell, it was me and Wayne who'd talked Mr. Denny into
doing demos in the first place. We were the first to do
demos in Nashville. The pioneers. But not without some
problems. Some of the Nashville clique had heard about the
sessions we were doing. And about us using outside musicians. Outside their clique, anyway. Grady Martin came in
Bradley's Quonset Hut one night during one of these
demos. We were using Brenda Lee's band, the Casuals, and
Grady told us all to get our asses out of there. Mr. Denny
told him to get his out. I could see a fight coming on. Mr.
Denny didn't back away from nobody. And Grady didn't
either. I told Wayne to get on the phone and call Mr.
Cooper, who was head of the musicians' union back then. I
told Grady he had a phone call. Mr. Cooper must have told
him we were legal and for him to get outta there and leave

us alone, 'cause he left, but not before throwing a Coke bottle through Billy Smith's bass drum. Demos became a necessary part of the business from that night on. Grady accepted the changes and played on most of our demos, and why not—he was the best.

Before Jan Crutchfield came along, Cedarwood hadn't been as open to new writers, or interested in developing young raw talents. When new writers would bring in songs, they usually were told by Dollie, who'd been instructed to do so, that Cedarwood had its own staff writers and wasn't accepting any new outside material. So the young hopefuls were sent away.

I heard some of their songs, and there were a number of pretty good ones. I thought that it was a mistake to have a closed-door policy like that—especially since several other Nashville publishing companies were making progress with an open-door approach. Today almost all Nashville publishers have that open door. It's much easier to get them to consider your song than it is to get a hearing in L.A. or New York.

I'd always been interested in business, even back when I dug earthworms and sold peanuts. I wasn't alone in that. For many years, country artists have been more open to business than most other performers. Maybe it's because for a long time it was hard to get country records into stores, so the touring musicians sold the records at shows themselves. And not only records. As time went by, that expanded to souvenirs. We've always had wonderful fans, loyal and intense.

I decided to try the music publishing business myself after Mr. Denny passed away. Wayne and I didn't want anybody screening our songs before we did the demos, even if they were qualified. Maryjohn left first. Her contract expired and she moved on. She immediately started her own country music publishing business—Buckhorn Music, she called it. Her son, Bucky Wilkins, had an instant smash, "Little GTO."

Then along came Kris Kristofferson, just out of the Army. He signed up to write exclusively for Buckhorn Music. We became big buddies and hung out at Maryjohn's house and at Buckhorn. Kris always wanted me to sing his demos. He didn't have that much confidence in his singing, and with good reason. His style of warbling hadn't been accepted yet, though it later was in a big way. I was glad to do it for him. Kris had come to town—a Rhodes scholar, a captain just out of the U.S. Army—with a heart full of songs and a family to feed. He drove a little Volkswagen Bug. One night he walked back from Center Hill Lake, eighty miles from Nashville, because he didn't like the company he was with. He said, "I don't like your attitude, so I'll just fade into the underbrush." He did, just disappeared. I didn't like the company either, but it wasn't our car and I damn sure wasn't walking back to Nashville. That was the night Kris wrote "Help Me Make It Through the Night."

When Kristofferson came to town, he asked for no quarter. He worked at the Columbia Records studio, which Columbia had bought from Owen Bradley. They built a whole new building around that old Quonset hut. He emptied the ashtrays, went to get beer and fast foods for the musicians and singers. Anything they needed, he did. I admired him for that. It goes back to what I said about not being a burden on anyone. And he wasn't.

One night, after a two-day roar, Kris asked me to ride up to Clarksville with him, about sixty miles away, to visit some old Army buddies of his. "Okay," I said—in my condition, I'd have agreed to almost anything—"but I got to go by and tell my bride where I'll be so she won't worry about me."

"Great," he said. "I've been wanting to meet Doris. You talk about her so much."

Kris drove me out to Lincoya Court, to the new house we'd just bought. We decided to have a few drinks at the house before we left for Clarksville, so he could get to know

Doris. I had several bottles of whisky in my arms, and Kris had the Cokes, orange juice, and bag of ice. Doris opened the door to let us in, and I said, "Doris, I want you to meet Kris K-K-K-" *Bam! Splash!* I dropped a whole quart of Seagram's V.O.

Well, I got down to clean it up, with Doris raising all manner of hell, and Kris said, "Hi, Doris, I've heard a lot about you. I was, ah, wondering if you'd let Melvin"— that's what he always called me—"go with me to—"

He never got it out. Doris said, "No, he can't go. Does he look like he's in any condition to go anywhere? And speaking of going somewhere, you can just leave."

Kris apologized for our grand entrance, then he left. I ran into him a few days later down on Music Row. He had cuts and bruises all over his body, at least what I could see of it.

I asked him, "What in the world happened? Doris didn't get hold of you, too, did she?"

"No, worse than that," he said. "I fell asleep on the way back from Clarksville, and totaled the Bug. The side you'd have been riding on was completely flattened. You'd have been killed for sure, Melvin."

Doris probably saved my life that night.

Kris moved on down to Louisiana. His songs weren't doing well, or his marriage, either. He got a job flying helicopters out to platformed oil rigs in the Gulf of Mexico. Ray Price cut "For the Good Times." Then "Bobby McGee" hit, and "Help Me Make It Through the Night" was a giant by Sammi Smith. The rest is history. I see Kris every so often out in Los Angeles or at some award show.

I still had quite a few years left to go on my contract with Cedarwood. I'd signed a twenty-year contract in 1961. That was the year I'd decided I could write just as well in Florida as I could in Nashville. I wanted a lake house and twenty acres of orange trees in Groveland, Florida, the place where my daddy lived his last sixteen years. Mr. Denny said he'd sign my note to buy it if I'd sign a ten-year contract. I said, "How 'bout twenty?" I was happy and not planning on going anywhere else. Cedarwood was a good home, I thought. I signed, and Doris and the kids and I moved to that lake house in Groveland, near Orlando.

My retirement was short-lived, but I did write some good songs while living on that lake. Fred Burch came down and we co-wrote two or three. "The Snakes Crawl at Night" was one, and "Atlantic Coastal Line" was another. They were back to back on Charlie Pride's first record. I wrote several more songs, fished a lot, messed with my bird dogs, played with the kids and with the kids' mama. Finally, bored with our slowed-down life, we moved back to Nashville. Doris was glad, and so were the rest of us.

After much thought, I left Cedarwood and rented a little one-room office in an old house the Dennys owned behind Cedarwood, on another street—Seventeenth Avenue South. I hired Red Hayes, a fiddle player from the Faron Young band, and also the writer of "Satisfied Mind," a great country standard, to head up the office.

Bill Denny told me I couldn't start a music publishing company because I was still under contract to Cedarwood. I told him I still planned to do all my writing for Cedarwood. The new songs I would publish would be by others. They would come in through the mail and with some luck and a little word of mouth, songwriters would come in off the streets, like the ones Dollie had been instructed to send away. I told him, "You're in the fast-food business as a sideline. Why can't I be in the publishing business as a sideline? I never did cheat or write under other names, and I'm not about to start now."

Most of the folks at Cedarwood doubted I could make a go of it and I don't blame them. I must confess that I don't respond too well when people tell me that I can't do something. Maybe it goes back to my stubbornness about beating the stuttering. I don't say much when people talk to me that way, but it does get me worked up and even more stubborn, more determined.

Now, I don't rush into things. I think about new projects for a long time—they sort of simmer in my head. And when I begin, I start small and careful. A big splash isn't my style, and I've worked too hard to toss money around foolishly. I don't even gamble when I work Vegas. So I set up shop in the music publishing business in that small office that I rented from Bill Denny. Among the people who wished me well was Jim Denny's widow, who's still a friend.

My respect for her and Jim Denny was one reason that I never tried to move any of my earlier songs from Cedarwood. I never lost my warm feelings for that company, which did so much for me over the years. I started with nothing but a name. I called the company Sawgrass, after a tough and plentiful grass that grows in the lowlands around Pahokee, and I affiliated it with BMI, since I was a BMI writer myself. Later on, realizing that I was losing songs from the ASCAP writers who were beginning to surface in Nashville (ASCAP stands for American Society of Composers, Authors, and Publishers), I decided to set up another company that was an ASCAP member. I named it Sabal Music—after a native palm tree that grows in Florida. Still later, I needed a third publishing house for songs of writers connected with still another performing rights outfit named SESAC (long a U.S. organization for licensing American music, but originally the Society for European Stage Authors and Composers). So I began a little company I called Guava, a delicious tropical fruit that Mama had used many times to make jelly. I guess I still had a feeling for the Glades.

Naturally, I was putting a lot of thought and hard work into my new music publishing venture. I wasn't gonna fail at this—not after so many people had said I would. And I was excited by the opportunities opening up for Mel Tillis and the Statesiders. As we built a name, bigger and better bookings began to drift in. It was slow but steady.

I hadn't broken through yet, but it looked as if I was really on my way.

As I was focusing on those career moves, I didn't notice that my marriage and family were paying a price. I thought that I was the only one who was paying, since I was working so hard on the road and just as hard at the new publishing efforts when I was in Nashville. Mr. Denny had set a mighty high standard for his writers. He'd treated each songwriter as an individual, and I wanted to do that, too. It was the right way. It was also a way that took a lot of time.

There were problems getting the right booking agent for our road engagements. I tried one, but they didn't have much faith in me as a performer because they thought of me as a songwriter. Then I tried another, but they had too many other acts. I needed some personal attention, I thought.

So I brought in a very bright young relative who meant well, but tried to do it all without drawing on my years of experience. He'd never been in the music business until then, and was too proud to ask for help, so he made a lot of mistakes before he suddenly quit to start his own company. I wish him well.

Now, if this was a hard time for me, it was an even rougher period for my children. It was a tough period for every American's children—the stormy 1970s. Values were being challenged . . . crazy life-styles were being experimented with . . . parents and the government were being criticized and defied . . . the rebellion was on . . . confrontation was the style . . . riots were commonplace . . . and drugs were showing up in every corner of the nation. It wasn't just the hippies who were messing with all kinds of dope. The stuff was everywhere.

Drugs had been around the music world a long time— years before country got to be big. The jazz people had been into grass in the 1930s and 1940s, and some jazz giants died of heroin in the 1950s. A wide assortment of drugs raced through the rock groups and some of their fans in the 1960s and 1970s, killing or doing brain damage or ruining more people than I like to remember.

Well, country musicians and singers weren't immune to all that. If lawyers in California and dentists in Florida and businessmen in New York are taking cocaine, it shouldn't be that much of a surprise that the entertainers in Nashville are, too. I can say that cocaine use is less than it was five years ago. I'm pleased with that, because I saw how much damage it could do. One good friend of mine was so disturbed by cocaine in Vegas one night that he actually thought he was God. I didn't know what I could do to help him. I told him he'd have to help himself, which should be easy, since he was so close to God. Well, he's off that devil's dandruff now and back in good health, both mentally and physically. Some other stars aren't that strong.

The first drugs to hit the country scene in the late 1950s and early 1960s were pills to keep people up, awake, and energetic. I think they were used by musicians driving cars and station wagons on long hops between one-nighters. Now people talk of those stimulant pills as speed. In the 1960s musicians called them "old yellers" because they were yellow. Their brand name was Simco. I didn't even know about them for several years, but I'd wondered how some performers stayed awake so long. I'm the kind who's even afraid to take aspirin. And my first experience with grass was enough to reinforce my caution about drugs— thank God. I'm a person who's normally "up," anyway— almost high-strung you might say—and who doesn't need those things. As for partying, I was still drinking hard liquor then, so why even bother with grass.

Marijuana was a new thing, and there were lots of opportunities and encouragement to try it. Almost everybody did—at least once—but I don't recommend drugs to anyone. I never did. It can do weird things to a person.

It sure did to me one night in Boise, Idaho, after a show

that I did there. A friend brought some grass to a post-performance party in the Governor's Suite at the Boise Hotel. This was before country musicians really knew much about drugs. The rock people were way ahead of us on that.

That man passed a joint around several times, but I wouldn't try it. One of the other guys at the party felt the same way. We were drinking whisky, and that was plenty for us. But two or three kept urging me.

I was facing the same thing that my kids had to cope with ten or twelve years later—peer pressure. If you're smart, you don't go along because it's what "everybody" is doing. I wasn't that smart.

"Aw, hell," I finally said. I was half drunk by then. "Give me a hit off that."

So I took a couple of drags and had a coughing fit. "This stuff doesn't affect me," I finally told them.

It didn't—for a while. But in about ten minutes I began to feel like I weighed a thousand pounds. It was like when you're a kid and somebody picks you up and turns you round and round—and then turns you loose as the world spins.

I began embarrassing everyone. I started pulling my clothes off. I was wild. I'd never done anything like that in my life.

Then I thought I was a duck. I quacked around that hotel room for a while. Since I was convinced that I was a duck, I wanted to migrate back to Lake Okeechobee. I turned the water on in the bathtub, filled it up to the rim, and jumped right in.

Well, I missed the tub and busted my head open. Blood poured down my face. Then I threw up and passed out on the floor.

That was back in '62 or '63. After that experience, I wasn't that interested in more experimenting with drugs. I wouldn't say that I never tried anything over the years

since, but it sure didn't become a regular part of my life. I
wouldn't let it. I don't need it. I'm not one to lecture other
grown-ups about how to run their lives, but my musicians
know damn well how I feel about this. I make that clear to
each new guy when he joins the band.

Well, how to deal with the pressure to do what
"everybody else does" was something a father could work
out with his kids if he were home enough. There are a lot of
other growing pains that he might help with, too, if he were
around every night. Unlike some parents, thank the Lord,
I didn't end up with my kids being ruined or killed by
"going along with everybody," but I might have done more
with them in those years of teenage rebellion.

All the touring musicians and entertainers with kids
faced the same problem then. And it hasn't changed. The
stormy '70s are gone, but the family's need to have a full-
time father is still here. It's something that traveling sales-
men or anyone who's away a lot—even ambitious guys who
never travel ten miles from home but work late night after
night to make more money for their families—have to face.
Mileage is only one kind of distance.

Like all the others, I assured myself that I was doing it
for my family and a better way of life. It was back then that
I invited my brother to work with me. Richard, a great
bread salesman and a wonderful companion, came out on
the road to take charge of our concessions and souvenirs.
He made a lot more money than he'd been earning as a
bread truck driver and salesman for bakeries. My brother
enjoyed traveling across America and Canada with our
show. He was doing it for *his* family.

Richard moved his family from Orlando to a house I had
bought as an investment, on Bell Road, near Nashville, so
he could be with them more when we came in off the road—
and so his family and mine could be closer. Later my two
sisters and their families came up from Florida so we could
all be near each other. Mama came, too. I wanted to help
them all.

But Richard didn't spend any more time with his children than I did with mine. The demands of life on the road wouldn't let him. He soon missed his family, as we all did. He was making more money than he could ever make in the bakery business, but sometimes I question whether I really helped him by asking him to join me on the road.

At the time, I thought I did.

Lord knows, I surely meant to.

CHAPTER

24

Five is enough.

That's what my wife said soon after our youngest, Carrie April, was born.

Doris felt that she'd done her duty, and she didn't want to be burdened with raising any more kids. Now that I was making good money and building a name in Nashville, and we had a nice house, she wanted more time to enjoy life.

So she asked me to have a vasectomy.

Well, I didn't exactly do handstands about that question. One mis-whack and it's goodbye Buford. I could see her point of view, though. She'd worked hard and hung in there through the tough times, and she'd been a good mother under some difficult circumstances. She was still a young and pretty woman and only in her middle thirties—I guess she yearned for a life that involved more than running a house. Many times she'd told me that she'd married too young and had missed out on lots of good times. I told her the good times were now with her family.

And five was a full family, I thought. Even though our marriage had had its ups and downs, I certainly wasn't considering leaving. We were a family, and that was important to me. If having my nuts cut on would make her happy and ease her mind, I'd do it. Dr. Hill in Madison, Tennessee, did the cutting and stitching. I couldn't wait to get home to try it out. It must have worked. She didn't get pregnant again.

But there was still the problem of my being away so much. I went on the road the next day, and do you know, I think that after that little operation, my voice got higher. Doris tried her best, but she and some of the other country singers' wives took it to mind that our out-of-town trips were nothing but partying, drinking it up, and messing with other women. That just kept troubling her.

Now, I wasn't one of the biggest drinkers, but I hadn't been one of God's little angels either—especially when I was still drinking hard whisky. I'd got into my share of predicaments. Some of them made funny stories, which spread like wildfire all over town. A number of those ditties were exaggerated or "improved" when told again and again and again. So, quite a few of the Mel Tillis escapades that people tell today aren't exactly accurate.

A good example involves a lady's negligee. That story comes in all kinds of versions, each wilder and woolier than the last. Here are the facts, folks.

Lester Vandore, a Nashville music publisher and record executive, now deceased, was promoting a country music show over at the Atlanta Speedway a day before the Firecracker 400. He asked Warner Mack and me if we wanted to go over with him a couple of days early to check on the advance ticket sales and help promote the show. Warner said he couldn't afford it, and I said I couldn't either.

"Come on with me, boys, and I'll foot the bill," Lester said.

We went home and told our wives, and since we were going to be on the show, they said it would be okay. We drove over in Lester's Cadillac the next day and checked into the Americana Hotel. It was getting late, about 9:30 P.M. We couldn't wait to get a shower, put on some clean duds, and get up to the bar on the roof and check out the scene. Lester had rented us three separate connecting rooms, very convenient for a party. We took the elevator to the rooftop lounge, and would you believe, it was completely empty except for the bartender and this old white-haired Negro piano player. We just looked at each other and laughed.

We got to talking about our wives and families and how lucky we were. Well, the more we talked, the more we drank, and the more we drank, the more our consciences hurt. Finally Lester suggested that we call our wives—Mazell, Doris, and Peggy—and tell them to go out and buy themselves new dresses and fly over to Atlanta to meet us the day of the show. They were really excited and said they would.

We didn't go to sleep that night, we just passed out.

Lester had us up at ten o'clock in the morning and announced that we were going to a lingerie luncheon with John Fox and Bill Johnson. Both of them worked for WPLO, the Number One country music station in Atlanta. John was to emcee the event. I had never been to one of those things before, but I was game.

There were a lot of people there, mostly businessmen and some women. We had lunch and several drinks, and then—show time. John got up and explained what was happening. He told the crowd that if they liked anything they saw, they could bid on it, right there on the spot. Lester told us he'd cover our bids.

We were still eating when the models came out. It was evening stuff, very late, late evening stuff. Things to make a lady look good and catch her husband's attention. It sure caught mine. It didn't affect my eating, but it did make me pay very close attention. So did just about all the other men and women, including waitresses and the hostess in charge.

I was in a good mood, relaxed by the company of my friends and the wine we'd been tasting. I went along with the program and bid on a cute little peach-colored negligee.

I hadn't realized she was the first model out. Well, no one bid against me. She smiled and left the stage. Later she brought me my purchase wrapped in a cute little box and presented me with the bill, which I handed to Lester. Lester paid her and then we helped each other out of that luncheon.

We were halfway to the hotel when I discovered that my purchased negligee wasn't all there. Holding it up, I said, "Hey, ain't there supposed to be more to this little thing than what I've got?"

Warner laughed and said, "Where's the bottom to it?"

"You boys are stupid," Lester commented, one of his favorite adjectives.

"I'll be damned if that's so, we're going back there and get the bottom," I angrily declared.

We went back and found the model. She apologized and gave us the bottom. John Fox talked about it on the radio for weeks.

We were all pretty well shit-faced when we arrived back at the Americana. None of us could believe our eyes. The lobby had at least a thousand women milling around. I asked a bellhop what in the world was going on. He said, "Hairdressers convention. Ten thousand men and women in town—eight thousand women and two thousand men who want to be women." It didn't take us long to trick several of those ladies up to my room. We told them we were entertainers from Nashville, so naturally they had to hear us sing.

Warner and I sang every song we knew and some of Webb's, too. Tired of singing, I showed them the pretty outfit I had bought Doris. They oohed and aahed and said, "Dare you to try it on."

It sounded like a good idea to me, so I disappeared into the middle room, squeezed into that little piece of nothing, and made my grand entrance. Everybody just died laughing. Warner laughed so hard one of his contact lens slid out. I really put on a show, until a knock came on the door.

"I'll get it," I gleefully shouted.

I twirled and made a perfect pirouette to the door. I opened the door halfway, and then closed it real fast. I couldn't believe my eyes. There were the wives. But they weren't supposed to be in until tomorrow, I said to myself.

I knew I couldn't, in my shock, speak the words to tell Warner, Lester, and the others that Doris, Mazell, and Peggy had come a day early. So I started singing, "Warner, your lovely wife, Peggy, is here, and Lester, so is your sweet wife, Mazell."

In about thirty seconds the party had moved to the middle room and then on over to the third room, leaving me alone. How could I explain the negligee? Oh, well, what the hell! I opened the door and said, "D-D-Doris, look what I bought you."

The wives thought it was the funniest thing they'd ever seen. I explained to Doris what had happened, then Warner and Lester came in and took their wives to their rooms. We all had a great weekend.

Some folks say that it was quick thinking on my part to come up with a lie like that—but I was talking straight. I had bought that outfit for Doris. I'd envisioned her with it on.

Others tell that story in different ways—some of them involving naked women. That sure makes a better story, but it damn sure wasn't the truth.

And I wasn't stuttering because I was scared or caught doing something wrong. I was stuttering because I stuttered.

I was stuttering really bad when I went out to Los Angeles to do my first semi-regular appearance on the "Glen Campbell Good Time Hour." It was a top-rated show. Doris and I were fussing as usual. I was trying to work show dates all over the country on the weekends. I'd beg the Campbell producers to let me come in on Tuesday so I could be with my family on Mondays. They understood and tried to work around this, but not many of my Mondays were spent at home. I was more than likely on a plane going somewhere.

While in Los Angeles, I'd stay in a motel across the street from the mammoth CBS television complex on Fairfax Avenue. Jerry Reed was my roommate. He was on the show, too. On my first time out, in that dreary room at the Farmer's Daughter Motel, I thought I was gonna die, I was so scared.

"What the hell are you scared about, Tillis?" Reed would say. "It's just a television show."

He'd already done a few of those shows and was talking like it was old stuff to him. But he wasn't fooling me. He didn't come across as warm in front of those network cameras as he did when he and I were just talking in our room. He was scared shitless, too.

Maggie Ward, of my office, had given me a couple of Valiums that first time out, before I left Nashville. I asked her what they would do.

"They'll calm you down if you get too nervous," she replied.

I never was too much on taking pills, even for staying awake on long trips. But I convinced myself to try them. About an hour before we were all to meet in one of those big rehearsal halls to read through that week's script, I took a Valium. I waited until the very last minute to walk across the street to all those waiting script writers, producers, directors, actors, singers, and CBS honchos. Fred Silverman was there. That good man has tried to help me as much as anybody. He's the one who okayed the miniseries called "Mel and Susan Together." It was on ABC. The Osmond family produced it at their beautiful new studios located in Orem, Utah. It was well planned and well done, but it just didn't make it. I think it was way before its time. Maybe a little too slick, I don't know. Susan Anton's a nice lady with a lot of talent. She did a great job.

Glen Campbell said, "Come on in, Melvin, and make yourself at home," as country people always do.

I tried to act unmoved by all the stares, but the truth of the matter was that I was just about to go to sleep. They invited me to sit down, but I refused. I knew if I sat down, it was all over for me. I had to stay awake. "Suit yourself," Glen said.

So I stood as the script was being read through. Several pages were read before I had a line. When it came my time to talk, I delivered my lines perfectly. Everybody looked at me with puzzlement in their eyes.

"Let's go back and try that again, Melvin," Glen said in disbelief.

Well, I read my lines again, and the same thing happened—perfect.

"What's going on here, Melvin, aren't you supposed to stutter? You're delivering your lines like Don Ameche," Glen said.

I confessed to taking two Valiums. (I'd swallowed the other one at a water fountain in CBS.)

They said, "No more Valiums, Melvin, you'll do this straight from now on."

And I did. I stuttered my way through seventeen "Glen Campbell Good Time Hours."

A lady who watched the show regularly wrote that my stuttering set a bad example for young people. Hell, I was young and trying to make a living the best I could.

Glen got real mad when he saw that letter. The producers had given it to him. Well, he read the letter on his next show that we taped. He said, "Here's a letter from a lady who says Mel Tillis's stuttering is a bad influence on our young people and shouldn't be allowed on television." Glen's answer to that was, "Why shouldn't Mel Tillis be on television? They let Ray Charles be on."

The next week hundreds of positive letters came in. CBS even did a warmth survey on guesting celebrities. I came in second. I asked Nick Savino, Glen's manager at the time, "Who c-c-c-came in first?"

"Kate Smith," he told me.

After the show ran its course, I went on to do other TV shows, like "The Tony Orlando Show," "The Dean Martin Show," all the talk shows including Johnny Carson, and "The Love Boat" and "The Dukes of Hazzard."

Burt Reynolds called me one day and asked me to do a small part in the film *W.W. and The Dixie Dance Kings*. I accepted. I played a gas station attendant. I had a few lines to say, and really had them down pat. I walked out before the cameras and spoke my lines to him perfectly. I hadn't been taking any Valiums, either.

Burt squirted me with a water pistol—scared the doo-doo out of me. I thought I'd been shot. He said, "You're supposed to stutter, Mel, you're being robbed."

Everybody had a good laugh, including me. I told him I'd memorized my lines real well and had gotten the rhythm down.

He laughed and said, "Well, get unrythmed." He rewrote my lines, and that worked. I tensed up and stuttered.

I've stuttered my way through nine movies: *Cannonball Run* and *Cannonball Two*; *The Villain*, with Kirk Douglas and Ann-Margret; *Every Which Way But Loose*, with Clint Eastwood; and *Smokey and the Bandit*, to name some. I know one thing—I like acting a lot better than I liked pulling that curtain at Pahokee High School.

Stuttering brings out some very strange reactions. It makes some folks feel nervous and uncomfortable, while others laugh because they find it funny. A lot of people think I'm putting it on. But I don't worry about that because people who stutter know I stutter. And that's what counts.

Yes, I've made a lot of money talking this way. But I didn't ask to be called that singer who stutters. Sometimes I feel the stutter is bigger than the song. I like to think that I have some God-given talent, too. During my first ten years in Nashville, I'd written enough songs for Doris, the kids, and me to live comfortably for the rest of our lives.

Then only the folks back home, the folks in Nashville, and people I might have met and forgotten along the way knew that I stuttered. The people who bought the records with my name on them didn't know. Folks didn't know Charlie Pride was black until they saw him, and they didn't care, either.

Television told the nation I stuttered. Millions watched each week as I stuttered my way through show after show. I'm glad they liked me. I'm still around, and I'm very thankful for that. My crowds are holding up and I'm making new fans through my movie work. I look on the stutter as an old friend—a f-f-friend that I have to live with.

Enough of that.

Going back to my modeling that negligee in Atlanta that night, Doris recognized that it was just another one of those crazy things I did when I had one drink too many—but it didn't seem to bother her that much. She knew I was innocent that night—women just know. But some other stories going around town about things I'd done—or was supposed to have done—made her uncool.

If I'd been home all the time and we had a normal family life, it might have helped. But we were getting more bookings all the time. That was good for my career, but bad for my marriage.

I don't know what happened to Doris and me. I do know, but then I don't. Maybe Mama was right when she told me to get on that train. That was the only time I ever questioned her wisdom. But I couldn't do that. I loved Doris and still hold a place in my heart for her. After all, she's the mother of my children, some flowers I planted long ago. I think about that a lot and the guilt that goes with it.

Mama failed to tell me a man could love two women at the same time. Bill Golden, with the Oak Ridge Boys, did. It was slightly out of pitch, but he got the message across. It was too late for me, though. I'd had my flings in and out of town, but nothing really serious, nothing that'd make a man leave home. Well, Doris suspected it more than once.

The fusses became a regular ordeal whenever I got home. I hated those quarrels. It was very upsetting for all of us—especially the kids. As for my falling by the wayside from Mama's good Baptist upbringing, I'll take the blame. I know I did wrong. And the reason could have been that I longed for the attention that I never got as a child, what with Mama working at the canning plant all kinds of hours, day and night, and Daddy gone much of the time. I never got much notice at school either, those early years, and when I did it was usually the wrong kind. It hurt. It was kinda like all the healthy chickens in a barnyard chasing and pecking the weakest one till they'd peck it to death. 'Course I didn't die, and nobody pecked me to death.

Doris had come from basically the same background—her daddy worked away from home and was gone a lot, times were hard—and that certainly didn't make matters any better.

I was starting to get some attention now—the good kind, and I liked it. Who wouldn't? My records were beginning to hit, one after the other. I think I had thirty-three straight top tens and about a dozen or so Number Ones. All the top TV show syndicates and networks were after me. My bookings on the road were full—Jim Halsey and his booking agency out of Tulsa, Oklahoma, were having to turn down dates, a booking agent's dilemma.

My publishing companies Sawgrass and Sabal were growing by leaps and bounds. Money was plentiful. I could do no wrong, I assured myself. Yes, I had caught lightning in a jar. Struck the mother lode.

Then came October 1976. That's a month I'll never forget. I was voted Entertainer of the Year by the CMA—Country Music Association. I never have figured out that one. How I even got nominated I'll never know. There was real stiff competition for the award that year. Willie Nelson, Dolly Parton, Waylon Jennings, Ronnie Milsap, and I were nominated. Now, that's heavy company, folks.

Waylon didn't show for the awards, as promised. He was

having his usual problems with the press. They were really on his case, whatever it was. The CMA members hadn't figured Willie out yet. This was just before Dolly was going to Hollywood, and Milsap was still new, although he did win the Male Vocalist of the Year award that year.

When I won, I couldn't believe it. I was sitting out in the audience with Doris and all the other nominees, smoking a pipe. I didn't really smoke, but I thought that it looked very distinguished. When Tennessee Ernie Ford announced the winner, he said, "The winner is M-M-Mel Tillis." The applause was deafening. All eyes were on Doris and me. She kissed me and I walked up to that stage at the new Grand Ole Opry House to accept my award. Was all this really happening to me? I thought. Is this for real? Are my kids at home with the baby-sitter watching their daddy on TV? That show was being telecast live across the United States, just as it is today.

A few weeks earlier, I'd been in Canada doing the "Tommy Hunter Show," a long-running country music show that's still in existence. Jimmy Dean was there, too. Jimmy—the man who gave me my first break into big-time television. We were talking and I told him I had been nominated for the biggie—a term used for the Entertainer of the Year. Jimmy said, "Tillis"—he never called me by my first name—"you'll win, it's your time."

"Well, what can I say if that happens?" I asked.

"Just thank 'em for helping you drive the bus," he answered.

What did he mean? I asked myself. I figured it out later, and it made a whole lot of sense.

After I accepted that award, all I could think about was that old fiddle Aunt Eula had bought for me years ago in Pahokee, the one I never could learn how to play. I thanked her for that fiddle and the encouragement she had given me. Of course, there were many others. Mama for sure—and Buck Peddy, Malcolm Millar, Jim Denny, Buddy Killen, Don Law, Dollie Denny, Minnie Pearl, Mary Claire

Rhodes, Mae Boren Axton, Louise and Bill McClellan, James and Juanita Simmons, Wayne Walker, Maryjohn Wilkin, Owen Bradley, Porter Wagoner, Webb Pierce, Ray Price, Maggie Ward, Carl Smith, Glen Campbell, Bob Wills, Paul Cohen, Jim Vinneau, Chet Atkins, Dick Howard, and Jim Halsey. There are more—all of Mama's sisters, Uncle Alvin, Uncle Wiley, Uncle Ernest, Uncle Clayton, Jellyroll, Carroll and Emily Williams, Mr. Miller, the man who gave that creed to me to read in Plant City, Richard, Linda, Imogene, and Johnny. I could go on and on, but I won't do that this time.

I put that pipe I was trying to smoke in the inside pocket of my rented tuxedo jacket and walked up on that stage. The pocket began to burn like hell—the pipe hadn't gone out. At first I thought I had the worst case of heartburn I'd ever had, then I saw the smoke finally finding its way out of my coat. After that startling discovery, I quickly said what I had to say—and I didn't stutter much, either—and got back to my seat, to Doris and some of my kinfolks from Dover who had come up especially for the event.

I was thinking about Judy, the new girl at the office that Maggie had hired while I was working up in Alaska a few months before. Doris had fired several of the girls who'd worked as receptionists for Mel Tillis Enterprises. I'd be out of town, and with all that wondering about me building up inside her, she'd come to the office and fire them right on the spot, especially if they had good looks and big boobs.

After several firings by Doris, Maggie, in desperation, hired a little country girl from Gallatin, Tennessee, with hardly any boobs at all. I guess you could say they looked more like a good bee-sting through her blouse. Maggie told somebody she walked like a goat and that Doris didn't have to worry about her. "Melvin wouldn't even look at her," she said.

While I'm out on the road, I usually call in to the office to check on the mail and see what's happening several times a day. We were in Anchorage, Alaska, this time. I called the office and the new girl answered, "Mel Tillis Enterprises, can I help you?"

I didn't recognize the voice, but that wasn't unusual. "Yes," I answered, "is the mail in?"

"No, he's not here, he's in Alaska doing a concert," she said.

"Well, let me speak to Maggie," I told her. When Maggie came on, I asked her, "Who in the hell is that girl who answered the phone?"

"That's Judy Edwards, the new girl I hired. Doris fired another one," Maggie replied.

Maggie told me what was in the mail and I hung up. I walked onstage that night in Anchorage and did my show. I was worried. You've got to have good secretaries to keep things in order, I thought.

When I got back to town, I had a few days off. I rested up at home with Doris and the kids. Doris apologized for what she'd done, and I accepted that. She promised to let me run the business from now on.

I went into the office the next day, wearing a pair of old blue jeans, a light windbreaker, and a little "go to hell" Jerry Reed golf hat with trout flies and spinners hanging from it. I sure didn't look like a publishing executive or a star, Judy told me later. She didn't even know who I was. She was into rock and couldn't care less about country music. She had taken the job because a friend had told her about the opening just after she'd lost her job with a little chartered airline that had bellied up.

I walked up front to the receptionist area, where Judy was busy answering the phone and doing some filing work that Maggie had put on her. I said, "You must be the new girl."

"Yes, sir, my name is Judy," she answered.

Judy's a real pretty girl with long brown hair that kinks up when it rains. She's got green eyes and enough personality for three people. I found out all about her in the weeks to come. I learned she'd got married right out of high school at the age of seventeen. She'd wed her high-school sweetheart, and that marriage had lasted for four years. Then she moved to Nashville from Gallatin, which was about thirty-five miles away. She told me she'd gotten lost on the interstate coming in, and had gone thirty miles past the city limits. She was dating now and again, but nothing really serious. I began to confide in her about my problems at home, and she'd listen and try to give me advice. Believe me, she was on the woman's side. She didn't tell me I was right when I was wrong. I liked that. I could talk to her.

One weekend I invited Judy and two of her girl buddies to come to Cincinnati to see our show. She didn't know about country music, and it was time for her to learn if she intended to work for me. So they drove up and arrived just in time for the show. Yes, they'd got lost and were fifty miles past Louisville, heading for Indianapolis, before one of them realized it. I got them seats in the orchestra pit, and they watched the whole show looking up. They all had cricks in their necks for three days, Judy said.

I sang my latest hits and some old ones, like "Who's Julie." I dedicated that song to Judy, and changed the lyrics to "Who's Judy." I think she liked that. The concert went well. Hank Junior was on the show, and afterward we had a big party at the motel. Hank's band, my band, and several ladies and Judy and her pals. We left the next morning, and Judy drove back to Nashville with her friends, still not sure about country music. She told Maggie it was different enough. The songs were real touching and had hit home more than once.

Then, a few weeks later, she came to Waldorf, Maryland. I was falling in love with her. I thought I could turn it off and on whenever I wanted to, but all I could think about was Judy, Judy, Judy.

Maggie Ward and Roger, my cousin that I'd brought up from Florida, suspected what was going on. Word was coming in off the road and spreading around town like the plague. Roger fired Judy. Well, that made me madder than hell. I went out to Gallatin, where Judy had moved into a real little house, more like a shack than anything. I told her everything was my fault and that I wanted her to come back to work. She finally agreed and moved to the Americana apartments.

Roger came into the office one day and told me he needed more space. He said he was starting a music publishing company with Don Williams. I'd brought Don to Roger as another act for him to book. We'd planned to build an agency together, Roger, Don, and I. Well, they moved out, and Judy came back to work, but not for long. Doris threatened to file for a divorce unless she left.

I was in pretty good with the folks at MGM—I was on their label and my records were doing well. They were opening up new offices and needed experienced help. I called Jimmy Bowen and told him about Judy. He hired her as Bob Alou's secretary. I wasn't too thrilled about her working for someone else, but I didn't have any choice.

Money was coming in faster now. I bought a King Air plane and started flying to my appearances. That plane was a blessing. It took me off the bus, and I was home more often. It saved a lot of wear and tear on my body, which I needed real bad.

Then I bought several connecting farms out in Montgomery County, near Henrietta. They had a few old houses on them and I hoped to build a new home there for Doris and me and the kids.

I'd take Doris and the kids out to the farm from time to time. The kids would go wild. They had horses to ride and woods to explore and fish to catch in the many little ponds on the place. Doris and I would walk and talk and I'd tell her about my plans to build us a home there. We'd usually end up in a fuss. She'd tell me I wasn't about to move her forty miles out in the sticks while I had my flings in town with Judy. We'd fuss all the way back to Nashville. I guess the kids were getting used to it. They never said much one way or the other. Our trips to the farm stopped, except for taking the kids once in a while.

One day when I was out on the road I called in, and Maggie told me that Glenn Ferguson, a Metro official, had called and told her that Robert Redford was coming to town that Friday night, and Billy Sherrill was having a cocktail party for him at his house. He said Mr. Redford wanted to meet Mel Tillis and Willie Nelson and nobody else. I couldn't believe it. What did he want? I asked myself. I found out later.

Doris didn't want to go to the party, but I talked her into it. It was a great party for about thirty people. Everybody had a fun time. Willie was there, and Robert Redford spent a lot of time talking to both of us, while Doris chatted with the other wives, probably about me. Robert Redford asked Willie and me to ride with him to the airport. He said he had to leave the party early and fly to New York on some business matters.

As we all three rode in a limousine to the airport, he talked to us about his interest in ecology and said that he would like our support on some of his projects. We agreed with his plans and promised to help all we could. He then got on his private jet and disappeared into the dark, rainy skies. I have waited eight years for him to tell me what I can do to help, but I haven't heard a word from him.

About a year after that meeting, Willie made a movie with Redford called *The Electric Horseman*. Now I knew what part of that meeting was all about. I saw that movie three times, and they both did a great job.

Doris and I left the party kinda late. We got into a real zinger on the way home. It was still raining. We began by talking about Florida and how much we missed that sunny state.

Doris told me in no uncertain words that I wasn't moving her back to Florida. Then the subject of Judy came up again, and it went on and on, even after we got home. She threw a hairbrush at me that night and hit me in the head, just missing my right eye. Boy, that hurt. That night I moved out of the bedroom. From then on, I slept with Sonny Boy or Carrie April whenever she was fussing, which was usually all the time. I wanted us to see a marriage counselor, but she wouldn't agree to that.

The older kids, Pam and Connie, were now in high school. They were bringing their share of problems home. Whatever Doris or I would tell them, they'd do just the opposite. Pam had a terrible car wreck that smashed her pretty face flat. She had to have several operations out in California to get her face back to looking nice. Then Connie had a wreck in my Blazer and it threw her completely through the windshield. That knocked her out for a while, but thank the Lord no other damage was done. The Blazer was totaled out.

Cindy and Sonny Boy were still in junior high and weren't giving us any problems. Carrie was still little, and we all loved her so much. She'd dance and sing for us. She'd play her little fiddle, using the Suzuki method. I let her play that little fiddle on "Pop Goes the Country" one time. Ralph Emery was the host of that TV show.

I guess Judy got fed up with the whole mess because she moved back to Gallatin, to her folk's house, and her daddy got her a job at the new nuclear power plant that the TVA was building in Hartsville. She drove a big dump truck or anything else that they needed driven. She told me that it was all over for us, that we could never be, so why go on like this torturing ourselves? She began dating other men, and I didn't like that one bit. But what could I do? She was free and I wasn't. She wouldn't answer my phone calls or call me. So I'd write her letters. Nothing can stop the U.S. Mail, I'd heard. She wouldn't write me back.

Now I was even more confused. I'd go home and hear more fussing. I'd go on the road and try to smile and be happy, but I'm sure my troubles showed through to the crowds. I'd come back home and Doris would accuse me of being with Judy. "Hell, she's in Gallatin and she's dating other guys now. I haven't even talked to her in two months," I'd tell Doris. That didn't seem to matter. I was catching hell from all directions.

Finally, one night in our bedroom, as Doris was hanging up a dress in her closet, I asked her for a divorce. She had filed several times before, but had always called it off at the very last minute, just before it went to court.

I moved out. I checked into a room at the Hall of Fame Motel. Most pickers call that place the Hall of Shame. I was more than hurt and ashamed, I was devastated. Judy was gone. Doris was mad. My marriage was all but over—too much stubbornness on both sides to save it. For the first time in my life I contemplated suicide. I quickly put that out of my mind, though. Too many people depended on me for their livelihood. (I had over seventy-five people working for me then. There's well over a hundred now, since the acquisition of WMML Radio in Mobile, and Cedarwood Publishing Company.) No, suicide was out of the question. I guess I was a little chicken-shit, too.

I stayed at the Hall of Fame Motel for about two weeks and then decided I had to get out of there. I'd been spending most of my time in the lounge listening to the band and drinking with a lot of other pickers who were having the same problems. I had to get away. I found a little house in Ashland City. I say it was little though it had five bedrooms, because it wasn't like the mansion I'd lived in with Doris, which had nineteen rooms in all. I bought a few pieces of furniture, just enough to get by, and moved in. Then I checked into the hospital for a few days. I was buying more property here and there and needed more insurance, so I had to have one of the complete physicals I have every year. (I'm lucky my health has been good.)

Well, Judy heard about me being in the hospital and she came to see me. I guess she felt sorry for me. She brought me some wildlife magazines. I told her about the divorce and that Dick Frank, my attorney, was in Europe, but

would be taking depositions as soon as he got back. She
didn't budge on the way she felt about things. She said the
divorce had been on and off so many times that she just
couldn't go on believing it would happen. She left and went
back to her dump truck.

As soon as she left, I got on the phone and somehow
found Dick in Europe. I told him to get back home and get
this thing over with. "I'm going crazy," I said, "and the
quicker the better. Enough is enough."

He finally returned from Europe and depositions were
taken. Then there were several meetings with Doris and
her attorney. Everything came out in those meetings. Dick
got an early hearing in Springfield, Tennessee. The divorce
was uncontested. We'd agreed on a pretty nice settlement.
I gave her all she asked for. I figured she had earned it. Her
settlement was based on earnings from 1976 and part of
1977. I think I netted about $750,000 that year.

Doris got the big house in Brentwood, a large cash settlement—tax free—which I was allowed to pay over a five-
year period. She receives monthly alimony checks and also
child support. Her alimony checks will continue until she
gets married again. But I don't look for that.

I pay for the kids' education as far as they want to take
it. Pam dropped out of the University of Tennessee and is
writing songs and recording for Warner Brothers. Connie
hasn't decided what she wants to do yet. She has a wonderful voice, and Harold Shedd, my producer, wants to do a
session with her, but she has to apply herself and get her
priorities in order. She will. I pray for her, and the Lord
answers prayers. I still pay for most of the clothes for the
children who are still in school. Carrie's in the sixth grade
now, Son and Cindy are away at college. Cindy says the
best thing about a divorce when there are kids involved is
that the kids get two birthday parties, two Christmases,
two homes—two of just about everything. That's one way
to look at it.

Doris and I are friends. I go by often, mostly if the kids

are there. The place doesn't look quite the same as I left it.
Doris has painted a mural on the solid-wall fence going to
the back area of the house. It's a depiction of me and the
kids playing in the yard. It saddened me when I first saw it.
She's turned the barn into a little studio apartment, which
she's rented out to some writer from England. The garage
has also been made into an apartment, and it's rented, too.
Then she's built a walk-in greenhouse onto the den. It's full
of plants and flowers.

Doris is good at antiques. She finds old furniture and
fixes it up for resale. She's opened a little shop, where she
sells those things. She's into sculpturing and oil paintings.
The sculptures aren't too bad, but she hasn't got the eyes
down on her portraits yet. She's beginning to grow now,
just as I did before. I wish her all the happiness in the
world and stand ready to help her with her investments, if
she'll let me. I'm good at that.

After the divorce, Judy was still not sure she wanted to
marry me. She'd been through enough. It took me quite a
while to get her even to go out with me again. Later I
talked her into quitting her job. I told her she didn't have to
drive a dump truck. It was unbecoming for a girl to do that.
She said, "It pays the rent."

Finally she quit her job and moved in with me at the new
house in Ashland City. We planned to get married as soon
as everything settled down. There wasn't much in the
papers or on the news about the divorce. Doris was good
about that. It was the best way.

Judy brought all of her plants and flowers and placed
them nicely around the house, as only a woman can. She
bought some more furniture and fixed the place real nice.
After about three months she asked me if everything had
settled enough for us to get married. She said she was
embarrassed to be living with me and that she didn't want
to keep her mama and daddy worried about her.

I kept putting our getting married off, mainly on account
of the kids. I loved Judy but still, I needed a little more

time. I'd just bought the King Air plane and wanted to go somewhere in it. Richard had met a man in Yakima, Washington, who had a little island off the coast of Belize (formerly British Honduras). He invited us to come down and spend a few days. So we went: Breadman; Raymond Hicks, my road manager, Bill Ray; the two pilots; and me. We had a great time.

We went to a nightclub in Belize called the Big C and got drunk as hell. There were a lot of available women, but I didn't participate. The place was full of British soldiers, who were there at the request of the Belize government. Guatemala had threatened several invasions, but with the British there, they had a good reason not to do so.

Breadman sold his cowboy hat to one of those soldiers for $200. He said, "Hell, let's go back home and get some more hats and come back. This is better than selling on the road."

Raymond Hicks also had a ball. That is, until he fell into an open septic tank up to his waist.

Those three days ended and we flew back to Nashville. Judy wasn't there to pick me up. I went out to Ashland City, to where Judy and I had set up housekeeping, and found her gone. I'd called her from Belize and she'd told me she was leaving because I wasn't serious about getting married. She took everything but her plants and flowers, and said she'd pick them up later, whenever I was out of town. I was home for about a week and I watered her healthy plants every day. I placed a little note that said "I love you" in every one of those plants. When I went out on the road, Judy came over to pick them up. They were all dead. I had killed them—too much watering.

CHAPTER

25

Judy and I were married on March 21, 1979, approximately twenty-one months after my divorce. It was a simple wedding, to say the least.

But let me go back to that house in Ashland City, before we were married. After I'd killed all of Judy's plants, I guess she figured anybody that stupid needed some help, so she moved back in. We lived there a few months, then moved to a new farm that I'd recently bought from a Baptist preacher. I had another eighty-acre farm about twelve miles away in Henrietta, Tennessee. I liked the preacher's farm and he liked mine. So we made a trade. The Henrietta farm was enough to cover his collateral, and I refinanced the balance of his farm with the original owners. We were both happy with the trade. He got 80 acres clear of debt, and I got 260 acres of beautiful rolling pastureland planted with fescue and red and white clover.

The new farm borders Sycamore Creek for about two miles and is lined with hundreds of giant sycamore trees. We named it Sycamore Acres. The creek is really a scenic beauty. It meanders its way through several middle Tennessee counties and finally joins the historic Cumberland River about five miles away from our farm. Mel, Jr., and I have caught small-mouth bass, large-mouth bass, blue gill, crappie, blue channel catfish, soft-shell turtles, and snapping ones, too. We love to eat turtles. We've gigged carp during the winter months, and big ole bullfrogs during the hot summer nights. There are red and gray squirrels, deer, quail, doves, and way too many beavers there to suit me. Judy has even seen a wildcat. There are also copperheads, rattlesnakes, and some moccasins, but they won't hurt you if you don't go messing with 'em. I damn sure don't.

I bought the two little farms on both sides of our property, and that brought the acreage up to about 460 acres. This was to be our home place. I would build our little cabin there among the great red and white oaks that grew majestically in a certain spot. We both agreed on the location.

Judy and I moved into a little two-bedroom house trailer that came with the trade, and together we set about fixing things up. First we gave the trailer a real good scrubbing inside and out. I patched the roof and Judy bought new curtains and rugs and things. I bought her some new plants and was kindly warned not to touch them. I promised I wouldn't, but only if she stayed for good this time. She said that was entirely up to me.

It wasn't too bad, and it was certainly different enough. We improved on what was there and got by just fine. We wanted to be around when our cabin was being built. We wanted to see every log put in its proper place, every stone laid, and every peg hammered into the ashwood floors. This would be the cabin I'd dreamed about during those lonely hours riding on the bus and lying around in uninteresting motel rooms. Yes, we would be there, at least one of us.

We started collecting different animals—dogs, horses, chickens, turkeys, a milk cow. One day I brought a little tomcat home on the plane with me from Illinois to give to Judy. I found him sitting out on the runway, waiting beside

Stutter One, after I'd finished working a show that evening. I picked him up and took him along. I gave him a name— Downwind. Now, that's a word used mostly by pilots and it seemed to fit, so that was what we called him. Judy was tickled to death when I came in with it.

We still weren't married. Judy didn't like the idea of us living together, although lots of people were doing just that, and it seemed to be acceptable. Nonetheless she felt like it was setting a bad example for my kids, and it was embarrassing for her mother and father as well as for her. I understood that and promised to marry her as soon as the guilt and hurt of the divorce had passed. But that never leaves, I found out.

One day, after several months of living in the trailer, Judy said, "Melvin, it's been almost two years now since the divorce. We've got to get our lives together. We can't go on living like this."

I agreed and told her to set the date.

She said. "How about next week?"

"Okay with me," I answered.

Well, Judy got all the premarital details in line, and then she announced to me that we could have our blood tests and marriage license and marriage ceremony all in the same day. I don't know how in hell she managed that, but she did. I've learned, though, that whenever I want something done, whether it's on the farm or in the office, if I ask Judy, and she believes in it, it gets done.

We were married on that Tuesday morning in March of 1979. We had to drive to Gallatin, which was about sixty miles away, but first we stopped to pick up Bob and Janet Younts, who live a few miles from our farm. Judy and I had stood up for them when they'd gotten married a few years back out at Lake Tahoe. Bob was playing drums for me then, but now he's the operational manager for Mel Tillis Enterprises, and he's doing a good job.

I drove about fifteen miles an hour on our way over to

Gallatin. Bob questioned our speed and said, "Hell, Mel, Louis and Clark made this trip quicker than us, and they were in canoes."

I wasn't talking hardly at all. My mind was on the kids and the early years of my marriage. Those were the good years, when the kids were little and life was simpler for us. Then came fame and fortune, and it was all gone. Just like a dream. I love Judy—I always will—but still, I had those thoughts about my first marriage. I wouldn't be much of a man if I didn't.

In Gallatin, I went through the blood test and marriage license proceedings and then we went before the judge. The folks at the courthouse let us go in front of some other couples who were there for the same reason. Two or three minutes and it was all over. I had a new wife and I loved her. We stopped on the way back home at a little country store and bought some bread, bologna, cheese, beer, and diet Pepsi. That was our wedding feast. I couldn't eat, so I just drank the beer.

Paul Harvey had it on his radio and television shows the very next day. Then the different news media picked it up, and it was all over the world in no time at all.

The kids heard about it on the news and were very hurt that I hadn't told them before. I didn't because I feared hurting them more than I already had. But that was wrong; I should have talked with them first. One by one they called me and said they still loved me and wished me well.

They started coming to the farm after that. Judy went through some pretty tough times with them. One time Sonny Boy put some live minnows in the ice trays and froze them as hard as rocks. Judy had filled our glasses with those minnowed ice cubes before she noticed them. We had a good laugh about it and it didn't happen again. She learned all their tricks, and sometimes even turned the jokes around on them. They liked it, and soon they were asking her advice on all sorts of things. They call all the time now, even the ones away at college.

My oldest daughter, Pam, had left the University of Tennessee and gone to San Francisco to live. She wanted to learn to write songs and develop her voice. She worked a show with the Ramsey Lewis Trio, a jazz group that's been very popular for quite a few years. She didn't want to follow in her daddy's footsteps and sing country. I didn't like it, but I admired her for making a decision. She's had one album out on Warner Brothers, and several of her songs have been recorded by others.

At this writing, I'm looking out across Lake Tahoe. I'm staying in Bill Harrah's Village, a huge complex of a home that's furnished to the entertainers who work Harrah's in Lake Tahoe. They really treat you first-class. I mean, a cook, a maid, a guard, and a Rolls-Royce to drive. Pam just called me from Nashville and told me she was thinking about going more country. I hope she's serious. She can sure sing pop or country equally well, and it would be a wise move for her, because she's living in Nashville now.

While she was living in San Francisco, Pam met and married a young man. His name is Rick Mason and he came from Iowa, a state I'd worked many times over. They moved back to Nashville and I let them stay in our house in Ashland City. That was my wedding gift to them. I was glad that I was able to do that, but I suppose both of them resented it in a way. Soon we were told that a baby was on the way. I couldn't believe it. I was going to be a grandfather.

Pam had picked up on some of those West Coast habits while living out there. It was herbal this and herbal that, sunflower seeds and all kinds of nuts. I had some garden seeds laid out for spring planting and they disappeared. I accused her of eating them. She laughed, but said she hadn't.

Rick and Pam weren't getting along too well. Pam was writing for Sawgrass Publishing Company, and she got a weekly draw from her songs, as I'd done with Cedarwood. Pam's doctor was one of those who believed in natural

births—no painkillers, no nothing, just let her fly and that
was it. Well, his office was way out in the woods near
Hohenwald, Tennessee, and the day finally came when
Rick took Pam for the delivery. She came home the same
day with a little baby boy. Ben Asher Mason had become a
part of our family. He was a real pretty baby. He looked a
little like Pam but more like Rick. About three weeks after
the baby was born, she and Rick split up for good and she
came to live with us in our trailer.

I was sorry about the breakup, but I was sure happy to
have a baby around the house (trailer) again. I had missed
that. Ben is a joy and smart as a whip. We love him very
much. He lives with his mother in Nashville now, but
comes and stays with us a lot. I'm learning a lot from that
kid. Judy wants a baby of our own, but Dr. Hill took care of
that about eleven years ago. We've talked about adopting
one, but haven't yet. Maybe I'll go back and get the vasectomy reversed. I've heard there are doctors doing that
now, with a pretty good success percentage.

Connie graduated from Overton High School and didn't
want to go to college, so I didn't make her. I should have,
but I didn't. She's worked in the publishing companies on
several occasions and has recorded several good demos.
She really has a great country voice. Connie married a
young man named Phillip Ray Hollingsworth, but everybody calls him Spooky because he was born on Halloween. I
liked him and still do. He's a plumber and a good one. I let
them move into one of our farmhouses that's not too far
from our log house. Connie got pregnant and had a little
boy, but she went to the hospital for her delivery. None of
that "no painkiller" stuff for her. Connie and Spooky are
divorced now and little Phillip is three and a half years old.
He's got really black curly hair and loves Michael Jackson.
He comes to visit us on the farm a lot, too, and it's really
"on your toes time" when both Phillip and Ben are there at
the same time.

Connie's working at other places now and is hoping to make a record someday. It's up to her, though, to put in her own dime.

Cindy is finishing up at American University this year and will probably stay in Washington, D.C., to work. Mel, Jr., will be a junior next year at the University of Florida, and Carrie April is into everything at her school—Franklin Road Academy. She runs track, plays in the marching band, and is an excellent student. I'm very proud of all my kids and love them very much.

CHAPTER

26

Now there were other problems cropping up in my life that I hadn't counted on. Problems that people I didn't even know brought us. That's something that nobody can prevent or predict.

I remember a time I was doing a Purina Dog Chow commercial with Jerry Clower—a good Christian family man, a great southern comedian, and a good friend of mine, I'm proud to say. We were half into the second day of filming when the producer came to me and said he'd received mailgrams from NBC and CBS saying they would not run the commercial, and then made reference to the stutter. I was really disappointed they felt that way. It was my first commercial and Jerry and I were having a ball. It was still planned to show the commercial in syndication in about 125 markets, but I was hurt by the networks' decision.

"Hell, I'm gonna be on the Johnny Carson show tomorrow night," I told my attorney, Richard Frank.

Dick thought about it for a few minutes, and then he said, "Well, Stutterin' Boy, we'll just ask them for a letter of apology, and if they don't send one, we'll find out who owns the company."

Both NBC and CBS wrote nice letters back to me.

I've done a lot of commercials in recent years with no trouble at all. There were some takes I did without stuttering, but, you know, they always used the ones with a little bit of stutter.

Anyway, when I was doing that Purina Dog Chow commercial, I hadn't had all that much national exposure. The advertising agency in charge of making the commercials had sent the storyboards up to CBS and NBC headquarters in New York. That's standard procedure. The storyboards are a row of panels—like a comic strip—carrying little drawings of what people will do in the commercials and spelling out what they're supposed to say. As usual, the commercial had to be okayed by a special department that checks to see whether it's airable, or whether it's immoral or in bad taste or against some network "standards." That makes sense, and like I said before, when I worked the "Glen Campbell Good Time Hour" on CBS, I found out that networks don't want to anger the audience—or the FCC (the Federal Communications Commission), which handles their licenses.

I guess the people who reviewed those Purina Dog Chow storyboards were only doing their jobs. When they read the stuttering lines I had to say, they turned thumbs down on the commercial immediately, and with good reason. One of the networks' standard rules is that you don't make fun of handicapped people of any kind. But country music was just as foreign to those people in the networks' headquarters as the opera would be to me (not the Grand Ole Opry, of course). They had no idea who I was and that I really stuttered. Those Purina folks didn't have to write the stutter in, anyway. I can't stutter on cue. I stutter where I stutter, and that's it.

The news got out on the talk shows I went on. Merv Griffin, Johnny Carson, Dinah Shore, Mike Douglas—all of those hosts asked me about the networks' letters. There was an uproar. It was in some trade papers, even on the radio news broadcast.

Now, I don't blame those people for what they did. Nobody knows everything. I don't expect the whole world to be familiar with me and my stutter. I realize that even more now. Country music is much more popular from coast to coast these days, but even so, there are still lots of folks out there who don't know about country artists. The fuss about the commercial finally died down, but recently I've had some more complaints.

One lady in Las Vegas didn't like the way they had my name on the marquee at the Frontier Hotel. It read, "M-M-M-Mel," in great big letters. That was all they had up there. But people must have known who I was because we really packed 'em at the Frontier.

Then a man in Dallas complained about the American Fina gas stations' signs. They read, "They're m-m-m-my kinda f-f-f-folks at F-F-F-Fina." Now, I didn't know about that. It was the advertising agency's concept, not mine. They quickly took down those signs.

Some folks think I'm deliberately teasing people with speech problems. Hell, I've been trying to get rid of the stuttering for years. Only about two years ago, I turned down some good bookings to go to a speech clinic in New York City. Maybe I was expecting an overnight miracle. I could have been hoping too hard . . . expecting too much too soon. Anyway, I didn't stay long. I had to go and do a movie *(Cannonball Run)* with Burt Reynolds, and he didn't care if I stuttered, or not.

The honest-to-goodness truth is that I know how much stutterers have to battle, and what they go through. It's just crazy to think that I'd mock them. I'm a stutterer—and I wouldn't make fun of me. After a lot of years and more hurting than I like to remember, I can talk about it lightly—which eases things a bit. It's a way of showing people that it hasn't licked me, so it doesn't have to lick others.

Now, that's mighty important. I've never thought of myself as any hero, but I am one of the living proofs that speech-handicapped men and women can live full lives. And thousands of people have seen how my speech has gotten better over the years—very slowly.

Sometimes stutterers or their relatives will come up to me after a performance and tell me how much of an inspiration I've been to them. I feel good when handicapped people say I give them encouragement—and I'm upset with those who accuse me of exploitation.

Another problem that I didn't expect was a result of our growing popularity. I'd been working for that so long, never thinking that it could be anything but all good. Well, what was so good for me and the Statesiders was starting to cost my brother money. He'd been doing a decent business with our T-shirts, records, tapes, and other souvenirs—especially since I was picked Entertainer of the Year in 1976. I had been honored often, as the Music City News Comedian of the Year, between 1971 and 1975, which was a real compliment. After all, the world of country has a lot of very funny people, including Minnie Pearl and Jerry Clower. But the impact of being chosen Entertainer of the Year was *much* bigger.

Now a lot more people wanted to buy Mel Tillis souvenirs at my concerts. Breadman had purchased thousands of copies of a souvenir book on Mel Tillis and the Statesiders. He'd invested his own money. That was the deal. He was an independent businessman, not an employee of mine.

He did all right until 1976. The souvenir books, which cost him less than a quarter each in bulk, were moving slowly but steadily. After October 1976 he sold them ten times as fast—moving thousands in six months at $2 each. And he even had the band helping with selling the various items, either at intermission or after a show. Naturally, those musicians who chose to sell got a commission.

Richard's ingenuity was a big factor in his sales success.

At one show in Pennsylvania, two ladies came up and one asked him for a certain recording. It was in a two-package LP selling for $10. That price soured the sale at first, but Breadman had a solution.

"Would you pay seven dollars?" he asked.

"Yes, sir."

And he turned to the other woman.

"Would you buy a Mel Tillis LP for three dollars?"

"I sure would," she answered.

So he took out his pocket knife and cut that hinged album cover right in half, sold each lady what she wanted, and collected the $10.

But quick as he is, the change in our success after 1976 affected his income in two ways. In the short run, it went up, but then the people who book our dates—the Jim Halsey Agency—began to get us different kinds of places to perform. Since there was more interest in us, we could fill bigger "venues." So we started to spend more time in places like the casino-hotels of Las Vegas and Atlantic City. Those kinds of dates are a lot easier on you physically and mentally. You know what to expect every night. A two-week stay in one comfortable, modern, air-conditioned hotel in a place where there is twenty-four-hour food service is hard to pass up. It doesn't wear you down like seven one-nighters, two shows a night, back to back in different towns. You don't have to sleep in bouncing buses or maybe a motel for only a few hours. You can sleep like a regular person does, get your laundry done—all those normal things. But most of the hotels won't let you sell your souvenirs, and that's understandable—they're in the gaming business.

Well, as the number of our appearances in those hotels went up, the income that Breadman was getting from his concession sales went down. What made it even rougher for him was that we were also playing in big coliseums and concert halls, where the owners usually demanded a large percentage of his concession money. I could see Breadman being squeezed out. He went out with us less and less, and finally not at all.

He sensed those days were over for him, and after failing in the worm and greenhouse businesses, he moved to Lafayette, Louisiana. He drove a bread truck for a while, but now he's got a real good job with an oil company. We talk on the phone once in a while and I see him from time to time. We all, including the band, miss his presence very much.

I'd like for him to come back and be with the rest of us near Nashville. I think a lot about our doing something together again, so the family would be reunited. As a result, I'm working on a plan now that could bring him back into my operations in a new spot.

CHAPTER

27

Since it was something that I'd yearned for since I was a boy living in small rented places in Florida, I guess there's nothing surprising about the fact that our cabin turned out to be a very large house. It isn't a southern mansion with columns—just a log house that's real comfortable to live in. That suits me much better.

Sonny Boy likes to kid about the fact that I wear simple clothes—with pretty fancy boots. I'm more comfortable in jeans than anything else, and the boots show my love for Western things—Bob Wills, cowboys, Texas, and the rest. He thinks that I should dress more like a businessman who runs several enterprises, as I do. When he came to work in my office last summer, it was strictly three-piece suits and ties for him. He looked fine and he did a good job, but I'll stick to my style and let others have theirs.

Now, there are all kinds of log houses you can build today. There are several kits for prefabs. They don't look bad, but they just don't have the sense of history, the connection with the South that I care so much about. Anyway, we decided to build from scratch. Before we finished our house, it was a whopper—seven thousand square feet.

The truth is, we never drew up any plans for that house. We never consulted an architect. Maybe it was because of my "put the dime in the slot yourself" upbringing, but I just reckoned I'd figure it out all right. Some folks thinks that I've got too much confidence and try to do too much without experts. I'm one of the few successful country performers who never has had a manager, except for that brief period with Buck Peddy. I have good people to advise me— lawyers and other specialists—and an able director of operations who watches day-to-day things and handles them well. That's been enough so far.

Things could get bigger and more complicated. I might find myself concentrating on some major new effort—such as the company I've organized to produce movies and television shows. I'd been thinking about that for years. Then I saw pretty Bo Derek in a terrible Tarzan picture. It was the worst I'd ever endured. If that movie got made and shown, I was convinced I could do better. And I believe that I will—when I've learned more. No way will I avoid mistakes, but I'm in no hurry.

As I was in no hurry when building our log house. I thought and thought about it—starting with the location, where the big oaks stood. Then I turned my mind to exactly what I wanted the new house to be. This was to be the first house I would ever build and probably the last. I'd been secretly pondering it for so many years.

One day I had it all worked out. "Come on, it's time," I said to Judy.

So we walked the 350 yards from our trailer and I pointed. "It's going to set right here," I said.

She looked, thought, and nodded.

Then I started to explain where each room would be. "I'll show you," I announced, and started walking. I paced off each room, and Judy put sticks into the ground as markers. Our ideas about where and how long and how wide the rooms should be matched. I'm grateful for that, since my feelings on the whole layout were strong. She did the kitchen and den and all the furnishings on her own.

Nobody sensible, I'm told, would go at building a house that way. But it didn't surprise too many people who knew me that I was doing that. Sinatra and Paul Anka may have the best known versions of "My Way," but it really should be my theme song. I can't help doing things like that. It's that drive—that will to do.

No, to do it *right*. Later on, when we were putting up a fence, I made sure that the best lumber was used and the posts were sunk in cement. I wanted the fence—and everything else about that farm—to be perfect. And I didn't want to have to do it over again. Those fence posts were pressure treated with salt water and guaranteed for fifty years.

After we had it all paced, staked, and talked out, we called in a builder. He was definitely startled when he found out that there was no architect, no written plan. We talked over what Judy and I wanted, and then a drawing was made.

I was real proud of myself when I mentioned the house to Webb Pierce. He asked me what it might cost.

When I answered, Webb shook his head. "About fifty percent more, Mel. Every damn house that's worth anything comes out costing fifty percent more than you expect."

He was right. We did have to redo some things. There was a problem with the roof. And I've got to admit that I added a few things as we went along. It took quite a while to find the big logs we needed from 150- to 200-year-old barns and houses that were scattered around the Tennessee and Kentucky hillsides, the hand-hewed timbers we used for the walls, inside and out. Some of those wonderful logs had been covered up by coats of paint or wallpaper for years, but we brought them back to their natural beauty. Many of the barns whose timbers we bought were abandoned, but some were still in use.

To pay for this and normal expenses, I was out with the Statesiders a lot. So Judy kept her eye on things day to day, while I inspected every time I came in from the road. Judy could deal with the touring. The road didn't threaten her.

We collected rocks from Sycamore Creek to build a forty-foot rock fireplace. At Judy's suggestion, we picked out furniture that would go with a log house. We have quite a few items—even appliances—that are from an earlier time. I don't mean two hundred years old, but we do have a refrigerator that's from the 1930s, with the original motor. She found several things at auctions, enjoying every minute of it.

Judy was getting impatient with how long it took those carpenters to get the whole project finished, and she made up her mind that we'd celebrate Christmas in our new house. She'd waited long enough. So the workmen went on extra shifts in December 1980. I was away, in Las Vegas, but that wasn't going to mess up her Christmas. She moved in all our furniture from the small house—everything but the couch—by *herself*. And the workmen were still connecting the electricity three days before Christmas, when she drove to the airport to pick me up—something she always does.

The tree was up and the house looked wonderful. There were a few touch-ups to do, but we really haven't had any trouble with that house.

It was a lot more hazardous getting the farm in shape. Fact is, I didn't know much about running a farm or its machinery. So I damn near killed myself—several times.

I was so pleased that I finally had a farm that I jumped into working the land with both feet., I was out one day with my son, who was about as happy as I was. He was all over the place—up in the trees and everywhere—as teenage boys will do. He was enjoying every second.

I had bought a Ford tractor and I had a Bush Hog—a mower that rides behind the tractor. I was smoking a big cigar while clearing a piece of the farm that was covered with sage brush, but I wasn't thinking about that. I was so content to be clearing the land, my land.

When I finished most of the cigar, I tossed it over my shoulder. Now, that wasn't something anyone who knew about farming would do. There was straw all over that Bush Hog right behind me, and sure enough it caught fire. I didn't even know it. So I'm going on in blissful ignorance, hearing sirens. I had no idea that they had anything to do with me. Some guys on a fire tower a couple of miles away had spotted it.

Well, I looked back a minute later. The whole damn pasture was on fire.

"I done it again!" I said.

But that wasn't all. I had to leave at noon to reach the Nashville Airport for a two o'clock flight to Los Angeles. I had to clean up, change my clothes, pack, and all that. When the fire crew came tearing out to my place, with their sirens going, they went right to work fighting what I'd started. But I couldn't help them because I had to leave. It was embarrassing.

"I hate to do this to y'all," I said, "but I have to go. I've got to be on a plane in two hours. I'm going to be on the Johnny Carson show tonight!"

They told me to go ahead and they'd put it out.

So I left them fighting my fire. They were very nice about it. Well, that fire cleared that piece of land just fine.

When I came back to work on the farm the next week, I decided to Bush Hog an old logging road that went down through the woods to the bottom land. That road hadn't been cleared out for forty years. The brush was really heavy. I started the Ford tractor inching down the road, and I could see what a deep drop it was over the edge. I could tell where the road was under all those briars, so I just kept inching and inching my way—avoiding the edge.

Then it happened.

Both front tires hit a slick wet slab of rock where a spring came out of the side of the bluff. And that tractor started easing over the side. When it did that, I jumped—went straight up in the air. The tractor slid out from under me. I could see that Bush Hog waving bye-bye at me as it went over the side. It dropped three hundred feet, and I fell into a tangle of blackberry bushes—a real briar patch. I felt like Brer Rabbit.

Falling on a boulder, the tractor broke completely in two under the impact. I'd have been killed for sure if I hadn't of bailed out.

Sonny Boy heard the noise, and he came a-hollering, "Daddy! Daddy! Daddy!"

"I'm all right, son," I told him, and explained what had happened. I looked like I'd caught the measles from those blackberry bushes. Judy picked thorns out of me for days.

Well, John Burdeshaw went down and pulled the two pieces of the tractor out of the gulley with a bulldozer. He put it back together later, and I still have it today.

Another time I was disking the field where my mama's house is now. She came to live on the farm from Henrietta a couple of years ago. We built her a nice little house, with a garden, where that old trailer had been. Behind that trailer—where Judy and I were living until the big log home was up—was a chicken house. No chickens—just an old storage place then. I wasn't an expert at running tractor, and you could tell it. I caught the back end of the disk on the corner of the chicken house and just about did it in. I knocked it sideways.

I got really mad. The harder I tried, the more I tore up. First I'd made a mess, and next I had to clean it up.

"The hell with that," I said, and got me a match.

I set the whole mess on fire. Well, all the old jars and bottles inside started to explode. They'd been out there for years and years—some with apple cider fermenting in them. They'd turned into bombs, blowing up and scaring the nearby grazing animals half to death. Cattle, horses, pigs, chickens—we've got all kinds of animals. Then there were more explosions—like the fake war we'd fought at National Guard Camp.

I had to move the tractor out of there fast. Judy hosed down the trailer to keep it from catching fire. When I got the tractor moving, I somehow managed to run over our water line and cut it.

"There's more," Judy says.

After we finally put the fire out, I got on the little riding lawn mower—and ran right into the house trailer. I knocked it about six inches off its blocks, and there was a scream. Judy was back inside at the time, wondering what I'd tear up next.

Judy has been real understanding about machines and me—and my fishing, too. She comes fishing with me—does pretty well. Some wives fight things like football and fishing, but not Judy. Once I took her up to the fish camp at Center Hill Lake at Smithville. There were a bunch of cabins on a cliff two hundred feet above the lake. We drove up, pulling our boat behind on a trailer. After I put the boat in the water, we went up to the cabins, where I disconnected the trailer from our station wagon.

I started to push it. But in about two seconds it was pushing me.

I had no idea that trailer was so heavy. Well, I fell down. When I did, it ran over me—over my arm. Why it didn't hurt me I don't know! It could have taken my arm right off, but it didn't. I hardly got a scratch. It rolled on—heading for one of the cabins and picking up speed. It would have gone through those little cabins like a train.

But somehow or other, it hit a rock and turned and spun. There were some big old telephone poles a-laying there, a barrier at the edge of the cliff. One of those poles slowed it down just enough, leaving the trailer with one wheel hanging over the edge. That was just an accident, of course. But

I learned one thing: never try to manhandle a boat trailer as heavy as that one was on a grade by yourself. It'll whip you.

I don't think I can be blamed for what happened with the golf cart. To help my mama (who is in her seventies) get around the farm, Judy had bought her an old motorized golf cart. I'm real pleased that she and·Judy get along so well. Of course, one reason is that Mama doesn't go around telling others what to do. Fact is, it's real hard to pry any advice out of Mama. She believes that grown-ups can figure things out for themselves.

Mama's real smart—country smart. One time when she was still living alone down in Florida, a bunch of strange guys with motorcycles, leather, and beards moved in next door. She couldn't tell whether they were harmless hippies or folks who could be dangerous to a person living alone. So she began hanging men's clothing and underwear on her clothesline to make them think that she wasn't living alone, that a man lived there. Never had any bother from those folks.

After she moved to the new house we had built for her on the farm, she was enjoying her garden. She's a very fit and lively lady, helps with all kinds of things and still does every bit of her cooking and housework, with spirit for more. She's especially fond of the lilies she grows in her front yard.

But her dog, Dolly, was digging them up, and that made her plenty mad. So Mama applied her down-home smarts. She filled a bucket with water and dropped in a handful of powerful red hot peppers to soak all day. Then, before she went to bed, she poured that "hot" water all around the lilies.

Worked just fine, too. When she woke up, she heard her dog thumping at the door. That Doberman had gone scratching around in the lily beds and started gnawing. All of a sudden, that fiery pepper water got to her. So she forgot all about those lilies. She just lapped up every drop of water in her dish, and wanted more. Mama gave her some. That dog never bothered those flowers again.

Mama's getting to like farm life. She wasn't always that comfortable with cattle, of which we have about 150. I can recall her mother giving us a milk cow back in Florida in the late 1930s. That cow's name was Curley. Well, Mama was scared to death of Curley. Having little experience and a real concern about being kicked, she'd have me and Richard tie that cow's hind legs together each time before she'd milk her.

Getting back to that golf cart that Judy bought for Mama at the auction, it didn't run right at first. One of my mechanics at the farm fixed it so it would go, but the only way you could stop it was to undo a wire from the ignition switch. I didn't know that. Nobody told me. I got on that crazy three-wheeler and it took off with me. All I could do was try to guide.

Before I could figure things out, the foot pedal to the accelerator came loose, and me and that golf cart were picking up speed. I was trying to stop that cart, but didn't know how. I could steer—but that's all. It ran around and around. I figured I'd get it to the barn, where I could maybe slow it down on something, somehow.

I think that was a mistake. I ran it into the barn, and we went in at full speed—right *up the wall*. It stopped up there—with me still on it, upside down. And the motor was still chugging. I couldn't get down off that thing, no matter how I tried. There were tobacco sticks all over me.

I began to holler, and Judy heard me. She came running into the barn, then stopped in her tracks when she saw me hanging there. I felt silly as hell. We still laugh about that. It's good to be able to laugh at your mistakes. Lord knows, I've made enough of them. What makes things easier is that we both accept the fact that I'm not too good with farm machinery.

But I do love the farm. It's my place of peace, where I refuel on nature's honest truths and beauties when I come home between tours.

I've seen a lot of good men, and some not so good, burned out on the road. Coming home to our farm in Tennessee—a beautiful place in a beautiful state—gives me the renewed strength to go on with the touring.

That road isn't going to beat me.

CHAPTER

28

After we moved into the log house, there were more changes in my life. It seems as if there always are.

Maybe I'm the sort who needs new goals, new growth, and new experiences. I am not the kind of person to rest on his laurels, that's for sure.

And maybe there are always changes in everyone's life— just the nature of things. And some things that need changing. Changes can be opportunities, not problems. My thinking is that we can make those opportunities—which I try to do.

Well, I was still concerned about my daddy. He was remarried and had a new family and had never come up to see his children and grandchildren living in Tennessee. But he was my father, and I loved him. After having been through the battering of a troubled marriage and divorce myself, I think I understood him better. I could see that in his own troubled way he'd loved us.

When I heard he was sick, I decided that this might be an opportunity. An opportunity to help him and show that we cared about him. An opportunity for me to come together with him after the long years. So, as I told you at the beginning of this book, we invited him up to see Nashville, the farm, and his grandchildren. Judy and I, as you know, flew down to Leesburg, Florida, and brought him back up in *Stutter One*. He was a little afraid of that airplane, but he came with us.

Nobody could predict how it might come out, but I had to try. I couldn't write off my own father. We talked about a lot of things on the flight up from Florida, but avoided the important questions. It wasn't the time, not yet. He seemed a little bit subdued—maybe it was age and his health—as we got out of the plane. Then we drove from the Nashville Airport to the farm.

After we had settled him in, we showed him around the big log house. He didn't say much at first, but I could see in his eyes that he was impressed. But was he pleased? That was hard to tell.

In the next few days we showed him all over the farm, and then we drove him to see his other children and his grandchildren. My children came out to the farm to be with him. He'd never met Carrie April before. They got along just fine—like any grandfather and his youngest grandchild should. He showed warmth for the other kids, too. Warmth I hadn't seen in him when I was a child.

We could all see that he wasn't well. He'd lived hard, worked hard, and time was running out for him. He was weary now, still strong-willed, but showing the fatigue of age and a tired heart. After a week he decided that it was time to go back to his home in Florida, the house I'd bought in Groveland years ago, where he lived. He got by on his Social Security and money I provided each month, and was comfortable.

I found it hard to ask the questions.

On the day he left, he provided the answers himself.

"You've done very well for yourself, Mel," he told me. "It's a beautiful home. I'd heard that you'd made it big, but

I never expected anything like *this*." He looked around thoughtfully and nodded. "Well, you did it," he said, "and without me."

I was all choked up—like that stutterin' teenager trying to talk back at Pahokee High School more than thirty years before. Where had the years gone? They'd passed so fast.

"This is much more than I ever expected, son."

And that was it. I had a hundred things more I wanted to say, but the words didn't come out. Somehow this was enough. Well, almost enough. We'd talk more when he came back again. He promised that he would. Even though the visits in the past had always been on our side, our going to see him, he said he would come back to see all of us.

So we drove him to the airport, and *Stutter One* took him back home. Wherever I was during the next months, on tour or at home, I kept thinking about what we'd do and what we would talk about when he returned. Now he *knew* that his stutterin' boy was neither a fool nor a failure. I had come a way.

One day shortly before Christmas he left his home and drove to the post office to pick up his mail. It was a bright, sunny morning and he was in good spirits. He collected his mail, walked back to his car, sat down, and died right there from a heart attack. He died instantly, they say.

I was in Forth Worth, Texas, doing Whataburger commercials when I got the news. I still had two days' shooting left to do. Judy told me to go ahead and finish my work and she'd handle the funeral arrangements with Imogene and Linda. I was not to worry. I didn't tell the Whataburger people about it until we were through. I knew that I'd never been his favorite, but I couldn't hold that against him. I hoped that the others might try to forgive him, too. He'd done the best he could.

It was a small funeral, a quiet one. Not all his children were there. Now he's finally at peace. I sometimes think about that second talk we never had. I wonder how it would have come out. I guess I will as long as I live.

CHAPTER

29

After Daddy died, I found myself thinking about how it had been growing up, remembering my early years as a boy in Florida. My memories were not sad ones—though there had been some hard times. Recalling the lake and the birds, the fish and other wonders of nature, my relatives and buddies, I had good feelings about Florida.

And then I found a novel that I couldn't put down. It was about the opening and development of the part of Florida that I knew—a big, bold saga set at the start of this century. Written by a very talented man named Richard Powell, *I Take This Land* had been a best-seller when first published by Charles Scribner's Sons in 1962. The sprawling, brawling story was rich in adventure and romance, conflict and human weakness. The people were dramatic—larger than life and fascinating. Well, that saga of my home state between 1895 and 1946 struck me as perfect for a movie. So I took out an option on the picture rights—the first step toward making my first feature.

I knew that there would have to be many more steps, and that it would be easy to stumble. In the language of the Hollywood folks, it was a project. From my earlier experiences and talks with movie professionals, I realized that about 499 out of 500 projects never make it to the screen. Since *I Take This Land* is a big story, it would have to be a large and expensive movie, or maybe a TV miniseries. So, as usual, I moved ahead slowly and carefully.

Several experienced people suggested that almost every beginner—and many who are not beginners—makes mistakes in film deals, and urged me to get my on-the-job training with a much smaller movie. I've been trying that. I found out how hard it is to get even a little picture going. There are a lot of very strange folks in Hollywood, guys who'll switch the terms of a deal in midstream or try to sell a new dreamer something they don't exactly own.

There are also plenty of honest and talented people. I've had an interesting and sometimes aggravating education. And the cost—in money for lawyers and writers—hasn't exactly been cheap. But I'm not the least bit discouraged. I made some mistakes in learning about songwriting, recording, music publishing, and touring on the road—so these bumps on the way to making a movie have only made me more determined.

In due course, I'll find the right writer and he or she will create a first-class treatment—an outline for the actual script. You can't get to major directors and actors without a good script. I've already talked with some talented actors I know, people who want to do *I Take This Land* when it's ready. In the meanwhile, I've set up a movie production company with Roy Clark. It's called Mel-Roy. We plan on doing a $3.5 million movie called *Uphill All the Way.* It's sort of a musical Butch Cassidy–Sundance Kid movie, except our names will be Ben and Booger. We hope to start filming sometime this year. I can't wait! The script's already been written, and it's funny.

The movie company was set up to bring my organization and me into movie production. I plan to do specials for television as well, in due course. The goal is to make quality films and tapes that enough people will like to make them profitable.

That could make it possible for me to spend less time on the road.

I'm definitely considering such a future, which would be better for me and my family. I'd like us to be together more. Family, as I've said, is very important to me.

Right now, my wife's dad is the man who runs our farm, Sycamore Acres. He does a wonderful job. He's a born farmer, a smart guy, and a person who cares about doing things exactly right. He had dreamed for years about running a big farm with the best equipment and a proper budget. Well, in making *his* dream come true, he did a whole lot for *mine*.

I've never seen a more dedicated man. Judy's parents live in a nice house on the farm. They get along fine with my mama, who recognizes and respects good people who work hard. Judy's mother and mine both help with a variety of chores that have to be done, such as pouring the sorghum syrup into jars.

In addition to our fourteen tobacco barns, the chicken houses, horse and cattle shelters, pastures, pig pens and houses, smoke house to make our own meats, and such, and acreage planted in various crops, we've got a syrup mill. That's what we use to grind and cook up the sorghum into molasses. Last year we sold about a thousand jars of Mel's Molasses at our gift shop, which is near Nashville's Country Music Hall of Fame.

There's a real nice couple running the shop, doing it well—Clifton and Pauline Totty. They're Judy's uncle and aunt.

Judy says that all this family togetherness is either going to be a huge success or we'll blow up and kill each other. So far, it's all success and family pleasure in a common effort.

Now, if someone takes a look at the label on Mel's Molasses, he'll see a picture of a mule marked J.T. on the right side. When my father-in-law came to help us out at the farm, he brought his mule, J.T., with him. So we're celebrating that four-legged, long-eared member of the family in a cheerful way. We let him plow the tobacco!

And I'm looking forward to the Tillis side of our family coming in actively. My daughter Connie and Sonny Boy have both worked at the office. She's doing her own thing now, but it looks as if Sonny Boy may come back on a full-time basis after he finishes college. I'm trying to persuade him that he should complete that education and take some proper business courses before getting into the music world.

He's had a taste of both sides of it—the Nashville office end and life on the road with me. He is a strong and healthy young man, and the pace of life on the road doesn't bother him a bit. It probably seems glamorous to him—in some ways, like a long football weekend of partying. He's handled himself well and managed to learn while having a lot of fun. Judy comes out on the road whenever (1) she has the time, (2) wants a change, (3) we are staying in the same place for a few days.

She's the hardest worker of all. That lady doesn't seem to stop. She runs and cleans our big house by herself, cooks and bakes and preserves and jars everything from fruit to grinding sausage to freezing vegetables. She takes care of the grandbabies and kids when they come to stay, and is in the office two or three days a week to pitch in there. Sometimes I think she's a wife and a half.

And she's my closest adviser. She's also very patient with a husband who's away a lot and who sometimes forgets things like anniversary presents until the last second. She never forgets such important dates. And I'm getting better at this—at least I'm working on it.

I don't believe that my two younger daughters will come into the business side, but Carrie April could be an excellent singer. Traveling not only can grind a touring performer down, but it can be dangerous. Quite a few artists have been killed in private or chartered planes. We had a scare ourselves last year when the electrical system in *Stutter One* went on the blink up near Newark, New Jersey. After that scare I sold it within a month. I'll fly on the airlines' big four-jet jobs from now on.

Not too long after I sold the plane, I bought something, something special. I'm still thrilled. The Cedarwood Publishing Company had been an important part of my career. No, of my *life*. That was where I grew up in music, where I made some wonderful friends . . . learned a lot . . . and laughed a lot, too. And the help that I got from the Cedarwood folks, especially Mr. Denny, was both warm and valuable.

For years after his death, Jim Denny's widow and his two sons ran the company. Then in 1982 Bill Denny—the older son, who was in charge of the business—left to become president of the Nashville Gas Company. Soon after that, word was out that Cedarwood was for sale.

Since Cedarwood was my musical home, and therefore not just a business to me, I wasn't about to let some out-of-town publisher or strangers get it. Several tried, but in October of 1983 I signed the papers for it. The Stutterin' Boy from Florida who'd come to Nashville twenty-seven years ago with a pregnant wife and a '49 Mercury with a hole in the windshield bought the company. In 1956 I'd had a $50-a-week "draw" at Cedarwood. In 1983 I owned it— with the help of my good friends at Commerce Union Bank, and good credit. An article in *Billboard* reported that the price was "in the neighborhood of $3,000,000.00."

Now, that's an interesting n-n-n-neighborhood. I can't help thinking how far it is from the little house in Dover where I nearly died.

The deal involved a catalogue of more than seven thousand songs—six hundred of them written or co-written by me. Those six hundred songs are more than words and music to me. They're practically a diary. Each still reminds me of a time and a place, of who I was when it was written.

In some ways I haven't changed, but in others I have. I feel more confident now. I have more security—material and mental. And the more security I have, the more independent I am, and the less I stutter. It took a lot of work to get that confidence and security. It's going to take years more work to keep both.

That's all right with me.

I still believe in putting that dime in the slot yourself. If you're not satisfied, it's up to *you* to do something about it. Even as a stuttering kid, I decided that if you're going to do anything, don't be a burden to somebody else. It's a question of self-respect, which we all need. If you're a burden to others, people think of you in a different way. I could never accept that. Mama raised us not to.

There are things that I know I've got to accept, though I just don't understand them. I'm a Baptist and I believe in a Supreme Being. I haven't been an angel, but I've tried to live by the Bible . . . the Ten Commandments. Still, I'm puzzled by why there's so much human misery. Maybe folks who've studied more than I have the answer. I don't, and it sometimes troubles me. Working within my small powers, I wrote a song called "Survival of the Fittest." It isn't well known, but it means a lot to me. It tells of the crippled, the weak. It tells how we preach peace, while thousands die in war. And each verse ends with the same sad truth; "Oh, wonder why God made these kinds of laws."

Infant turtles racing to the sea,
Seagulls screeching crying hungrily,
Twisting, kicking, jerking in their craws,
Oh, wonder why God made these kinds of laws.

Now the preacher's preaching loudly on the street,
While the deaf and dumb men cannot hear nor speak,
Twisted legs can't chase a bouncing ball,
Oh, wonder why God made these kinds of laws.

Well, the carney's barking to the crowd, "Let's go,"
While the geek's a-waiting to do his sickening show,
Freaks a-standing 'round, some fat, some tall,
Oh, wonder why God made these kinds of laws.

Now I don't mean to criticize
The works of the Master's plan,
But after all the faith I have in him
I still can't understand.

'Cause Moses teaches us thou shall not kill
While the cannons roar aloud on foreign hills.
The strong will stand, the weak will surely fall,
*Oh, wonder why God made these kinds of laws.**

I'm not setting myself up as a preacher or great author-
ity, just a mortal with questions. I've been able to avoid
any delusions of grandeur over the years—which is important for performers. It is real easy for men and women in
my line of work to lose their perspective and get swelled
heads.

I try to avoid that because it's not needed, and you can
make a real fool of yourself right fast. I recall a football
game in Tampa not so very long ago. I was sitting in the
stands with my friends, watching the activities on the field
and listening to the radio at the same time. The announcer
was filling time before the players came out, and he started
talking about "celebrities" in the crowd.

"And Mel Tillis is here!" he announced.

There was a great roar, so I stood up and took a bow,
smiled, and waved at seventy thousand people.

The shout was for the Tampa Bay Buccaneers charging
out onto the field. As soon as I realized that, I sat down—
feeling really stupid. The Lord had given me another well-
deserved lesson in humility. I still laugh when I remember

it. If I forget it, there are some helpful pickers in my band who're kind enough to remind me.

I hear that there's a wise proverb carved on the U.S. Archives building in Washington. They say it reads, "What's past is prologue."

You know, I feel exactly the same way.

So whenever I ask myself that question—"Well, Stutterin' Boy, is *that* all you've got?"—I've got the answer.

Hell, no! There's plenty more. And I'm looking forward to every b-b-b-bit of it.

To be continued . . . . .

DISCOGRAPHY

SINGLES

Release Date	Record Label	Selection Number	Title
February, 1957	Columbia	4-40845	It Takes a Worried Man to Sing a Worried Song/Honky Tonk Song
April, 1957	Columbia	4-40904	Case of the Blues/It's My Life
June, 1957	Columbia	4-40944	Juke Box Man/If You'll Be My Love
October, 1957	Columbia	4-41038	This Heart/Take My Hand
January, 1958	Columbia	4-41115	Lonely Street/Teen Age Wedding
June, 1958	Columbia	4-41189	A Violet and a Rose/No Song to Sing
November, 1958	Columbia	4-41277	The Brooklyn Bridge/Finally
June, 1959	Columbia	4-41416	Sawmill/You Are the Reason
November, 1959	Columbia	4-41530	Georgia Town Blues/Till I Get Enough of These Blues
March, 1960	Columbia	4-41632	Loco Weed/It's So Easy
November, 1960	Columbia	4-41863	Walk on By/Say
March, 1961	Columbia	4-41986	Hearts of Stone/That's Where the Hurt Comes In
December, 1961	Columbia	4-42262	If I Lost Your Love/Party Girl
June, 1962	Decca	31445	How Come Your Dog Don't Bite/So Soon
January, 1963	Decca	31474	Don't Tell Mama/Half Laughing, Half Crying
January, 1963	Decca	31528	Couldn't See the Forest for the Trees/It's No Surprise

Release Date	Record Label	Selection Number	Title
February, 1964	Decca	31623	I'm Gonna Act Right/It'll Be Easy
July, 1965	Ric	158	Wine/Mr. Dropout
May, 1966	Kapp	K-764	Mental Revenge/Guide Me Home My Georgia Moon
August, 1966	Kapp	K-772	Stateside/Home Is Where the Hurt Is
December, 1966	Kapp	K-804	Life Turned Her That Way/If I Could Only Start Over
December, 1966	Kapp	K-881	All Right/Helpless, Hopeless Fool
December, 1966	Kapp	KL-1514	Life Turned Her That Way/The Old Gang's Gone
December, 1966	Kapp	KJB-120	Life Turned Her That Way/ Stateside
May, 1967	Kapp	K-837	Goodbye Wheeling/At the Sight of You
June, 1967	Kapp	K-867	The Old Gang's Gone/Survival of the Fittest
February, 1968	Kapp	K-905	Something Special/You Name It
May, 1968	Kapp	K-941	Destroyed by Man/I Haven't Seen Mary in Years
August, 1968	Kapp	KJB-122	Destroyed by Man/Something Special
August, 1968	Kapp	KJB-123	I Haven't Seen Mary in Years/ Lonely Girl
September, 1968	Kapp	K-959	Who's Julie/Give Me One More Day
January, 1969	Kapp	K-986	Old Faithful/Sorrow Overtakes the Wine
May, 1969	Kapp	K-2031	These Lonely Hands of Mine/ Cover Mama's Flowers
May, 1969	Kapp	KJB-124	These Lonely Hands of Mine/Old Faithful
November, 1969	Kapp	K-2072	She'll Be Hanging 'Round Somewhere/Where Love Has Died

DISCOGRAPHY 255

Release Date	Record Label	Selection Number	Title
February, 1970	Kapp	K-2086	Heart Over Mind/Lingering Memories
October, 1970	Kapp	K-2103	Too Lonely, Too Long/Memories Made This House
February, 1971	Kapp	KJB-98	Heart Over Mind/She'll Be Hanging 'Round Somewhere
March, 1971	Kapp	K-2121	One More Drink/I Could Never Be Ashamed of You
May, 1970	MGM	14148	Heaven Everyday/How You Drink the Wine
August, 1970	MGM	14176	Commercial Affection/I Thought About You
January, 1971	MGM	14211	Arms of a Fool/Veil of White Lace
April, 1971	MGM	14255	Take My Hand/Life's Little Surprises
June, 1971	MGM	14275	Brand New Mister Me/Brand New Wrapper
August, 1971	MGM	14303	Living and Learning/Tangled Vines
November, 1971	MGM	14329	Untouched/I Went a Ramblin'
January, 1972	MGM	14365	Anything's Better Than Nothing/Then It Will All Be Over
March, 1972	MGM	14372	Would You Want the World to End/Things Have Changed a Lot
July, 1972	MGM	14418	I Ain't Never/Burden of Love
October, 1972	MGM	14454	Neon Rose/It's My Love
November, 1972	MGM	14472	Happyville/Back to Life
March, 1973	MGM	14522	Thank You for Being You/Over the Hill
June, 1973	MGM	14585	Sawmill/Mama's Gonna Pray
September, 1973	MGM	14660	Let's Go All the Way Tonight/In the Vine

Release Date	Record Label	Selection Number	Title
December, 1973	MGM	14689	Midnight, Me and the Blues/ Modern Home Magazine
March, 1974	MGM	14714	Don't Let Go/Why Not Do the Things They Say We Do
March, 1974	MGM	14720	Stomp Them Grapes/Hang My Picture in Your Heart Dear
August, 1974	MGM	14744	Memory Maker/Second Best
October, 1974	MGM	14776	You Are the One/I See Heaven in You
January, 1975	MGM	14782	Best Way I Know How/Honey Dew Melon
May, 1975	MGM	14803	Mr. Right and Mrs. Wrong/Just Two Strangers
May, 1975	MGM	14804	Woman in the Back of My Mind/ Kissing Your Picture
September, 1975	MGM	14835	Looking for Tomorrows/ Tennessee Banjo Man
February, 1976	MGM	14846	Mental Revenge/My Bad Girl Treats Me Good
May, 1976	MGM	14850	Come on Home/Always Just a Memory Away
May, 1976	MCA	40559	Love Revival/Gator Bar
September, 1976	MCA	40627	Good Woman Blues/You Can't Trust a Crazy Man
December, 1976	MCA	40667	Heart Healer/It's Just Not That Easy to Say
March, 1977	MCA	40710	Burning Memories/Golden Nugget Gamblin' Casino
August, 1977	MCA	40764	I Got the Hoss/It's Been a Long Time
December, 1977	MCA	40836	What Did I Promise Her Last Night/Woman You Should Be in Movies
April, 1978	MCA	40900	I Believe in You/She Don't Trust You Daddy

Release Date	Record Label	Selection Number	Title
August, 1978	MCA	40946	Ain't No California/What Comes Natural to a Fool
December, 1978	MCA	40983	Send Me Down to Tucson/ Charlie's Angel
June, 1979	MCA	41041	Coca Cola Cowboy/Cotton Mouth
September, 1979	Elektra	E-46536	Blind in Love/Black Jack, Water Back
January, 1980	Elektra	E-46583	Lying Time Again/Fooled Around and Fell in Love
April, 1980	Elektra	E-46628	Your Body Is an Outlaw/Rain on My Parade
August, 1980	Elektra	E-47015	Steppin' Out/Whiskey Chasin'
March, 1981	Elektra	E-47116	Million Old Goodbyes/Louisiana Lonely
June, 1981	Elektra	E-47157	Texas Cowboy Night/After the Lovin'
August, 1981	Elektra	E-47178E	One Night Fever/Time Has Treated You Well
November, 1981	Elektra	E-47247	Play Me or Trade Me/Where Would I Be
February, 1982	Elektra	E-47412	Long Way to Daytona/Always You, Always Me
May, 1982	Elektra	E-47453	The One That Got Away/Why Ain't Life the Way It's Supposed to Be
August, 1982	Elektra	7-69963	Stay a Little Longer/Dream of Me
February, 1983	MCA	MCA-52182	In the Middle of the Night/Even at Her Worst She's Still the Best
June, 1983	MCA	MCA-53347	Cowboy's Dream/After All This Time
October, 1983	MCA	MCA-52285	She Meant Forever/Try It Again
April, 1984	MCA	MCA-52373	New Patches/Almost Like You Never Went Away

ALBUMS

Release Date	Record Label	Selection Number	Title	Producer
March, 1961	Columbia	CS-8616	Various Artists Album	Don Law
June, 1961	Columbia	CS-8524	Heart Over Mind	Don Law
June, 1964	Harmony	KH-31952	Heart Over Mind	Don Law
May, 1966	Kapp	KS-3493	Stateside	Paul Cohen
December, 1966	Kapp	KS-3514	Life's That Way	Paul Cohen
October, 1967	Kapp	KS-3535	Mister Mel	
March, 1968	Kapp	KL-1543	Let Me Talk to You	Paul Cohen
March, 1969	Kapp	KS-3594	Who's Julie	Paul Cohen
August, 1969	Kapp	KS-3570	Something Special	Paul Cohen
November, 1969	Kapp	KS-3589	Greatest Hits	Paul Cohen
December, 1969	Kapp	KS-3609	Old Faithful	Paul Cohen
March, 1970	Kapp	KS-3639	Mel Tillis/Bob Wills	Paul Cohen
April, 1970	Kapp	KS-3630	She'll Be Hanging 'Round Somewhere	Paul Cohen
June, 1970	MGM	SE-4681	One More Time	Jim Vienneau
September, 1970	Harmony	HS-11170	The Great Mel Tillis	Don Law
February, 1971	MGM	SE-4757	Arms of a Fool/ Commercial Affection	Jim Vienneau
June, 1971	MGM	SE-4788	Live at Sam Houston Coliseum	Jim Vienneau

Release Date	Record Label	Selection Number	Title	
August, 1971	Kapp	KS-3653	Mel Tillis' Greatest Hits, Vol. II	Paul Cohen
July, 1971	MGM	SE-4800	Living and Learning/Take My Hand	Jim Vienneau
September, 1971	MGM	SE-4806	The Very Best of Mel Tillis	Jim Vienneau
January, 1972	MGM	SE-4841	Would You Want the World to End	Jim Vienneau
June, 1972	Vocalion	VL-3928	Walking on New Grass	Jim Vienneau
September, 1972	MGM	SE-4870	I Ain't Never/ Neon Rose	Jim Vienneau
March, 1973	MGM	SE-4889	Onstage, Live in Birmingham	Jim Vienneau
September, 1973	MGM	SE-4907	Sawmill	Jim Vienneau
November, 1973	MGM	SE-4937	Let's Go All the Way Tonight	Jim Vienneau
March, 1974	MGM	SE-4960	Midnight, Me and the Blues/ Stomp Them Grapes	Jim Vienneau
June, 1974	Harmony	KH-31952	I Ain't Never/ Heart Over Mind	Don Law
September, 1974	MGM	SE-4970	Mel Tillis' Greatest Hits	Jim Vienneau
October, 1974	MGM	SE-4987	Mel Tillis Featuring Best Way I Know How	Jim Vienneau
February, 1975	MGM	SE-5002	M-M-Mel and the Statesiders	Jim Vienneau
November, 1976	MGM	MG-1-5021	Best of Mel Tillis	Jim Vienneau

Release Date	Record Label	Selection Number	Title	Producer
November, 1976	MGM	MG-1-5022	Welcome to Mel Tillis	Jim Vienneau
November, 1976	MGM	MG-2-5402	24 Greatest Hits	Jim Vienneau
June, 1976	MCA	2204	Love Revival	Johnny Virgin/ Mel Tillis
February, 1977	MCA	2252	Heart Healer	Jimmy Bowen/ Johnny Virgin
October, 1977	MCA	2288	Love's Troubled Waters	Jimmy Bowen
June, 1978	MCA	2364	I Believe in You	Jimmy Bowen
January, 1979	MCA	3077	Are You Sincere	Jimmy Bowen
June, 1979	MCA	3167	Mr. Entertainer	Jimmy Bowen
September, 1979	Gusto	GT-0047	The Great Mel Tillis	Various Producers
November, 1979	Elektra	6E236	Me and Pepper	Jimmy Bowen
December, 1979	MCA	3208	M-M-Mel Live	Jimmy Bowen
March, 1980	Elektra	6E271	Your Body Is an Outlaw	Jimmy Bowen
August, 1980	Elektra	6E310	Southern Rain	Jimmy Bowen
February, 1981	MCA	3274	The Very Best of Mel Tillis	Jimmy Bowen
April, 1981	MCA	2-4091	The Best of Mel Tillis	Jimmy Bowen
June, 1981	Elektra	5E-549	Mel Tillis and Nancy Sinatra	Billy Strange
April, 1982	Elektra	EL-60016	It's a Long Way to Daytona	Billy Strange
September, 1982	Elektra	EL-60192	Mel Tillis' Greatest Hits	Jimmy Bowen/ Billy Strange
March, 1983	MCA	5378	After All This Time	Harold Shedd
April, 1984	MCA	5472	New Patches	Harold Shedd

INDEX